To Jack and Luke (JA) and to Jessica, Sophie and Zachary (SB)
with all our love.

Contents

List of tables and boxes

List of tables

List of boxes

Preface

While there is a growing body of research on young carers, there has been little published to date specifically on children caring for parents with severe and enduring mental illness. The Young Carers Research Group (YCRG) in the Centre for Child and Family Research, Department of Social Sciences, Loughborough University (to which the authors belong) has been conducting research on young carers and their families for the last ten years. This book arose from a project which started in January 2000 and which aims to fill the gaps in knowledge and understanding of children caring for parents with severe and enduring mental illness.

We were fortunate to have an excellent working partnership with the National Schizophrenia Fellowship (NSF, since renamed Rethink) who, with us, applied to the National Lottery Charities Board (now the Community Fund) for a grant to conduct research on this topic. We must acknowledge our gratitude to the NSF, and in particular to Martin Kinsella who was instrumental in the original application and who chaired the Advisory Board, and Gary Hogman, who was our day-to-day contact at NSF. We are also indebted to the Community Fund for making funding available from their health and social research grants programme to conduct this study.

The research was ably assisted by an Advisory Board who offered advice and guidance throughout the two-year research period. We are grateful to: Sarah Byford, Harriet Clarke, Jeff Cohen, Chris Dearden, Jenny Fisher, Liz Fletcher, Gary Hogman, Ilan Katz, Martin Kinsella, Richard Olsen, James Wade and Cassie Wragg. We also sought specialist advice from a number of others who we would like to acknowledge: Adrian Falkov, consultant child and adolescent psychiatrist; John Russell, pharmacist; Fiona Becker, NSPCC child protection training consultancy; David Deacon, Communication and Media Studies, Loughborough University; Simon Cross, Centre for Mass Communication Research, Leicester University; and to the many others who shared with us their ideas through formal and informal discussions. Two anonymous referees made helpful comments about the first draft of the manuscript.

It would not have been possible to undertake this research and to select our sample without the help of the many dedicated young carers and NSF projects across Britain. We thank the project workers for taking the time and trouble to assist us in identifying families where children were caring for parents with severe and enduring mental illness and in helping us to recruit these families. We are indebted to the families themselves for agreeing to be interviewed about their lives and experiences. For many of the parents and children this was their first opportunity to talk openly about what were sometimes very difficult and painful experiences. We are grateful to them for their honesty and for their trust in us to deal sensitively with the information they gave us. These families also identified their key workers who we also went on to interview, and our thanks go to them for giving up their valuable time.

Chris Dearden, a research fellow in the YCRG from its inception, played an instrumental role in the data collection process and we are grateful to her for the important contribution she made to the study. Richard and Pat Silburn also assisted with some data collection and interviews and we thank them for their valued input. Our thanks finally go to Dawn Rushen and others at The Policy Press for all their help and support.

Jo Aldridge and Saul Becker, December 2002

Introduction

About half of those with severe mental illness live with family or friends, and many others receive considerable support from them. Carers of service users, including young carers, should be involved in their own assessment and care planning process, which takes account of the state of their own mental and physical health needs, and ability to continue to care. (*National service framework for mental health*, DH, 1999a, p 69)

A number of authors (for example, Göpfert et al, 1996; Falkov, 1997) have drawn attention to the lack of research, information, and knowledge about the specific experiences and needs of children caring for parents with severe and enduring mental health problems. While there is an established medical literature on the impacts of parental mental illness on children within families, there is very little medical or social research that has focused on children *caring* for parents in these situations. Chapter One reviews the relevant and available literature, that is, medical and social research, and child protection and contemporary young carers' studies.

This volume is the first in-depth research study of children caring for parents with severe and enduring mental illness. Data were collected from 40 families and interviews were conducted with parents, their children who cared for them and the key professionals in contact with these families. A full discussion of the methodology involved in this study can be found in Appendix A.

The chapters that follow present the accounts and experiences of each of these three respondent groups. Chapter Two presents the parents' perspective; the perspectives of children are presented in Chapter Three. Chapter Four looks at the role of professionals and their relationships and interventions with parents and young carers. We contend that, to understand why and how children care for parents with mental illness, we must understand what goes on within families by reference to the perspectives of those who provide and receive family care, as well as those professionals who are charged with the formal care and support of vulnerable parents and children. This is the first ever study to give this three-way perspective. The study also benefits from a dynamic element, which was achieved by a two-phase interview approach, whereby families and professionals were interviewed and then re-interviewed ten months later. This allows us to present throughout the book data on the *changing* needs and experiences of families and the implications of these for policy and practice. In Chapter Five, we discuss the findings from our study and locate them in a broader context of how professionals might identify and respond to the needs of parents with mental illness and children who may have to care for them. We offer a model, or mapping device, which we hope will be of practical use to professionals in these fields, to help them intervene more appropriately and sensitively in meeting the needs of families where parents have mental illness and children provide care.

In order to adequately understand the experiences of parents, young carers and professionals, we must also make reference to the legal and policy framework that influences heavily experiences and outcomes for families and for the professionals who work with them. Appendix B presents a chronology and guide to the relevant law and policy relating to parents with mental illness, young carers and the professionals in contact with these families. We hope that readers interested in the detail of law and policy will find the chronology and guide useful in informing their understanding of how policies have developed over time. Throughout the book we refer the reader to specific entries in the chronology where they illustrate or illuminate our own data and narrative.

We use the term 'young carer' as shorthand throughout the book for children caring for parents with severe and enduring mental illness. We acknowledge that some people may find the term 'young carer' difficult. However, this term is in common use in much of the legal and official policy documentation, as well as in the established research literature. We use the term in a quite deliberate and specific way. Thus:

> Young carers are children and young persons under 18 who provide, or intend to provide, care, assistance or support to another family member. These children carry out, often on a regular basis, significant or substantial caring tasks and assume a level of responsibility which would usually be associated with an adult. The person receiving care is often a parent, but can be a sibling, grandparent or other relative who is disabled, has some chronic illness, mental health problem or other condition connected with a need for care, support or supervision. (Becker, 2000, p 378)

The definition we use has a number of important elements. Certainly, many young carers are commonly defined by professionals with reference to the *amount* of care that children do – the notion of 'substantial and regular' care. Our definition, while retaining this quantifiable element, also includes reference to the *significance* of care. In other words, we recognise that, while care giving may not always be substantial and regular among children, the contributions they make – and the outcomes of care giving – may nonetheless be highly significant and important to families themselves.

While many children living in families with parental mental illness will undoubtedly be affected by their parents' condition (see Chapters One and Three) not all of them will be, or will become, young carers. In using this definition, we wish to draw attention in this volume to a particular group of children who provide care to parents with mental illness.

We are also mindful that the term 'mental illness' can be problematic in its association with a medical model of understanding people's mental health problems. Again, we use the terms 'mental illness' or 'mental ill health' interchangeably because of their widespread usage in the health and social literatures and in policy documents, even though they are not adequately defined in mental health law. The parents in this study had all been diagnosed with *severe and enduring* mental health problems. As shorthand in the text, we do not repeat the 'severe and enduring' aspect of their mental health problems; rather, the reader needs to be reminded that this aspect is key in defining those parents we selected and recruited for the study (see Appendix A for our methodology).

This volume will not be the last word on young carers and mental illness. We hope it offers an opening into a hitherto hidden and neglected area for research, policy and practice. Other issues will require attention in the future, including, for example, issues of race, gender, social class and specific types of mental illness, which may have distinct outcomes for parents and children. We hope that this volume will help to further knowledge and understanding about parental mental ill health and the contribution that many children make to care work within families.

ONE

Parental mental illness and young caring: research and prevalence

What is the first step we must take in order to fully understand the impact of parental mental ill health on children, and to consider the potential consequences for children who, by choice or *election* (see Aldridge and Becker, 1993a), undertake caring responsibilities for their parents? The first step must be to *contextualise* adult mental ill health. In this chapter, we do this by reviewing some of the early medical investigations that have helped shape current understanding about symptomatic behaviours and outcomes. At the same time, it is also important to look more broadly at what social research tells us about the impacts of mental ill health on children. The first part of this chapter reviews this medical and social research. The second part reviews data on the incidence of young caring, and in particular on the prevalence of children caring for parents with mental illness.

Representations of mental illness

Medical research to date has contributed to our current understanding about mental ill health and its impacts on individuals and the family. It has also, to some extent, informed the political and public perception of mental illness both in an institutional and community setting. Furthermore, it has helped inform the social and political framework that has shaped the lives of people living with mental health problems.

The body of medical research and its subsequent literature is useful in a number of ways: in clinical and pharmacological settings; in terms of improving our understanding about diagnostic methods, the nature of particular illnesses and prognoses; generating clinical evidence that may lead to new and effective treatments. However, the usefulness of this body of research in informing us about outcomes for individuals and families that are not exclusively clinical but, rather, are psychological, psychosocial and even political is more problematic. And yet, this medical work has undoubtedly been both expositional and influential in all of these areas.

In addition to this medical evidence, we must also recognise the influence of the media in shaping public perception of people with mental health problems living in communities today. Certainly some print and broadcast media have tended to link adult mental illness, particularly those with psychotic illnesses, with danger to the public (see Philo and Secker, 1999; Murray, 2000). Considering the media's emphasis on risk association, as well as the predominantly negative consequences for individuals with mental illness and their families represented in medical and social research, it is easy to understand why adults with serious mental health problems have become cemented in the public (and, to some extent, professional) consciousness as both *defective* and *infective*.

Medical investigation in Britain was conducted for many years in a political climate that demonised the mentally ill and removed them from society by institutionalising them in asylums. However, more recent clinical studies, certainly from the 1960s to the late 1980s, have to a greater or lesser extent continued to reinforce negative representations of adults with severe mental health problems. Recent social research, and child protection studies in particular (discussed in detail later in this chapter), has further compounded the association of parental mental illness with the developmental delay, neglect and even abuse of children.

In this chapter, we consider how these medical and social literatures – and to a lesser extent the media – have influenced perceptions of adult mental ill health, and what this means for children when these adults are also parents. As we have said, medical research, from the 1960s to the late 1980s, describes mental illness only in general terms of negative outcomes for affected adults and, more particularly, their children (see Boxes 1.1 and 1.2). This literature records the often 'bizarre' behaviour of those affected, their maladaptive responses and the psychological as well as physical degeneration, which 'infected' all aspects of family life. Anthony (1970) described these outcomes more generally as "the dynamics of deterioration".

Within these dynamics, *parental* mental illness was circumscribed by notions of risk:

- the risk of decline into insanity, institutionalisation or suicide among parents themselves;
- the risk of divorce and family disintegration;
- the risk to children of symptomatic assimilation, role disorder, maladaptation and maltreatment and abuse.

Other researchers that looked at the effects of a range of mental illnesses, including schizophrenia, unipolar and bipolar disorders and neuroses, concurred with Anthony (1970) in respect of outcomes for individuals and families (see Boxes 1.1 and 1.2).

More recently, as people with mental health problems have become de-institutionalised and have been moved into community settings, perceptions of risk associations have, if anything, increased. It is here where representations of adults with severe mental health problems become amplified and where discriminatory or prejudicial attitudes, particularly among local communities, can generate. Philo and Secker (1999, p 140) have argued that "the media play a significant part in shaping these public attitudes and perceptions"; the media also play a part in reproducing negative stereotypes of people with mental

Box 1.1: Effects of parental mental illness on parents and mothers as described in the medical literature (from 1960s to late 1980s)

Outcomes for affected parent	Outcomes for affected mother
Onset: seen as deviant behaviour; escape from the pressure of everyday life.	*Onset:* seen as deviant – even hysterical – behaviour; escape from the pressure of everyday life and motherhood.
Role transformation leading to: behavioural changes, 'bizarre'-type behaviour, hostility, rejection, disaffection, disruption, withdrawal.	*Role transformation leading to:* behavioural changes, periods of 'bizarre'-type behaviour, disruption, hostility, rejection, disaffection.
Psychological impacts: self-preoccupation, denial, increased psychosomatic tendencies and hypochondria.	*Psychological impacts:* withdrawal, fearfulness, sadness, increased psychosomatic tendencies and hypochondria, self-preoccupation, denial.
Resolution: hospitalisation or death; regeneration can only occur with (formal and informal) support from others and acceptance of illness.	*At increased risk of:* delivery complications, higher levels of mental and physical illness, 'retardation', transference of illness to child(ren), maltreatment and abuse of children.
Domestic impacts: 'substandard' orderliness and cleanliness.	*Resolution:* hospitalisation or death; regeneration can only occur with (formal and informal) support from others and acceptance of illness.

Note: These outcomes are derived from a review of the medical research cited throughout this chapter.

health problems (see Table 1.1). To some extent, this has also engendered fear of mental illness and crime and fostered a 'not in my back yard' attitude toward mental health facilities located in communities (Sayce, 1995; Baker and MacPherson, 2000).

Such predominantly negative representations of adults with mental illness – particularly the reporting of violent crimes committed by the mentally ill – also generates concern among those affected by mental illness as well as those working with and on their behalf (see Philo et al, 1994; Philo and Secker, 1999, p 136). Some research suggests that people with mental health problems are themselves aware of how disparagingly they are represented in the media (Baker and MacPherson, 2000). There is also some evidence to suggest that young television viewers are being socialised into stigmatising perceptions of people with mental illness (see Wilson et al, 2000). In this respect, children

Box 1.2: Effects of parental mental illness on children as described in the medical literature (from 1960s to late 1980s)

Outcomes for children
Onset in parent seen as physical, psychological, social, and educational crisis for children. Role transference and transformation leads to maladaptive behaviour, sacrificing contact with reality to maintain contact with ill parent; hiding feelings; role assimilation (child takes on 'idiosyncratic' roles such as 'caretaker', 'baby', 'patient', 'mourner', 'recluse', 'escapee', 'good child', 'bad child', and can function in an amalgamation of these roles); maladaptive behaviour; less responsive and spontaneous (younger children).

Psychological impact: increased risk of psychopathy (adopting intra-psychic defence mechanisms); denial; reaction formation; suppression; projection; incorporation; identification and repression.

Increased risk of depression and schizophrenia (withdrawn schizoid type or hyperactive asocial delinquent type); extreme stress (anger, guilt, grief, confusion).

At increased risk of: lower birth weights, poorer obstetrical status, poorer performance on newborn measures; developmental delay (especially in language); maltreatment and neglect; assimilation of illness in later life; underachievement at school.

Resolution: continuing crises until removal from family home occurs. Regeneration can only occur if children: show a resistance to being 'engulfed' by the illness; show intellectual curiosity about the illness; have an objective yet sympathetic approach to person who is ill; have the support from others in the environment and an ability to speak for themselves.

Note: These outcomes are derived from a review of the medical research cited throughout this chapter.

Table 1.1. Media coverage of mental health/illness, April 1993

Output category	Number of items	Percentage of total
Violence to others	373	66
Prescriptions for treatment/advice/recovery	102	18
Harm to self	71	13
'Comic' images	12	2
Criticism of accepted definitions	4	1
Total	562	100

Source: Philo and Secker, 1999, p 137.

who use disparaging language (the language of prejudice and social exclusion) may also add to other children's negative and isolating experiences of living with, and caring for, parents will mental illness.

As a result of such negative representations, mental health campaigners, and others working with and on behalf of adults with mental illness, often fear knee-jerk, coercive responses in respect of mental health policy formulation. Such fears have been realised to some extent in more recent legislative changes. For example, in his foreword to the Department of Health's *Modernising mental health services* (1998a), the then Secretary of State for Health, Frank Dobson, wrote:

> We are going to bring the laws on mental health up-to-date. In particular to ensure that patients who might otherwise be a danger to themselves and others are no longer allowed to refuse to comply with the treatment they need. We will also be changing the law to permit the detention of a small group of people who have not committed a crime but whose untreatable psychiatric disorder makes them dangerous. (DH, 1998a; see also Appendix B: 1998 (i) of this volume for a full discussion of this document)

This theme – of protecting society from mentally ill people, and protecting the mentally ill from themselves – is a dominant characteristic of mental health legislation and policy[1].

Birds of a feather

Medical investigation from the late 1950s described the outcomes of mental illness for affected adults in terms of 'mental retardation', and 'abnormal' and maladaptive behaviours and responses (see, for example, Arnaud, 1959). Here a 'deficiency' in one family member was seen to have *infective* consequences for all other members of the family, and particularly children (see Boxes 1.1 and 1.2). In 1970, Anthony was busy 'unroofing' his patients and bringing them "collectively to our research center, where they appear in their best clothes and best behavior" (1970, p 61). He described the families who 'shelter' a chronic patient as 'birds of a feather', all generating the same climate of deviance toleration and encouraging and fostering 'abnormal trends' (p 62).

The inevitability of atrophied parenting skills was also seen to be one of the main consequences of parental mental illness, and this in turn is described as leading to significant role modifications for each family member – and children in particular (see Box 1.2 above). Sturges noted children's "idiosyncratic role enactments" and how they "function in an amalgam of roles, sometimes shifting back and forth between opposite role positions, for example caretaker and baby, prisoner and escapee" (1978, p 535).

Anthony saw these and other role transformations among all family members as evidence of a decline in family relationships and values. In this way the onset of parental mental illness translates as a crisis for all the family:

We therefore find families that are disorganised, suspicious, chaotic and fluctuating .... Within the interpersonal matrix, a great deal of psychopathology can develop insidiously within individuals, especially children, without it's becoming recognisable. Abnormal attitudes and behaviour are assimilated and symptoms are exchanged with sometimes extraordinary facility. In this sort of setting, some small psychological epidemics frequently occur. (1970, p 62)

Anthony also suggested that in these situations "Family life becomes coarsened and the dirt and disorder are no longer noticed" (1970, p 62). Furthermore, the only real chance families had of recovery or regeneration was when:

- the affected parent died or was permanently removed from the family home;
- the family had evinced strength during previous crises (see Boxes 1.1 and 1.2);
- the family talked and supported each other throughout the period of illness (Sturges, 1977; Hatfield, 1978).

Although Anthony's investigation was highly influential, it echoed the work of many other medical researchers who tended to regard a range of mental illnesses as having similar outcomes (for individuals and families). More significantly, researchers at this time were investigating the outcomes of parental 'handicap' per se by considering the loss of physical and mental function *together*. Anthony's work was typical of this type of inclusive approach. His study on the impact of mental and physical illness on family life looked at the effects of a range of affective disorders – schizophrenia, depression, and so on – alongside, in the following case, tuberculosis:

An adolescent girl said to me: 'You cannot believe what it's like to wake up one morning and find your mother talking gibberish'.... The child of a tuberculous parent may have to adjust to a sudden restructuring in the pattern of the relationship .... The parent has to keep a proper distance and strongly discourage demonstrations of affection directed toward him. One father was so rigorous in the maintenance of this 'distance' that when he became sputum- and culture-negative, he went home joyously on a weekend, opened the door of his home, and ran forward to embrace his young son. The child became panic-stricken and raced off down the road. (Anthony, 1970, p 62)

Clearly, what Anthony's work (and other similar studies that looked at the consequences of parental mental illness for families) failed to recognise was the *nature* of a particular condition as an important variable in determining the type and duration of outcomes for individuals and families. Therefore it is problematic to arrive at firm conclusions when different populations are studied (see Roy, 1990).

Beginning in the early 1970s, medical researchers investigated patients with single diagnoses and how these affected patients and their children. In 1977, Sturges concluded that "the *nature* of the illness and the child's relationship to the person who is ill will influence his or her reactions and concerns" (1977, p100, emphasis added). Nevertheless, Sturges' later work, which has undoubtedly influenced subsequent medical research, continued to emphasise the negative consequences for families, and particularly children, where parents were affected by mental ill health. Evidence from contemporary medical research[2] also suggested an inevitable causal relationship between parental impairment and the risk to children of a range of adverse, and damaging childhood experiences (see Boxes 1.1 and 1.2).

Furthermore, there was a tendency during this period for researchers to 'laboratorise' their subjects by attempting to scientifically 'measure' mental illness and its outcomes (see Sameroff and Zax, 1973; Connors et al, 1979; Winters et al, 1981). However, the nature and consequences of many mental health conditions often manifest themselves as the very antithesis of this systematic and precise approach. Although 'testing' enabled clinicians to categorise their patients, the *social* consequences of this categorisation or labelling has been challenged more recently among social scientists (see Philo and Secker, 1999) and even from within psychiatric practice (see, for example, Perkins, 2000).

Many journals, such as *The American Journal of Mental Deficiency*, *Mental Retardation* and the *Journal of Abnormal Child Psychology*, continued in the early 1980s to publish work that focused on (mainly pessimistic) outcomes for 'mentally retarded' parents. Changes to medical terminologies have subsequently occurred, thanks to the campaign strategies of disability and mental health lobbies, as well as a more sensitised political climate. These changes reflect the growing realisation and understanding that our choice of language is important. Indeed, the labels and language used to categorise and describe people are part of a process that has much wider personal, social, and political implications for individuals, as well as society.

'Marginal people' and 'mentally dull mothers'

Up until the mid 1980s, women (as mothers) were often the subject of medical investigation, particularly in respect of outcomes for children of maternal mental illness. Once again, the consequences of mental illness among women (as mothers) were described as detrimental and seemed in part to reflect the gender assumptions of the (predominantly) male investigators. These assumptions perceived women (as mothers) as 'natural' child rearers, the lynchpins of domestic harmony, routine and cleanliness. When women 'succumbed' to mental illness, therefore, this was often described as 'hysterical' behaviour or as an 'escape from duty' (see Box 1.1).

Women were more often defined in terms of the roles they fulfilled (in other words, as mothers), than their status as patients. It followed, then, that women were 'intellectually handicapped mothers' (Rosenberg and McTate, 1982), 'mentally dull mothers', 'retarded mothers', 'deviant', 'marginal people' and 'mentally slow'. As mothers-to-be, women with mental illness were investigated for their part in increasing the risk of delivery complications during labour and for increasing developmental risks once a child was delivered. Their performance during pregnancy and childbirth was also seen to be inferior to the childbirth capacities of women who were well:

> Besides the effects of the patient's incompetencies and anxiety during the pregnancy, there are complex interactions during the delivery itself which increase the risk of complications. Anxious women tend to have a longer labor and less uterine motility. (Sameroff and Zax, 1973, p 197)

The notion of compulsory sterilisation gained some support for a time as a recommended strategy to prevent women with mental health problems transferring their illness to their children. Sturges has asked:

> In the interest of less vulnerable, better adjusted children, should not chronically ill, psychotic mothers who require intermittent hospitalisation be maintained in alternate institutions while stable surrogate mothers are provided? Should not certain chronically ill psychotic females be sterilised to prevent the birth of more children who are at risk? (1977, p 107)

Significantly, the subtext of much of the medical literature belonging to this time is centred, as we have said, on the perception of the mother as lynchpin of domestic family life. Once this key figure 'succumbs' to mental ill health, her performance in the mother role becomes the subject of medical scrutiny besides the effects of the condition itself.

More recent evidence suggests that women have a higher rate of neurotic disorder and psychoses than men (Meltzer et al, 1995; see also Chapter Two of this volume). Furthermore, women, when they become mothers, are more likely to be the subject of investigation by clinicians because of the incidence of postnatal depression. However, as Cleaver et al argue:

> One might question whether the variance in reported rates of mental illness is due to real differences in prevalence, in how mental illness manifests itself, or in methods of assessment and recording. (1999, p 12)

The key consequences of mental illness for women themselves, certainly in the medical literature from the 1960s until the mid to late 1980s, were poor domestic functioning and inadequate role functioning. This in turn was seen to increase the risk to children of maladaptation, role disorder, developmental delay and maltreatment (see Box 1.2; Sameroff and Zax, 1973; Schulsinger, 1976; Seifer and Sameroff, 1981; Rosenberg and McTate, 1982). Interestingly, the role of the father and external dynamics (such as poverty and the availability of alternative support and kinship networks) tended to be overlooked by the same medical research. O'Neill's (1985) case studies illustrate the emphasis on the dysfunction of women in their mother roles while suffering mental ill health, as well as the failure to consider other key factors (such as the absence of the woman's partner) that could also contribute to negative outcomes for children. The following case studies by O'Neill also indicate how children can be drawn into care and how they can sometimes replace (healthy) fathers who could care but who often choose not to (see Aldridge and Becker, 1993a):

> Some children take the parent's role very early in their lives: Ken's mother said he had helped her ever since he was 5 when his father left. His third grade teacher said 'He was responsible for all of them, mother too .... He helped Mama along and looked after her'.
>
> Lyle's mother depended on him ever since his father died when Lyle was 4. His mother said: 'I think I used him more than I would when he was older'. His younger sister said, 'He was more like the father. He ran the house'. This precocious competence sometimes stands in the way of adult fulfilment. (O'Neill, 1985, p 259)

The medical literature consistently underlines the consequences of a woman's mental ill health for her 'proper' functioning as a mother. This, more than the absence or loss of the father role as well as other social and professional support systems, is perceived as the root of family problems. Indeed, men as partners and fathers are either absent from the parameters of investigation or are defined, not in terms of their ability to perform as a competent parent, but in the role of the *non-ill*. They are often compared favourably to their mentally 'defective' partner even when they might be seen to be performing poorly in their various roles as husbands or fathers. For example, Zetlin et al (1985) make extensive use of case studies in their work on diversity, shared functioning, and the role of benefactors. Here, men as partners and/or fathers are either absent from the investigation or they are presented as 'saviours' (even when their role as effective partners would appear to be dubious). They describe the case of Debbie, who "has deafness in one ear and mental slowness", and who "married Michael, a *normal* man who supported her" (Zetlin et al, 1985, p 76, emphasis added). However, the fact that 'normal' Michael is later found "beating [Debbie] and involving himself with another woman" is not considered significant in terms of the chronicity and perpetuation of Debbie's symptoms, nor in relation to wider family relationships.

Cleaver et al also recognise the emphasis on women's roles as mothers in child protection work: "What does become evident is that irrespective of which parent figure was representing the problem, professionals involved in the child protection process directed their attention to working with mothers" (1999, p 4).

The influence of risk assumptions

It is not unrealistic to suggest that the negative tone of this earlier medical research could be translated within medical practice as assumption or misconception about the nature of mental illness and how it affects families, and particularly children, when parents become ill. In their 1983 review of the medical literature regarding the impacts of physical and mental impairment on families, Buck and Hohmann proposed:

> Most generally and obviously the presumed effects on children are just that – assumptions without empirical basis. The predictions of identification theory also are based on two premises, both of which are not supported by research: (1) it is assumed that individuals with disabilities are psychologically maladapted, and (2) children identify only with the parent, an assumption that disregards other role models in the child's environment (eg relatives, friends, teachers) …. After descriptions of children with disabled parents appear in the literature and are subsequently quoted, they may be repeated often enough to be taken as 'gospel'. As a result, few have investigated the question empirically in order to determine if the deleterious effects on children actually occur. (Buck and Hohmann, 1983, p 210)

Therefore, it may be equally valid to suppose that this negative tone has also passed out of medical research and, to some degree, helped to shape public (and professional) perception about what it means for individuals and families to be mentally ill. Buck and Hohmann concluded:

> It is commonly assumed by both professionals and the general public that all psychological effects of disability are negative, ie disruptive, dissatisfying and disorganising. (1983, p 211)

We can account in a number of ways for the perpetuation of the assumption among medical scientists concerning the impacts of mental illness for individuals and families. First, studies themselves often demonstrated clear methodological limitations. By the beginning of the 1980s, social and medical researchers came to a number of conclusions when reviewing the medical literature on the impacts of parental mental illness on families and children:

- studies often drew firm conclusions from second hand evidence;
- there was a tendency for researchers to 'laboratorise' their subjects;
- studies often failed to use adequate controls in relation to the contexts in which mental illness occurred.

At the time, Schilling et al argued that studies were "weakened by small sample size, lack of control and inadequate measurement of the critical variables of IQ, parental competence and child maltreatment" (1982, p 201). In looking at the medical evidence on the risk factors that predispose the children of impaired parents to psychological vulnerabilities, Roy found that the evidence was far from satisfactory or conclusive, commenting that "Paucity of well designed research in this field is responsible for this state of affairs" (1990, p 118).

Roy was also interested in studies that drew firm conclusions about the (negative) impacts of parental mental illness on children in particular. He found that "reports of children's difficulties were mostly based on subjective observations of the parents ... minimally questions can and should be raised about the reliability and validity of such observations" (1990, p 119)[3]. It is certainly true that, where the medical and social research considers the consequences of parental mental illness for children, children themselves are rarely consulted or used in sample surveys (see Alderson, 1995; see also Appendix A of this volume).

What is interesting – and our evidence also confirms this – is that, while much social and medical research (and practice) does not include children, conclusions are frequently drawn and specific examples are given about a wide range of consequences for children when parents have serious mental health problems (Box 1.2; see also Chapter Four of this volume). Given that children often are not included in research processes, we must assume that outcomes here are based on the presumptions of the researchers themselves.

Another way we can account for the predominance of negativity in the medical literature, and how such negativity becomes a matter of perpetuation and inheritance within the medical sciences, is recognising medicine's heavy reliance on biological determinism. This means that the influences of external social, ecological and political dynamics in determining adults' vulnerability to mental illness, as well as the impacts of these conditions among individuals, are consistently overlooked. Therefore, until the mid to late 1980s the medical literature failed to consider the consequences of mental illness for parents and families beyond aetiology and intra-familial deterioration. Thurman noted the absence of any ecological perspective in the medical literature during this time, and suggested that "affective disorders do not exist, or occur within, the vacuum of the family" (1985, p 35).

Thurman's work reflected an increasing convergence between medical and social research in trying to understand mental illness in a wider, ecological context. Discussing the concept of ecological congruence in a study of families where parental impairment occurred, Thurman asserted that, "like the early researchers concerned with mother–child relations, we have overlooked the fact that there is a mutuality of effect between the individual and the environment" (1985, p 36)[4].

This idea shifted the focus away from looking primarily at the (mainly negative) risk associations of parental mental illness and childhood to a wider view of family life, which could also be affected by a range of other factors:

No human behavior is inherently deviant as a valid basis for the conceptualisation of deviancy. The judgement made about a particular behavior or set of characteristics can be made relative only to the social context in which it has occurred. (Thurman, 1985, p 38)

From the mid to late 1980s, research increasingly focused on wider issues that were relevant to families and individuals who are also affected by mental ill health. Medical research has also taken on board ideas about aetiology, for example, that are not only located in clinical evidence, but also acknowledge the significance of environmental and other factors (see Jones, 2000; Murray, 2000). We now know, for instance, that the causes and outcomes of a range of mental illnesses are not simply biologically determined, but in fact rely on a complex interplay between neuro-developmental factors and the environment in which the illness first occurs. Schizophrenia, for example, is increasingly seen as a multifactorial condition, "like diabetes or coronary heart disease [resulting] from the cumulative operation of a number of risk factors, some but not all of which are neuro-developmental" (Murray, 2000). However, it seems – and our evidence confirms this – that this broader understanding about the causes and effects of adult mental illness from a medical perspective are not necessarily filtering down to health and social work professionals on the 'front line' of service delivery. Rather, these professionals continue to make assumptions about outcomes for children and families in such cases. This is something we discuss in more detail in the following chapters of this volume.

Evidence from child protection studies on the effects of parental mental ill health on children

It has been observed that, outside medical studies, research on the prevalence and impact of parental mental illness is "sparse" (Cleaver et al, 1999, p 12). Therefore, considering the inherited medical assumption that children are at risk when their parents are mentally ill, how do we ensure that professionals and practitioners (in children's services, for example):

> achieve a mental health perspective which includes an increased awareness of the impact of parental psychiatric disorder on child development and on child care practice decision making? (Falkov, 1997, p 2)

It would seem that looking to the conclusions of child protection studies here may prove as problematic as relying on 'evidence' from medical investigations. In reviewing the child protection literature, Cleaver et al show that a "significant proportion" (1999, p 13) of children who come into the child protection system are from families where there is parental mental illness, drug or alcohol dependence, or domestic violence. In multi-problem families (where more than one of these issues is present, and domestic violence especially), children are often even more vulnerable to abuse. As suspected cases of child abuse go through the formal child protection system (and as the case is considered increasingly serious), a large proportion of confirmed abuse cases are found to be of children with parent(s) with mental illness.

In his review of the same literature, Falkov (1997) also noted the link between parental mental illness and child abuse. He cites O'Hagan (1993) who asserted that, "where parents have a mental illness, the emotional and psychological abuse of children will be inevitable" (O'Hagan, in Falkov, 1997, p 2). Furthermore, women with mental ill health are often the subjects of investigation in child protection studies, but it is their role as mothers that is scrutinised, particularly their importance in terms of (negative) outcomes for children[5].

While the child protection research clearly shows an association between parental mental illness and child welfare concerns, in particular with the most serious forms of abuse and neglect, this association is complex and far from 'causal' in nature. We must remember that child protection studies often focus on families where there are extant child welfare concerns, rather than drawing their samples from the general population (where a risk has not already been either established or assumed).

Mental illness is found in many families and among many parents (the prevalence of mental illness is discussed in detail in Chapter Two of this volume). Child protection research shows that mental illness is particularly prevalent in families where there are serious child welfare concerns and where child protection investigations and interventions are underway. We also know, however, that child protection interventions can often represent knee-jerk approaches that are based more on the individual concerns of the professionals involved and a lack of adequate information on the families concerned, than on concrete evidence that the children of mentally ill parents are being neglected or abused (Schuff and Asen, 1996).

It is also important to note that, as well as parental mental illness, other 'common' social characteristics can also be found in many 'abusive' families, such as poverty, low income, social exclusion and other disadvantages (Becker and MacPherson, 1988). However, *most* poor and disadvantaged people, and *most* parents with mental illness, do not abuse or maltreat their children. Nor, might we add, do *most* children of parents with mental illness (or physical illness or disability) become young carers. If this was the case, these children would be a far more prevalent and visible group.

According to Cleaver et al, "much research indicates that in isolation problem alcohol/drug use or mental illness of a parent presents little risk of significant harm to children" (1999, p 23). They argue:

> The best predictor of adverse long-term effects on children is the co-existence of mental illness or problem drinking with family disharmony. Where families remain cohesive and harmonious, the children generally grow up relatively unharmed. (Cleaver et al, 1999, p 23)

Our evidence appears to confirm this (see Chapter Two of this volume). However, even in disharmonious homes most children may not show any problems:

> It is important that professionals do not pathologise all children who live in families where a parent suffers from mental illness .... As we have already noted, although these issues serve to qualify children as 'in need' a significant proportion show no long-term behavioural or emotional disturbance. Nonetheless, the health and development of a considerable number of children living in these circumstances are adversely affected and would benefit from services. (Cleaver et al, 1999, pp 44-5)

The National Society for the Prevention of Cruelty to Children (NSPCC) survey of the experiences of a national sample of young people (Cawson, 2002) also confirms this analysis:

> Most studies which identify mental illness as a factor [in child maltreatment] give figures for occurrence of approximately a quarter to a third of maltreating families, so that although it is clearly important for some families, it cannot be the primary explanation for most abusive acts to children, or for neglect. (Cawson, 2002, p 23)

A recent inter-agency guide to safeguarding and promoting the welfare of children (DH, HO and DfEE, 1999) makes clear that, while parental mental illness may lead to some parents being neglectful or abusive of their children, many parents with mental illness do not behave in this way and their children do not suffer from any long-term, damaging, consequences (see Appendix B: 1999 (iv) of this volume for a full discussion of the inter-agency guide). It is equally important to understand these situations – that is, where parental mental illness has no or few negative consequences for children – as it is to understand why and where it plays a damaging role:

> Mental illness in a parent does not necessarily have an adverse impact on a child, but it is essential always to assess its implications for any children involved in the family .... The adverse effects on children of parental mental illness are less likely when parental problems are mild, last only a short time, are not associated with family disharmony, and do not result in the family breaking up. Children may also be protected when the other parent or a family member can help respond to the child's needs. Children most at risk of significant harm are those who feature within parental delusions, and children who become targets for parental aggression or rejection, or who are neglected as a result of parental mental illness. (DH, HO and DfEE, 1999, p 9)

The literature on young caring – evidence from research

Research on young caring began more than a decade ago, during a time when both medical and social scientists had begun to look at the wider issues influencing the consequences for families of parental mental impairment (see DeChillo et al, 1987; Feldman et al, 1987; Lynch and Bakley, 1989). At this time, methods and systems of supporting parents with mental illnesses based on family-oriented policy interventions were also being considered (see Gorell Barnes, 1996; Kavanagh and Knapp, 1996; Marlowe, 1996; Falkov, 1998; Cleaver et al, 1999).

Within this new environment, researchers looking more closely at young caring in general as a 'welfare issue' (when parents had a range of mental and physical impairments) were trying to gauge the extent of the issue on a national level. However, estimating the numbers of young carers in this way has often proved problematic. There are a number of reasons for this:

1. Early small-scale studies (rather unhelpfully) suggested young caring was relatively uncommon. Indeed, O'Neill compared the incidence of young caring at the time to that of serious traffic accidents: "If adult caring is on a comparable scale with unemployment, young caring is probably on a similar scale to severe road accidents" (1988, p 2).

2. Identifying young carers in order to gain some insight into their numbers often proved difficult because families were wary of divulging the circumstances in which they had to rely on their children for care (see Meredith, 1991; Aldridge and Becker, 1993a).

3. Identification of cases in practice relies on the perceptiveness and understanding of professionals in recognising the triggers for young caring. Research evidence consistently points to failures in this respect (see SSI, 1995; see also Chapter Five of this volume).

4. The stigma often associated with adult mental illness might also suggest that parents affected in this way may be less open about the nature of their illnesses and how their domestic care arrangements are organised (see Frank et al, 1999).

The prevalence of young caring

However, it is possible to extrapolate figures from a number of different studies and data that tell us something about the numbers of young caring. In the UK, almost three million children under the age of 16 (equivalent to 23% of all children) live in households with one family member "hampered in daily activities by any chronic physical or mental health problem, illness or disability" (Eurostat, 1997, cited in Becker et al, 1998, p xii). We cannot be precise about how many of these children are young carers because studies conducted to date have been largely unable to provide reliable estimates of a potential national population of children with caring responsibilities. This difficulty has been compounded by the fact that there has been no uniformity in the definition used by researchers, or in the 'age-band' being studied. Becker et al (1998, Chapter 1) review critically the early attempts by researchers to calculate the number of young carers. National estimates have ranged from 10,000 young carers, to between 15,000 and 40,000 (Mahon and Higgins, 1995), with the latest estimate by the Office for National Statistics (ONS) being between 19,000 and 51,000 (ONS, 1996).

The ONS calculation is for the number of young carers aged 8-17 in Britain who provide substantial and regular care. This would mean – based on the national figure of just under seven million 8-17 year-olds – that around 0.27% (low), 0.46% (mid) or 0.72% (high) of all these 8-17 year-olds would be young carers. Put another way, the ONS calculation would suggest that anywhere between one quarter of 1% to three quarters of 1% of all children aged 8-17 are young carers at any one time. However, as Becker et al (1998, pp 17-18) point out, the way in which the ONS definition of young carers has been operationalised, and the way in which the data have been collected, analysed and interpreted, all give some cause for concern.

Secondary analysis of 1985 General Household Survey data, conducted by Parker (1992, 1994), indicates that the number of children involved in care-giving may be considerably higher than the ONS figures suggest. Parker was able to determine that 17% of carers aged 16-35 had caring responsibilities before their 16th birthday, and that one third of these had been assisting their parents:

> This means that of the 1.2 million carers aged 35 and under in 1985, some 212,000 had been providing care since before the age of 16 and, of those, around 68,000 for a parent. (Parker, 1994, p 9)

More recently, the Scottish Executive has calculated that 1% – that is, 6,000 – of *all* family carers in Scotland are under the age of 16. This is the first 'official' national estimate for the number of young carers in Scotland, based on data from the Scottish Household Survey 1999 (Scottish Executive, 2001). If this proportion was to be applied across Britain as a whole, with its 6.8 million carers aged 16+ (2000 General Household Survey data; see Maher and Green, 2002), then around 68,000 might be counted as young carers under the age of 16.

Evidence from child maltreatment studies

Indications that the extent of young caring in Britain may be greater than previously thought also come from a recent NSPCC study of the prevalence of child abuse and maltreatment in Britain (Cawson et al, 2000). Nearly 3,000 young people aged 18-24 (1,235 men, 1,634 women) were asked about their childhood experiences. The findings are "representative of the total UK population of 18-24 year olds" (Cawson et al, 2000, p 7).

The young people were also asked about the responsibilities they had to take on during their childhood. Almost three quarters (74%) said that the amount of independence and responsibility they had experienced during childhood was 'about right'. One in ten said they had too much (3% said 'far too much') and a slightly greater proportion (13%) said they had too little responsibility (2% said far too little):

> In total 14% said that they regularly had some form of adult responsibilities in their childhood. Although there were some gender differences, the marked differences are in social grade, with respondents in C2 and DE grades at least twice as likely to have had these responsibilities than those in AB grades. With a sample of 18–24 year olds, this is likely to reflect the respondents' reduced educational opportunities due to carer responsibilities. (Cawson et al, 2000, p 16)

Some of the 'adult' responsibilities identified by the young people have much in common with the tasks and responsibilities performed by young carers. Table 1.2 identifies the specific adult-like responsibilities that some young people undertook during their childhood, as identified in the NSPCC survey. Almost 4% of *all* young people (4% of boys and 3% of girls) said that they *regularly had to care for someone in their family who was ill or disabled*. This group could be

Table 1.2: Experience of adult responsibilities in childhood

	Total	Male	Female	AB	CI	C2	DE
		Sex			Social grade		
Unweighted base	2,869	1,235	1,634	435	944	627	847
Weighted base	2,869	1,434	1,435	416	1,101	594	744
	%	%	%	%	%	%	%
Regularly had to care for someone in your family who was ill or disabled	4	4	3	2	2	5	5
Often had to look after self as parents had problems of their own (such as alcohol and drug abuse)	3	2	4	I	3	3	5
Parents regularly depended on you for support for emotional problems (arising from divorce, separation, bereavement, for example)	8	6	10	5	8	9	10
Regularly had to look after self because parents went away	2	2	2	0	2	I	3
None of the above	82	82	82	91	85	81	74

Source: Cawson et al, 2000, p 17, Table 8.

considered to be 'young carers'. Five per cent of young people in the 'lower' social grades (C2, DE) provided regular care, compared to only 2% in the 'higher' social grades (AB, C1). In other words, those in the 'lower' social grades were more than twice as likely to take on regular caring responsibilities for an ill or disabled family member than those in the higher social grades.

Another 3% of all young people said that they *often had to look after themselves as their parents had problems of their own*, such as alcohol or drug abuse. Girls were twice as likely as boys to have to do this, and those in the lower social grades were also far more likely to have to do this than young people from the higher social grades.

Another 8% of all young people said that *their parents regularly depended on them for support for emotional problems.* Young people brought up in DE social grade households were twice as likely as young people from AB households to provide emotional support to distressed parents, and girls were more likely than boys to do so.

The NSPCC researchers suggest that:

> Almost a fifth [of young people] had regularly to shoulder responsibilities at an early age because their parents were ill, disabled, had substance abuse problems or had needed emotional support through divorce or bereavement. (Cawson et al, 2000, p 20)

Box 1.3: Sources of data on illness/disability and caring during childhood

Findings (%)	Numbers involved	Source (reference)
Proportion of children aged under 16 living in families with one family member hampered in daily activities by any chronic physical or mental health problem, illness or disability: **23%**	Approximately three million children under 16 live in families with illness/disability in the UK	Eurostat, 1997 (Becker et al, 1998)
Proportion of all 8-17 year olds that will be young carers: **0.27%-0.72%**	19,000–51,000 young carers (aged 8-17) in Britain	Office for National Statistics (ONS, 1996)
Proportion of all 18-24 year-olds who will have regularly cared for an ill or disabled relative during their own childhood: **4%**	173,040 young people aged 18-24	NSPCC (Cawson et al, 2000; Cawson, 2002)
Proportion of carers aged 16-35 that had caring responsibilities before their 16th birthday: **17%**	212,000 adult carers (aged 16-35) cared during their own childhood	1985 General Household Survey (Parker, 1994)
Proportion of all family carers in Scotland who are young carers: **1%**	6,000 young carers aged under 16 in Scotland	The Scottish Executive (Scottish Executive, 2001)

These data suggest that some form of caring by children – for ill or disabled family members, or self-care – and particularly emotional support for distressed parents, is far more common in childhood than had previously been thought. This does not mean, however, that all these young people could be described as young carers. Indeed, over half of all these young people would not generally be considered to be young carers (particularly the 8% of young people whose parents regularly depended on them for support for emotional problems arising from divorce, separation or bereavement).

What is clear, however, is that around 4% of the young people in the NSPCC survey could be defined as young carers because, during their childhood, they regularly had to care for someone in their family who was ill or disabled.

Making sense of the data

It is hard to reach definitive conclusions about the prevalence of young caring since each of the studies reported above relate to different groups of people – that is, some refer to carers, others to young people in general – and to different age bands. Box 1.3 summarises and compares the findings from these different studies.

The different sources and their findings cannot be reconciled because they each measure different things. However, the recent NSPCC survey of a nationally representative sample of 18-24 year-olds may be the most reliable source of data to date, and the most useful in *indicating* the extent to which young people *in general* are likely to have had *regular caring responsibilities during their childhood*. The NSPCC data suggest that about 4% of 18-24 year-olds will have been regularly caring during their childhood for a sick or disabled family member. These young people can be considered to have been young carers. Put another way, young people aged 18-24 have a 4% chance of being a young carer in their childhood. These data show that regular caring in childhood is far more common than previously thought, and would indicate that the ONS figures of 19,000–51,000 young carers are likely to seriously underestimate the prevalence of young carers in Britain.

The prevalence of children caring for parents with mental illness in the literature on young caring

Our knowledge of the *extent* of young caring in the context of parental mental illness has been extended in particular by three quantitative studies conducted between 1995 and 2001. As more specialist young-carer projects have evolved and developed (from just two in 1992 to around 120 or so within a decade), it has become possible to conduct large-scale national and regional surveys of this group of children, drawing on the projects themselves as a source of data.

The first two large-scale national surveys of young carers, which also presented in-depth profiles of children caring for parents with mental illness and other conditions, were conducted in the second half of the 1990s. In the first of these, Dearden and Becker (1995) collected data on 641 young carers in contact with 26 specialist projects across Britain. A few years later these same researchers, and using the same methodology, were able to collect data from 69 projects, compiling information on a far larger sample of 2,303 young carers (Dearden and Becker, 1998). More recently, the London Young Carers Workers Forum (a forum for the two dozen dedicated projects across London Boroughs) conducted a regional survey of young carers in contact with London projects, as well as providing an overview of the projects themselves and the types of support they offer (Brook Chen and Baker, 2001). Together, these three surveys provide a valuable statistical profile of young carers in contact with specialist projects and also of those young people looking after parents with mental illness.

In Dearden and Becker's two surveys (1995, 1998), over one quarter (29%)

---

of young carers in contact with projects across Britain were caring for family members with mental health problems (including drug and alcohol misuse), and in most cases the person receiving care was a parent. This equated to 681 young carers out of 2,303 in their second study (Dearden and Becker, 1998, p 13). Our analysis of the data presented in the London Young Carers Workers Forum report (Brook Chen and Baker, 2001) shows that around 24% of those receiving care were identified as having mental health problems (which would equate to just under 600 people), with another 6% (around 133 people) having drug or alcohol misuse problems. Therefore, in the London survey, 30% of people receiving care from young carers had mental health problems or misused alcohol and drugs – an almost identical proportion to that found in Dearden and Becker's two national surveys (1995, 1998). The London figure (2001) is also very similar to the proportion of young carers looking after parents with mental illness cited in a number of evaluation reports conducted for some London projects in the late 1990s. For example, in the London Boroughs of Westminster and Southwark, evaluation reports have shown that nearly one third of the families in contact with projects experienced mental health problems (Mumoz, 1998; Newton and Becker, 1999).

The London 'average' of 30% (derived from Brook Chen and Baker, 2001) disguises the considerable variations that exist in the proportion of people with mental illness who are known to individual projects. The data show, for example, that in some London projects the proportion of people identified specifically with mental health problems and being cared for by children can be as low as 10%, while in others it could be as high as 40%. While considerable local variations exist, the three surveys reported above do indicate that, on average, just under one third of young carers known to specialist projects are likely to be caring for family members (mostly parents) with mental health problems (this figure includes those family members who misuse drugs and alcohol). It is possible to relate this figure to data on the incidence of young caring (Box 1.3). Therefore, one third of the 4% of young people aged 18-24 who had regularly cared for an ill or disabled relative during their own childhood (Cawson et al, 2000) are likely to have cared for a parent with mental health problems. This would mean that young people aged 18-24 have a 1.3% chance in their childhood of caring for a parent with mental illness. Using the ONS (1996) data, it is also possible to suggest that at any one time between 6,000 and 17,000 young carers will be looking after mentally ill parents.

Outcomes for children when they care

Recent quantitative *and* qualitative surveys based on *known* young carers have provided us with a statistical profile of young caring, as well as some general characteristics about these children and an indication of some of the consequences for them when they care (see Table 1.3, Boxes 1.4 and 1.5).

While we now have greater insight into the outcomes for children of caring for parents who have physical impairments, less is known about the specific

Box 1.4: Some characteristics of young carers in the UK

- Average age is 12
- 86% are of compulsory school age
- 57% are girls, 43% are boys
- 14% are from minority ethnic communities
- 54% live in lone parent families
- Most young carers (63%) are caring for someone with physical illness; 29% are caring for someone with mental health problems; 14% are caring for someone with learning difficulties; sensory problems account for 4% of young carers
- 12% are caring for more than one person
- One quarter receive no other professional support except for contact with a young carers project

Source: Dearden and Becker, 1998

Box 1.5: Outcomes for children when they care unsupported

- Restricted opportunities for social networking and for developing peer friendships (Bilsborrow, 1992; Aldridge and Becker, 1993a; Dearden and Becker, 1995, 1998).
- Poverty and social exclusion (Dearden and Becker, 2000a).
- Limited opportunities for taking part in leisure and other activities (Aldridge and Becker, 1993a).
- Health problems (Becker et al, 1998; Hill, 1999).
- Emotional difficulties (Elliott, 1992; Dearden and Becker, 1995, 1998).
- Educational problems (Marsden, 1995; Dearden and Becker, 1998; Crabtree and Warner, 1999).
- Limited horizons and aspirations for the future (Aldridge and Becker, 1993a, 1994).
- Stigma 'by association', particularly where parents have mental health problems or misuse alcohol or drugs, or have AIDS/HIV (Elliott, 1992; Landells and Pritlove, 1994; Imrie and Coombes, 1995).
- Lack of understanding from peers about young carers' lives and circumstances (Aldridge and Becker, 1993a, 1994; Dearden and Becker, 1998).
- Fear of professional interventions leading to family separations (Meredith, 1991; Aldridge and Becker, 1993a, 1994; Dearden and Becker, 1998).
- Young carers' silence and secretive behaviour because of the fear of public hostility or punitive professional responses (Aldridge and Becker, 1993b; Crabtree and Warner, 1999; Frank et al, 1999).
- Difficulties making a successful transition from childhood to adulthood (Frank et al, 1999; Dearden and Becker, 2000a).

Table 1.3: Percentage of young carers performing various caring roles, 1995 and 1997

Caring tasks	1995	1997
Domestic	65	72
General	61	57
Emotional support	25	43
Intimate	23	21
Childcare	11	7
Other	10	29

Source: Dearden and Becker, 1995, 1998.

experiences of children who care for parents with severe and enduring mental illnesses. Although it is recognised that in some families where there is parental mental illness, children "may take on caring responsibilities within the family as a result" it is also clear that "often little attention is paid to this issue" (Cleaver et al, 1999, p 99).

Until recently (and until the outcomes of our study, for example, are more widely disseminated), the consequences for children of living with and caring for a parent with mental illness have been based on past medical and child protection studies. These studies suppose that:

> With both mental and physical illness in a parent, children *may* have caring responsibilities placed upon them inappropriate to their years, leading them to be worried and anxious. If they are depressed, parents *may* neglect their own and their children's physical and emotional needs. In some circumstances, some forms of mental illness *may* blunt parents' emotions and feelings, or cause them to behave towards their children in bizarre or violent ways .... (DH, HO and DfEE, 1999, p 9, emphasis added)

Conclusions from the NSPCC survey data on the experiences of children and the prevalence of maltreatment indicated that:

> Young carers who said they often had to look after a sick or disabled family member rarely regarded themselves as maltreated. But research assessments [by professionals, of young carers] indicated that many of them experienced maltreatment, especially physical abuse and absence of physical care. This was usually attributed to parents' mental health problems rather than to physical illness or disability. (Cawson, 2002, p 48)

However, the report also suggested that, "Being a young carer was not in itself defined as neglect" (Cawson, 2002, p 36). While a number of young carers in the NSPCC survey *did* report that they had suffered from neglect or abuse, and in some cases sexual abuse, this was certainly not the experience for *most* young people who had caring responsibilities during their childhood.

A number of other studies have been conducted into children's experiences of living with and caring for parents with mental illness. However, these surveys have either focused on retrospective analysis of case study work, have been large-scale statistical investigations about young caring in general, or, where qualitative work has been carried out these studies have been small-scale and, therefore, more problematic in terms of drawing any firm conclusions about outcomes for children.

In respect of child protection work, it is important to be aware of the different perspectives that children and professionals have of childhood experiences and what constitutes maltreatment. One must also be careful not to confuse cause and effect, and the extent of the problem. Many children who are subject to child welfare or child protection concerns *do* live in families with parental mental illness, and many young carers are also subject to child welfare concerns – especially in families with parental mental illness. However, there is no evidence to show that, by itself, parental mental illness *necessarily* causes child maltreatment or *necessarily* leads to children taking on caring responsibilities, even though in some families with mental illness either or both of these experiences do occur for children.

In Dearden and Becker's study of 60 young carers' transitions to adulthood (2000a), one third of the parents had mental health problems. When it came to leaving home, Dearden and Becker noted that:

> In families where a parent had a severe and enduring mental health problem, young carers' spatial transitions were sometimes premature and traumatic if, for example, the young person reached crisis point or had to be received into public care. (2000a, p 2)

Data from Dearden and Becker's 1997 survey of more than 2,000 known young carers found a number of significant associations for children who were caring for parents with mental health problems. The first was that these children were more likely than other young carers to provide emotional support to their parents. The second was that they were less likely to be providing intimate caring or general nursing type tasks. The third association was that most young carers whose parents have mental health problems did not receive an assessment of their own needs or of their ability to provide care and support (see Chapter Four of this volume).

Two small-scale *qualitative* studies to date have looked at children's particular experiences of caring in the context of parental mental ill health (Elliott, 1992; Landells and Pritlove, 1994). From these investigations it would seem that stigma – and coping with the behavioural consequences of mental ill health – can be significant factors in young carers' lives, perhaps more so than for those children whose parents have a physical, chronic illness or disability. For example, Elliott suggests that:

> Children of a parent with mental health problems have the added difficulty of dealing with bizarre behaviour. This behaviour is difficult for adults to

comprehend but for children trying to make sense of their parents it is at best confusing and at worst impossible. (1992, p 25)

Children's concerns about the behavioural outcomes of schizophrenia are also reported in Landells and Pritlove's (1994) study of young carers. This study also found evidence of young carers being "taken into the parent with schizophrenia's delusional system" (1994, p 4).

However, these studies, as we have mentioned, were relatively small-scale investigations (for example, Elliott's study involved just nine young carers). Although they represent important first steps in this previously uncharted field of study, they perhaps contribute less to our further understanding of the nature of relationships between young carers and their mentally ill parents. Neither do these studies explore the nature of professional relationships nor any differences between young caring in the context of parental mental ill health and parents with physical illnesses and disabilities.

However, perhaps the lesson we *can* learn from these, and other, studies (and Elliott's in particular) is the need for caution when looking more closely at children's experiences of caring for parents with mental illnesses. For although Elliott concluded that young carers require "information, support and social contact" when their parents have mental health problems, he also suggested they are in need of "*better parenting*" (Elliott, 1992, p 2, emphasis added). In this respect it is perhaps unwise to question the efficacy of parenting on the basis of diagnoses and without reference either to control studies or to clearer definitions about what 'better parenting' is or might be.

Conclusion

We have seen how negative and damaging associations between children's experiences and the presence in families of parental mental illness have been reinforced by medical and, to a lesser extent, social research in this area. However, in reviewing evidence from these sources it becomes clear that sound empirical proof has yet to be produced to confirm the validity of the suggestion that children are at risk of neglect or serious harm and abuse simply on the basis of a parent's diagnosis. As Roy has argued: "Overall, the answer to the question of risk factors has to be viewed as very incomplete" (1990, p 19).

Negative and sometimes deterministic medical research, alongside some child protection studies and other social research, has contributed in part to current public perceptions about what it means to be a parent with mental ill health. However, it is important to point out that other agencies, such as current health and social care organisations, have also been implicated in the perpetuation of negative associations. Göpfert et al talk about the risk of intensifying "the negative effects of pathologising commonly associated with professional responses to serious mental health problems" (1996, p 2). Service users themselves have also talked about dehumanising mental health services (see Perkins, 2000). And in his follow-up work with 32 mental health service users, Philo (1996) found that respondents were undermined by a medical diagnosis that they understood, largely from *media representations and mental health service delivery processes*, to be stigmatising.

Research investigating the nature and effects of caring on children, which began more than a decade ago, has contributed in part to our understanding about consequences of care for children whose parents are impaired in some way. However, we know less about the specific outcomes here for children whose parents have severe and enduring *mental* health problems. Our evidence would suggest that in this context the picture of co-residency and care, as well as children's inter- and extra-familial relationships (with parents, other relatives and with professionals), is a complex one. It is these relationships as well as children's other experiences that we wish to explore in the following chapters of this volume.

Notes

[1] See Appendix B: 1983, 1991 (i), 1992 (ii), 1994 (ii), 1994 (iii), 1995 (iv), 1996 (i), 1998 (i), 1999 (ii), 2002 (ii) of this volume for specific examples.

[2] See, for example, Rieder, 1973; Sameroff and Zax, 1973; Schulsinger, 1976; Hatfield, 1978; Seifer and Sameroff, 1981; Schilling et al, 1982; Orvaschel et al, 1988.

[3] Social scientific investigation that has considered the impacts of parental impairment from a child's perspective – particularly in the work on young carers – has been increasingly based on qualitative work with the children themselves (see Becker et al, 1998).

[4] This growing understanding that ecological and other external factors can strongly influence, if not determine, the nature of family relationships (both intra- and extra-familial) has not been confined to medical researchers and their understanding of the nature and impact of mental illness. A Department of Health report, *Framework for the assessment of children in need and their families* (DH, 2000), also considers environmental factors to be crucial in determining the nature and extent of children's needs (see also Appendix B: 2000 (i) of this volume). We return to this report in Chapter Five of this volume.

[5] Falkov cites studies that have found that 'depressed mothers' demonstrate constricted behaviour and expression, and flat speech. He also refers to Weissman and Paykel's 'seminal' work (1974), which found that "at the simplest level, the helplessness and hostility which are associated with acute depression interfere with the ability to be a warm and consistent mother" (Weissman and Paykel, 1974, p 1).

TWO

The effects of mental illness on parents and relationships with their children

"I don't want my son to end up like I have. I mean, really, I don't think I'm a fit mother for him ... but I love him to bits. I've tried to be a good parent. I've tried everything I can. I've really had to bring the three boys up on my own. Since the two oldest ones was four and five. I think out of their 20-odd years, they've only had a dad for five, on and off, and Adam [who has a different father] for three months ... about that time. I tried my best I could with them. Which has just not been good enough has it?" (Lone parent, aged 47 and mother of three, suffering from depression, epilepsy, asthma and thrombosis)

This testimony exemplifies the concerns and fears many parents experience when their lives are affected by mental illness. The evidence from our study of 40 families where parents have mental illness (Table 2.1) clearly shows that the prime concerns of parents with mental health problems relate to the prognosis of their illness and, more significantly, how this will affect their children in terms of their development and their transition into adulthood. Many parents, as we have just read, also feel that the onset and chronicity of their mental illness seriously undermines their parenting skills. This effect is heightened when they do not receive effective treatment or support. Some parents recognise that others, not least professionals and those in local communities, consider the parenting skills of adults with mental illness to be inadequate or ineffective *because of the presence of mental ill health*, and that parents in these contexts are unable to protect their children from harm or neglect (the stigma associated with mental ill health when *parents* are thus affected is discussed later in this chapter).

It is clear from our evidence – and elsewhere, in fact – that mental illness in and of itself does not *necessarily* put the children of parents thus affected at increased risk of physical or psychological harm (see also Chapter One of this volume). However, we know that children's experiences of caring for, and co-residency with, parents who have mental health problems can be negative. We also know that adverse experiences here can also be influenced by a range of other mediating factors that can have serious consequences for children and family life (see Chapter Three of this volume). In this chapter we examine further the caring and filial relationships parents share with their children when parents have mental health problems and children are providing care.

Table 2.1: Profiles of parents and family composition from first- and second-round interviews

Details	First round	Second round
Age (range)	31-57	31-57
Average age	40	41
Median age	40	41
	Number of cases	**Number of cases**
Female care recipients	35	25
Male care recipients	5	3
Mothers cared for by daughter	24	15
Mothers cared for by son	11	10
Fathers cared for by daughter	3	2
Fathers cared for by son	2	1
Two-parent families	15	11
with single co-resident child	6	5
with more than one co-resident child	9	6
Lone parent families	25	17
with single co-resident child	9	5
with more than one co-resident child	16	12
Care recipients in paid employment	1	0
Care recipients subsisting *only* on benefits	30	22
Care recipients whose partners were in paid employment	9	6
Housing		
Owner occupiers	9	4
Private rented	1	1
Housing association	8	5
Rented council	21	17
Part own/rent	1	1

Furthermore, we want to understand the factors that can cause and perpetuate mental illness and thereby create impediments to effective parenting *from the point of view of the parents themselves* who face these obstructions on a daily basis. These factors include:

- *genetic susceptibility* to mental illness (individuals are more at risk of inheriting mental illness from a first-degree relative);
- *expeditious factors* (for example, bereavement, divorce, parental separation, parent relationship problems, onset of other health problems);
- factors that are of an *enduring* nature (ongoing housing or financial problems, lack of effective support inputs, chronicity of other health problems, and so on).

First, however, we want to examine the prevalence of mental illness among adults and parents.

The prevalence of mental illness among adults and parents in the general population

The most reliably comprehensive, up-to-date, and nationally representative source of data on the extent of mental illness is the Office for Population Censuses and Surveys (OPCS) Survey of Psychiatric Morbidity in Great Britain, conducted between 1993 and 1994 (Meltzer et al, 1995). The survey provides information about the prevalence in Britain of psychiatric problems among adults, including parents, as well as their associated social disabilities and use of services.

The research obtained prevalence estimates for the relatively numerous, minor psychiatric disorders (neurotic psychopathology) and for the less frequently occurring major psychiatric disorders (psychotic psychopathology). Cleaver et al (1999, pp 24-6) present a useful description of these most common forms of mental illness, and in particular they highlight the impacts of symptoms on the daily lives of parents (see also Chapter Three of this volume).

Minor psychiatric disorders (neurotic psychopathology)

The OPCS survey of adults living in private households found that 160 per 1,000 of the adult population (that is, 16% of all adults, or nearly one in seven) experienced a neurotic disorder during the survey week. The neurotic disorders included fatigue, sleep problems, irritability, worry, depression, anxiety and so on. Table 2.2 shows the prevalence of neurotic disorders among the adult population.

Women are considerably more likely than men to experience any neurotic disorder. Lone parents and people living alone (or without close relatives) have the greatest chances of having neurotic symptoms compared with people living in couples with no children. Having children increased the prevalence of many of the symptoms, notably irritability. Unemployment is also very strongly associated with the prevalence of almost all neurotic symptoms. Indeed,

Table 2.2: The prevalence of neurotic disorders

Type	Rate per 1,000 of the adult population	Rate (%)[a]
Mixed anxiety and depressive disorder	77	7.7
Generalised anxiety disorder	31	3.1
Depressive episode	21	2.1
Obsessive compulsive disorder	12	1.2
Phobias	11	1.1
Panic disorder	8	0.8
Overall prevalence of neurotic disorder	160	16.0

Source: Meltzer et al, 1995, p xii.

[a] Figures are the rate per 1,000 of the adult population recalculated as a percentage (of 100).

the odds of having many of these symptoms are twice as high among unemployed people as those in full-time employment (Meltzer et al, 1995, pp xi–xii).

Major psychiatric disorders (psychotic psychopathology)

The OPCS survey also presents data on the extent of the more serious psychiatric disorders, including functional psychoses, and alcohol and drug dependence. These are summarised in Table 2.3.

The survey found that psychiatric disorders are strongly related to two factors in particular:

> The first, employment status, was related to most disorders: compared with those working full time, the odds of having most disorders were more than doubled among unemployed and economically inactive people. The second factor, age, was particularly related to alcohol and drug dependence, with the odds of these disorders decreasing with age. (Meltzer et al, 1995, p xii)

Mental illness among parents

Another key factor which strongly influences psychiatric morbidity, and one which is particularly relevant to our current study, is the type of family unit. The OPCS data show the prevalence of any neurotic disorder and functional psychoses are highest among families with children – either two parent families or lone parent families. Table 2.4 summarises the OPCS data on the prevalence of mental illness among parents. As the table illustrates, there is a higher rate of mental illness (of all types, including alcohol and drug dependence) among lone parents than for adults living as a couple with children. For example, lone parents are almost three times more likely than couples with children to have more serious, functional psychoses or drug dependence, and are almost twice as likely than couples with children to have some neurotic disorder.

Table 2.3: The prevalence of other psychiatric disorders

Type	Rate per 1,000 of the adult population	Rate (%)[a]
Functional psychosis (such as schizophrenia, manic depressive psychosis and schizo-affective disorder)	4	0.4
Alcohol dependence	47	4.7
Drug dependence	22	2.2

Source: Meltzer et al, 1995, p xii.

[a] Figures are the rate per 1,000 of the adult population recalculated as a percentage (of 100).

Table 2.4: The prevalence of mental illness among parents in the general population

	Couples with children		Lone parent with children	
Type of mental illness	Rate per 1,000	Rate (%)	Rate per 1,000	Rate (%)
Neurotic disorder	155	15.5	281	28.1
Functional psychoses	4	0.4	11	1.1
Alcohol dependence	27	2.7	38	3.8
Drug dependence	9	0.9	24	2.4

Source: Meltzer et al, 1995, Table 6.8, p 83 (adapted)

Other OPCS data show that there is a gender differentiation here (Meltzer et al, 1995, Table 6.8, p 83). Men living either as a couple with children or in lone parent families have a lower rate of neurotic disorder, functional psychoses and drug dependence than women in similar situations.

Additionally, mental illness is also strongly associated with social class. Those in unskilled and manual occupations have the highest rates of neurotic disorder and functional psychoses (Meltzer et al, 1995, Table 6.7, p 82). It has been suggested that vulnerability to mental disorder may be the result of social class-related factors, including adverse life events such as poverty, sexism or racism, and other forms of social disadvantage or oppression (Cleaver et al, 1999, p 12).

What is clear from the OPCS data is that a considerable number of children are living in families where at least one parent is suffering from a mental illness, and that lone parents are especially vulnerable to mental ill health.

Our sample

Table 2.5 presents a list of the range of the symptoms of mental illness described by the respondents in our study during the first- and second-round interviews. We can see that despite the nature of a patient's formal diagnosis (first column), the symptoms parents describe (second column) are often shared across different illnesses (for example, schizophrenia and personality disorder). Some of these symptoms seemed to be indicative of diagnoses other than the one that respondents had been given. For example, several respondents who had been diagnosed with depression also described hearing voices and experienced psychotic episodes and anxiety. This might suggest a need for diagnostic reassessment, but is perhaps more likely to be indicative of the ways in which the symptoms of mental illnesses present themselves and the fact that diagnoses rely on patterns of recognised symptoms or behaviours (which can and do fluctuate and transform over time). This may also account for the fact that some respondents had waited some considerable time for a firm diagnosis and that others had received more than one diagnosis since they had first become ill.

Table 2.5: Symptoms and incidence of mental illness and co-morbidity among parents in our sample

Mental illness/clinical diagnosis	Symptoms described by parents	First round (number of cases)	Second round (number of cases)
Unipolar disorder (depression) Severe and sometimes enduring episodic depression – lack of motivation, unhappiness, tearfulness and tiredness	Antisocial behaviour, agoraphobia, irritability, alcohol misuse, low self-esteem, unable to be alone, aggressive, self-harm, voices, psychotic episodes, audio and visual hallucinations, suicide thoughts and attempts, lack of motivation, eating disorders, panic attacks, tiredness, lack of concentration, over-compensation, tearfulness, insomnia, short tempered	29	20
Bipolar disorder (manic depression) Severe and sometimes enduring episodic depression with mania – includes hyperactivity, insomnia, irritability, psychotic symptoms and episodes, extravagant behaviour	Rapid cycling, ups and downs, suicide thoughts and attempts, difficulty maintaining friendships, anxiety, argumentative, picking on people, lack of motivation, verbally aggressive, poor concentration and memory, self-harm, alcohol misuse	8	6
Schizophrenia 'Disconnected' personality, inability to separate personal internal world from external world – accompanied by a lack of concentration, hallucinations, hearing voices, delusions, withdrawal, personal neglect	Suicide thoughts and attempts, voices, paranoia, auditory hallucinations, depression	3	3
Paranoid schizophrenia More common form of schizophrenia – see above	Alien voices, voices, suicide thoughts and attempts, aggression, paranoia	4	4
Personality disorder Enduring behaviours which may be seen to be inappropriate or intransigent in a range of personal and social situations – emotionally unstable, anxiety, dependency, antisocial behaviour, aggression, alcohol or substance misuse,	Self-harm, suicide thoughts and attempts, alcohol misuse, drug misuse, self-neglect, confusion, agoraphobia	2	2

Table 2.5: contd.../

Mental illness/clinical diagnosis	Symptoms described by parents	First round (number of cases)	Second round (number of cases)
Borderline personality disorder (see Personality disorder)	Suicide thoughts and attempts, self-harm, intolerance, obsessive cleaning, voices, memory loss	5	4
Obsessive compulsive disorder Anxiety disorder with obsessive compulsive behaviours	Obsessive locking of doors and windows, fearfulness, anxiety	3	2
Body dysmorphia Anxiety disorder typified by self-loathing (particularly of body part/s) – also paranoia	Self-loathing (of body parts), self-harm, obsessive behaviour, paranoia	1	1
Anxiety disorder Anxiety and fearfulness accompanied by physical symptoms (irritability, fearfulness, panic, insomnia, tension) – physical outcomes include: dizziness and fainting, excessive sweating, muscle spasms and pains, shortness of breath, heart flutters	General anxiety, fearfulness, with accompanying physical symptoms of insomnia, sweating, heart flutters	3	2
Post-traumatic stress disorder Anxiety and fearfulness following trauma	Anxiety, fearfulness, overwhelming sadness, panic attacks	1	1
Co-morbidity More than one mental health diagnosis		18	15
Co-morbidity and other combinative physical health problems		11[a]	15
Total number of parents		40	28

[a] Includes six cases of alcohol misuse.

Total number of cases of single mental health diagnosis and no other mental or physical health problems: 11 (depression: six cases; manic depression: four cases; schizophrenia: one case).

We can also see that, although depressive illnesses (unipolar and bipolar disorders) are the most commonly occurring mental disorders (37 cases recorded), it is important to note that these were not all single diagnoses. What is significant here is the incidence of co-morbidity (where more than one mental health diagnosis has been given – 29 cases recorded), and co-morbidity alongside other combinative physical health problems (11 out of the 29 cases; see Tables 2.5 and 2.6). In those cases, where only one mental health diagnosis had been given (11 cases), 10 of these included unipolar or bipolar disorders (and one case of schizophrenia). In circumstances where parents had been given more than one diagnosis (for example, schizophrenia and depression) parents often considered one to be their main or predominant illness, but were being treated for both with medication and other interventions.

Table 2.6: Incidence of physical illness among parents in our sample

Physical illness	First-round number of cases	Second-round number of cases[a]
Alopecia	1	0
Angina	1	1
Arthritis	3	2
Asthma	4	5
Back problems	2	2
Bowel disorder	1	1
Cerebral palsy	1	0
Cervical cancer	1	0
Crohn's disease	1	1
Diabetes	2	2
Dyslexia	2	1
Epilepsy	3	0
Fibromyalgia	1	3
Heart problems	1	0
Hypothyroidism	1	0
Joint problems	1	0
Migraine	1	1
Osteoporosis	3	0
Stomach problems	1	1
Thrombosis	1	0
Visual impairment	1	1

[a] In the second round, new physical health problems included: recurrent chest infections, Irritable Bowel Syndrome, renal problems, various physical health problems as a result of road traffic accidents, cellulitis, severed arm (self inflicted).

Risk of transmission and genetic susceptibility to mental illness

Much evidence suggests that the risk to individuals of developing any mental disorder is increased should any first-degree relative be affected by mental illness, or where there is a family history of mental ill health (see, for example, Jones, 2000; Murray, 2000). Figures from our own study indicate that inherited mental illness was unlikely to be the cause of the parent respondents' own mental health problems: only one of the 40 parents said that there was a *known* family history of mental ill health. However, if we consider the *range* of mental illnesses and co-morbidity represented in our sample, then it is perhaps likely that family medical history could be a significant factor for transmission (respondents may not have always known about their parents', or other relatives' illnesses, particularly mental disorders). This might be particularly true of schizophrenic illnesses (which carry a greater risk of transmission to children; see Falkov, 1998). The causes of schizophrenia remain inconclusive, and its onset can be delayed in children until later life, but the effects of which can be both severe and enduring.

It is also important to note other statistical risk relationships. As we have seen, the OPCS data (Meltzer et al, 1995) show that women are more susceptible to mental illness than men, and other factors are also strongly associated with a vulnerability to mental illness. More recent statistics tell us that one in four people will experience mental illness of some kind in the course of one year (www.mentalhealth.org, 2002). While there is a significant risk to adult populations it is also necessary to consider the *increased* risk factors, such as genetic inheritance and other influences that put *children* (and families) at particular risk. While we do not suggest that the effects of parental mental illness are necessarily the same across the range of mental health conditions, it is clear that, for whatever reason, statistically and evidentially, the children in our study were at increased risk of inheriting mental disorder because their parents were mentally ill. Considering evidence from earlier medical work and child protection studies (see Chapter One of this volume), it would appear that these children are also at increased risk of emotional and even physical harm or neglect (discussed later in this chapter).

While few of the children in our study appeared to be concerned about the risk of transmission of mental illness (see Chapter Three), some parents were clearly worried about outcomes for their children. Eleven out of the 40 parent respondents said they were concerned about their children inheriting the illness or assimilating 'learned behaviour'. Furthermore, nine parents said they thought they had witnessed their children mimicking their own behaviours. One parent talked about their child who "gets down when I'm down". Another said her daughter, had "moods and threatened to slash her wrists". Others said their children sometimes "seemed depressed". However, some parents could also relate their children's behaviour to other factors. As one parent said: "I can see that some of it might be learned behaviour, but also some of it is down to adolescent angst".

Expeditious factors in the onset and chronicity of mental illness

Understanding the effects of parental mental illness for children is made more problematic by the complex cause and effect relationships between genetic – that is, inherited – indicators for the (risk of) onset of mental illness (for adults and children) and expeditious and enduring factors. It is clear that, just as mental illness can create new and enduring difficulties for mentally ill adults – for example, when they are employees, members of local communities and when they are *parents* – extant social, economic and personal difficulties can become precipitating factors in the *onset* of a range of mental health conditions. Expeditious factors here can also contribute to the enduring or chronic nature of mental illnesses themselves.

Our sample of 40 families included parents whose personal lives had been affected by past trauma or significant life events – expeditious factors (including bereavement, marital disharmony and breakdown, past emotional and sexual abuse) – which had contributed in part to the onset of their mental health problems. Respondents also experienced ongoing economic, social and personal stresses and concerns that in many cases helped to perpetuate the symptoms and chronicity of illnesses themselves – that is, enduring factors. Significantly, 23 out of the 35 mothers in our study said they thought their mental illness had been triggered, or precipitated, by past sexual, physical or emotional abuse. Fourteen female respondents said they had been sexually abused (including rape), but only one of these women had sought and received help for these past traumatic experiences (from a sexual abuse survivors group). The other female respondents said they had either told only one or two people (including the researcher) or said they had told no one about their abuse experiences prior to the interviews taking place. In this respect what these women considered to be the root cause of their illness (and other problems) was not being addressed in any therapeutic sense.

Nine female respondents said they thought their mental health problems had been triggered by past physical or emotional abuse by a family member, including fathers, mothers, and husbands. Bereavement was seen as the trigger for a further six respondents' mental illness, including two children's deaths. Six respondents said they had been ill since childhood; four mothers suffered post-natal depression, and one related their mental illness to being bullied at school and because of a family history of mental illness. Of the five fathers included in the study, one could not identify what triggered his illness; another said his illness had been caused by childhood epilepsy; a further respondent said his illness had been caused by the break up of his marriage; one said his father's violence had triggered his illness; and a further respondent said he had been ill since childhood.

While we would not suggest that there is a corresponding intergenerational risk of sexual abuse for children when their parents have been abused in this way, it is perhaps more likely that children are made vulnerable here by the secondary effects of the abuse their parents suffered (such as poverty, isolation, or lack of self-esteem). Conversely, however, our evidence suggests that past traumas, such as sexual or emotional abuse, were sometimes considered by parents to be *protective* factors in respect of their own children's welfare and susceptibility to mental health problems for two main reasons:

1. *Abuse as a trigger was seen to negate the risk to children of the genetic transmission of mental illness.*

   "I don't worry about my kids being mentally ill because I feel it is symptomatic of the abuse and neglect I suffered as a child and my kids haven't had that."

2. *Parents' past experiences of abuse seemed to make them more protective of their own children's physical and emotional security.*

   "I was sexually abused when I was a child [by an uncle] so and that like started when I was eight and it carried on right through more or less up to getting married ... you know it's made me like really protective over, I mean I don't know what I'd be like if I'd had a girl but I'm so protective over [my sons]."

   "I was abused sexually, physically and mentally by my father for a long time and I always said I was never going to let that happen to any of my children."

When expeditious factors have enduring influence

In some cases parents believed that the triggers for mental illness related to more than one particular traumatic life event (for example, sexual abuse as a child and domestic violence from a partner during marriage). The emotional distress caused by the combination of these events had become enduring contributory influences in the chronicity of the mental illness itself. In these contexts, other social, personal and economic problems had 'trailed in the wake of the illness' and life post trauma. While there is a recognised link between mental illness and the onset of alcohol misuse (Cleaver et al, 1999), some of the parents in our study had started to drink (and subsequently become alcohol dependent) almost as a form of 'treatment' for the symptoms of their illness (to counter the effects of depression and mental distress caused by past trauma). However, in most cases parents had found that drinking only exacerbated symptoms, as the following case illustrates.

> Sandra is a 36 year-old lone mother of two daughters. She said her chronic depression followed post-natal depression after the birth of her youngest daughter who has cerebral palsy. Sandra said she started drinking heavily to try to control – or mask – her depression, particularly during 'bad' or psychotic episodes. She subsists on benefits and recently underwent a course of Electro-Convulsive Therapy as part of her treatment. Her anti-depressant medication was stopped as it 'didn't mix' with her drinking. "I have cut down [drinking] a lot but I do drink a lot. But there's quite a lot of days when I've not had any and some days where I've just had, you know, low volume. There's odd occasions when I've had too much and then I get in a bit of a state. Er, well when I've cut down it's just like Hooch's ... and if it, I do get really down it's like Special Brews and they're quite strong. No [spirits], well I do have wine but I daren't drink Vodka or 'owt because it makes me violent."

A further example of how expeditious facts can have enduring consequences is in respect of parent's mutual relationships. In our study, marital breakdown was seen to be the *main* trigger for the onset of mental illness in just a single case. However, marital discord and relationship problems between parents had often arisen as a result of the onset and continuity of mental illness in one partner, and had then become an enduring factor in the perpetuation of symptoms as well as additional family difficulties. Marital discord and breakdown, however, can in itself have quite profound emotional and behavioural consequences for children (see Pound, 1996), and thus becomes a further risk association in this respect.

Looking at our sample, of those who commented about their relationships with their partners (nine out of the 15 two parent families), only one said their relationship was close and supportive. Of the others, some said the illness itself had caused the break up of relationships while some related a number of factors to the disintegration of their relationships with partners. The following respondent's marriage had ended by the time the second phase of interviews took place. During the first interview she said:

> "We're [husband and I] really struggling at the moment. You know it's touch and go as to whether we're going to carry on, I think. But it's not just the depression – it's other factors like social services withdrawing this care, this Home Care and the wheelchair I think up to a point. But [depression] definitely has affected our relationship."

In other cases, parents' mental illness had seriously affected their intimate relationships with their partner. One parent said: "We're close and loving, but since I've been depressed I've had no interest in sex". Another said she had been unable to have sex with her boyfriend since the trauma of her past mugging and rape, which had triggered her depression. In severe cases, relationship difficulties had escalated into domestic disputes and violent episodes. The combination of parental mental illness and other problems, such as domestic violence, can have more serious consequences for children in these families (see Cleaver et al, 1999; see also Chapter Three).

Loss of employment is another expeditious factor in the onset of mental illness that can also have long-term or enduring consequences for affected parents. No more than 13% of people who have severe and enduring mental health problems are in paid work, a figure which is lower than for any other disability group (www.mentalhealth.org, 2002). Loss of paid work can be an expeditious factor in the onset of mental ill health among adults (lone parenthood *and* unemployment can be significant factors in women's susceptibility to depression; see, for example, Falkov, 1998). However, continued unemployment – and, for some, the accompanying loss of self-esteem – can become an enduring factor in the chronicity of mental illness. In such instances, the consequences of unemployment and of perpetuating mental illness (that can also make it difficult for those affected to *secure* employment) become indistinguishable. Therefore, it is not surprising that there is such a strong association in the general population between mental illness, unemployment, and living on benefits (Meltzer et al, 1995).

Only one of our parent respondents was in paid work. Table 2.1 shows us that of the 15 two parent families in our survey, nine (well) partners were in full-time paid work. It also tells us that three quarters of the 40 parents interviewed in the first round were subsisting only on benefits, including Disability Living Allowance, Income Support, Incapacity Benefit, and Child Benefit. Although many of the respondents felt their illness prolonged their reliance on benefits and impeded their ability to take on and sustain paid work, five out of the 40 initial respondents said they wanted to work but had been unable to secure jobs because of discrimination they had encountered among employers. As one respondent (diagnosed with manic depression) commented:

"I'm actually, I'm unemployed at the moment. I did work up until last May [at the local police station] but I had another breakdown and as soon as they discovered I'd got mental health problems they got rid of me. I feel well enough to work now, er, but it's just finding something suitable and finding an employer that understands that's the problem. I've been campaigning for quite some time for people with mental health problems to be able to get employment .... I've even been to see my MP about it as well. On one occasion, I'd only been in a job one day and somebody recognised me and told the boss that I was a mental health patient and he got rid of me that day."

Enduring factors in the onset and chronicity of parental mental illness

Lucy is 34 and has depression and obsessive compulsive disorder (OCD). Her depression is cyclical but she says she feels "down most of the time, it's just that some days are worse than others". Her OCD means she becomes exhausted by her obsessive behaviour – constant door locking, checking windows are shut and locked. She has four children of her own and is also caring for her ten year-old nephew who came to live with her because of his own parents' substance dependency and other problems. Lucy does no paid work and subsists on income support and child benefit. She lives in a rented three-bedroom council house. She was trying to get rehoused at the time of the first interview because of the cramped conditions at home. Although she has effective Care Programme Approach (CPA) support, she says she has to cope during difficult times on her own with her illness and relies on her 12 year-old daughter for care when "times are bad". She thinks her illness may have been triggered by physical abuse from her ex-partner (the results of which led to hospitalisation on a number of occasions), particularly the nature of her OCD. She says she often feels suicidal and thinks that she isn't "a normal mother, but I want to be". She thinks that the negative effect of her illness for the children (aside from them witnessing her ex-partner's violent behaviour) means that "there's no joy for the children". Despite CPA support, she says she feels her circumstances mean she has a lot of responsibility to shoulder on top of her illness, and this sometimes makes her illness worse. "It's only me isn't it so at the end of the day, you know? [Youngest daughter's father] said he never wanted to see her and he doesn't support me financially. I don't think his family even know about her, and the other children's dad, he's actually in prison at the moment .... He had my children at knifepoint so I don't want him around at all and I think maybe with my doors and things because he used to come you know even after he left here he used to come and kick all the windows and everything in so maybe that is where I get my OCD from. Now there's no one else to sort of diffuse the situations [when I'm feeling bad and I have to look after the children] is there when you're on your own really, it's not like you can just go out of the house and you know and let someone else take charge is it if you're feeling like that that's the thing. Really, there's no wonder I'm depressed."

We have shown, to some extent, how genetic susceptibility and other expeditious factors can cause and contribute to the onset of mental illness among adults. Lucy's case study also illustrates how these factors can influence onset here. This example also reveals how symptoms can persist because of, and in conjunction with, other social, economic and personal circumstances. We refer to these influences as enduring factors, and recognise that some, all, or a combination of these enduring principles can also be expeditiously influential at times. However, it is enduring factors that adults with mental illness and their families face on a daily basis that can have particularly detrimental consequences for parents and children alike, as well as for the processes of recovery and regeneration.

Enduring factors include:

- The nature of mental illness and its treatments (for example, symptomatic outcomes for affected individuals, medication and its effectiveness, side effects and incidence of co-morbidity);
- The environment (for example, housing, neighbourhood and community relations, including discrimination or prejudice);
- Economic and financial factors (for example, employment status, debt issues, access to and adequacy of benefits);
- The nature and effectiveness of formal and informal interventions and support (the range and effectiveness of support services, the availability of family support, support to children as well as help and assistance from neighbours, friends and relatives);
- Family concerns (fear of separations, hospitalisation).

The nature of mental illness and treatments

Looking at Tables 2.5 and 2.6 we can see that a range of mental and physical illnesses were represented in our sample, although some symptoms as described by parents could be similar irrespective of the specific diagnosis. Box 2.1 describes the chemical medications and other treatments and interventions identified by parents. In all, 30 different chemical medications were referred to and used by the respondents in our study.

We also know that 30 out of the 40 (first round) parents had been prescribed more than one medication for their illness (see Table 2.7). Fifteen respondents were undergoing other treatments, including cognitive therapy, dialectical behaviour therapy, group therapy, counselling, art therapy, self-help group, transactional analysis, anxiety management, motivational enhancement therapy, relaxation classes, occupational therapy, family therapy (one case), healing, and herbalism. The reported effectiveness of all of these ranged from good to poor.

The most commonly occurring treatment was the use of medications (particularly anti-depressants). Respondents recorded a range of outcomes:

- "Medication eases symptoms but doesn't cure them, or prevent episodes" (six cases);
- "Drugs are effective" (eight cases);
- "Some of the drugs work and others don't" (four cases);
- "None of the drugs work" (one case).

Other respondents either did not know whether or not their drugs were effective, or felt unable to comment.

Those respondents affected by co-morbidity (18 and 15 cases in the first and second rounds respectively) and other combinative physical illnesses (11 and 15 cases, respectively) were often on a 'cocktail' of medication and treatments.

Box 2.1: Treatments represented in the sample of 40 parents

Unipolar disorder (depression)
- Anti-depressant medication
- Therapies including psychotherapy, cognitive behaviour therapy, counselling, dialectical behaviour therapy, social therapies (group work, art therapy, and so on)
- Those affected by psychotic episodes may be treated, for example, with anti-psychotic drugs and electro-convulsive therapy

Bipolar disorder (manic depression)
- Anti-depressant and medication for phases of mania (such as Lithium)
- Psychotherapies and other treatments (see Unipolar disorder)

Schizophrenia and paranoid schizophrenia
- Anti-psychotic medication
- Medication (such as Procyclidine) to counteract symptoms caused by anti-psychotics (which cause Parkinson's-type symptoms)
- Cognitive behaviour therapy

Personality disorder (and borderline personality disorder)
- Anti-anxiety medication
- Some anti-psychotics

Obsessive compulsive disorder
- Anti-anxiety and anti-depressant medication
- Behaviour therapies

Body dysmorphia
- Anti-anxiety, behaviour therapy

Anxiety disorders
- Anti-anxiety medication
- Sometimes low doses of anti-psychotic medication
- Cognitive behaviour therapy

Agoraphobia
- Anti-anxiety medication
- Psychotherapy

Alcohol misuse
- Anti-alcohol medication (Antabuse)

In most of these cases, respondents said that their medication eased their symptoms but did not prevent impulses, particularly self-harming or self-destructive behaviours. (Of the 40 respondents, 17 were self-harming and 27 had attempted suicide; over ten months, two parents had made further suicide attempts.) One parent, being treated for paranoid schizophrenia, commented:

"[The medication] keeps things under control and [the voices] stop enough for me to get it under control, they're not so intense. [But sometimes] I need to distract the voices and the only way I can do that is to hurt myself, you see they constantly want me to do nothing but kill myself so like if I

Table 2.7: Range and combination of medication and treatments

Type and combination of medication	Number of cases
Anti-depressant	7
Anti-psychotic	I
More than one anti-depressant	5
More than one anti-psychotic	3
Anti-depressant and hypnotic (sleeping tablets)	3
Anti-depressant and anti-anxiety	4
Anti-depressant and anti-psychotic	5
Anti-depressant and medication for phases of mania (bipolar disorder)	2
Anti-depressant, anti-anxiety and anti-psychotic	I
Anti-depressant, hypnotic and anti-psychotic	2
Anti-depressant, anti-anxiety and hypnotic	2
Anti-depressant, anti-anxiety and anti-alcohol	I
Anti-psychotic and hypnotic	2
Did not know	2
Total number of cases	40

hurt myself badly enough it convinces them, they stop a bit and then I get in control so it's a balancing act."

Most of the parent respondents said that they complied with treatments although there were occasions when self-administration became more difficult (in one case a child was administering medication and in another a partner was taking responsibility for this). Other co-morbid respondents, who also had combinative physical health problems, were confused by their range of medication (because there were "so many tablets to take"). It seemed that some medicines could be contra-indicative, especially when taken together. (We need to ask why, for example, five parents were taking more than one anti-depressant medication? See Table 2.7.) Another parent was being treated by her doctor with steroids for Crohn's Disease and antibiotics following a stomach operation. She had also been diagnosed with depression by her psychiatrist and was on anti-depressants. These were changed regularly because she felt that the steroids (and frequent antibiotic use) exacerbated her depression.

Changes in medication were common. Of the 28 parents who participated in the second round interviews, 20 had been prescribed new or different drugs. The changes not only reflected the incompatibility of medications with some parents' conditions, but were also indicative of pharmacological advances. New anti-depressant medications are regularly introduced on the market. At the time of writing, increasing attention focuses on the use of Seroxat in the treatment of depression which, like Prozac, is a Selective, Serotonin Re-uptake Inhibitor (SSRI), and a range of other non-specific symptoms including sadness, insomnia and anxiety. While SSRI medications appear to be successfully treating a growing number of patients with a range of symptoms, reports have also increased of disadvantageous side effects. Fifteen of our respondents were taking SSRI medication, some successfully; but once again, symptoms were only eased in some cases, and unwanted side effects were reported. Indeed, 25 of the 40 respondents in our study described a range of side effects from SSRI and other medications that added to their list of extant symptoms. (Side effects included headaches, itchy skin, ticks, insomnia, weight gain, lactation, inability to concentrate, drop in sodium levels, loss of libido, sweating, shakes, stiff joints, vomiting, tiredness, loss of appetite, and aggression.)

In some cases it seemed that the reported side effects of medications were almost as damaging symptomatically as the original illness being treated, particularly where violent or aggressive behavioural outcomes or increased suicidal tendencies were recorded. In this respect, we can see how medication itself can become an *enduring factor* in the chronicity of parents' mental illness, and how it may also serve as an *expeditious factor* in the onset of new and distressing symptoms.

Enduring environmental and economic factors

A range of interrelated environmental and economic factors can contribute to the enduring consequences of mental illness, the perpetuation of symptoms and the recurring, episodic nature of some conditions. Unemployment, lone parenthood, large families and inadequate housing – all of these issues (and others) can be both independently and cumulatively influential in terms of the negative experiences of parents, children and families when parents experience mental ill health.

Table 2.1 shows us that 25 of our parent respondents were lone parents at the time of the first-round interviews. The highest proportion suffered from depression. We have already said that only one of our respondents was in paid work. Furthermore, 30 families were living in rented properties that many parents considered to be inappropriate or too small in relation to family size. Thirty families were also subsisting on benefits alone, and money problems were more common where financial support was missing from other family members, for example, husbands, ex-husbands or partners. (Of the 25 lone parent families, only two parents said they received some financial contribution from their ex-partners.)

Tables 2.1 and 2.5 also tell us that the majority of respondents were mothers with some form of depression, being cared for, in the main, by their daughters. Twenty-five parents in our study had more than one child, and 21 of these were mothers. We have already said that women with young children are more vulnerable to depression. Falkov also found that "the factors which protected women against depression included a confiding relationship with a partner and paid work outside the home" (1998, p 35).

We have said that access to paid work is often denied to adults affected by mental illness not just because their illness prevents them from obtaining and keeping a job, but because their illness sometimes means they are discriminated against when they do work, or when they want to work. Furthermore, relationships can also break down as a result of the onset of mental illness. It is in these contexts that parents with mental illness – and women in particular – can become more tied to home, more reliant on their children for care and support, and more permanently based in local communities where discrimination or prejudice about mental illness can be most prevalent (see Box 2.2). Furthermore, parents with mental illness often try to conceal the fact of their illness from neighbours and others in local communities (because of the fear of discrimination and abuse), which often only leads to further isolation and social exclusion. Those parents affected by depressive and psychotic illnesses, which can commonly be associated with antisocial behaviour, can also become further isolated, marginalised, and lacking in social opportunities. Our evidence shows that discrimination from neighbours, friends, family members and professional communities was a significant factor in parents' enduring mental health problems: 14 parents described being fearful of discriminatory attitudes, while 32 of the 40 respondents described actual experiences of discrimination.

Box 2.2 clearly demonstrates parents' fears and concerns about the attitudes of others in respect of mental illness. Actual experiences of discrimination can exacerbate parents' low self-esteem and their tendency to hide the fact of their illness. It can also mean that they are treated with suspicion by those in local communities and workplaces, particularly when they are parents, as the following example from a parent with paranoid schizophrenia illustrates:

"Stigma takes many forms, yeah, stigma is about attitudes as well I believe, but there's stigma around here [local community]. If they knew my background here, because you hear of discrimination, you hear of the guy up the road that I know, now I know that he's [mentally ill] because I've had contact with him at the hospital, the day hospital because I do a little, a session there for MIND once a month and people round here you know, he suffers immensely because of the way they speak to him, about him, and the kids sort of throw things through his windows, he's constantly got his windows boarded up. You know, and in the past when I've done radio shows and television shows and I've come off there and you know people in the community have heard it or seen it … because I've worked a lot with young people, I've always been asked 'Am I safe with young people?' Does that suggest I'm a paedophile, you know? There's that kind of stigma."

Furthermore, prejudice can enhance parents' fears about their children's experiences in schools and among their own friends and neighbours. In at least seven of the cases where parents experienced actual discrimination, children were also involved (Box 2.2). Furthermore, children's experiences of stigma by association (with their mentally ill parents) can also compound their own desires to conceal the severity of their parent's illness. Consequently, this makes it more difficult for professionals to identify children's role adaptations (as carers) and needs. (Children's experiences of stigma are discussed in Chapter Three of this volume.)

Box 2.2: Parents' fear – and actual experiences – of discrimination

Fear of discriminatory attitudes
- People think parents with mental illness will abuse their children
- Being thought of as a paedophile
- Will not tell anyone because of fear of discrimination (seven cases)
- People think parent will harm children
- Frightened of being stared at (three cases)
- Not getting children back after being in care (one case)
- People are ignorant
- People think parent is not a 'normal' mother

Experiences of discriminatory attitudes
- Discrimination by welfare professionals and legal professionals (hospital staff, psychiatrists, child protection teams, police) (four cases)
- Ridicule/abuse in community (nine cases)
- Lack of understanding of mental illness in general (two cases)
- Ridicule by family and friends (three cases)
- Lost friends because of mental illness
- Lost custody of child because of mental illness
- Mental illness used in divorce proceedings to try and get custody of child
- Caused marriage or relationship breakdown (four cases)
- Children in care because of mental illness
- Humiliation of having to be 'locked in' in psychiatric hospital
- Children embarrassed by parents' behaviour (two cases)
- Children faced discrimination by association from friends and friends' parents (two cases)
- Discrimination from work colleagues

The nature and effectiveness of formal and informal interventions and support

Our evidence tells us that effective professional interventions can play key roles in the ways in which adults with mental illness experience and resist the enduring influences that can affect the nature and severity of their mental health, as well as their experiences of parenthood. On the other hand, ineffective or inconsistent professional support can also be influential in terms of the perpetuation of mental ill health among parents. For these reasons alone we examine parents' relationships with mental health and other professionals in a separate chapter – Chapter Four. There we also consider the circumstances in which services change or are withdrawn, and the longer-term implications of these changes for individuals and families.

Fundamentally however, our evidence points to the continuing division between adult and children's services. It suggests that, while adults with mental illness frequently have access to multi-agency interventions, children are often supported by single agencies, whose staff often have little training in mental health or child welfare or protection issues. In this respect, parents' concerns about children's lack of support, particularly when they are carers, can also become an enduring facet of parents' mental ill health and can create further crises for the whole family.

Most of the parent respondents in our study had access to other, informal support networks (see Table 2.8). These included members of immediate and extended families and friends. (Although many of these relatives and friends often did not live close enough to lend support on a regular basis, they often helped out during times of crisis, such as looking after children when parents were hospitalised.) Thirteen parents were reliant on the support of just one friend or family member (three parents received no other informal assistance). However, what is significant here is the type of support relatives and friends

Table 2.8: The range of informal support available to parents with mental illness

Type of informal support available	Number of cases
Just family members	5
Family and friends	8
Friends only	4
Just one close-by family member	5
Just one friend	8
No other informal support	3
Neighbours	1
Samaritans	1
Total[a]	35

[a] Five respondents did not comment.

offered which tended to be emotional help for parents rather than domestic or practical assistance or help with parenting (except, as we have said, during times of crisis).

What is notable is that children often provide a range and type of assistance and care that is not available elsewhere. Our evidence showed that parents with mental illness were far more likely than their children to be supported by a range of both formal and informal agencies and individuals. However, parents also remained at times quite heavily reliant on their children to provide *immediate* and *consistent* support (in other words, flexible care, outside those times when children were at school). This was because:

- professionals could not respond to parents' needs as quickly or provide flexible services;
- professionals and support services changed or were withdrawn (see Chapter Four of this volume);
- other relatives and friends often did not live close enough to lend immediate and flexible assistance;
- friendships were rarely formed among immediate neighbours because of parents' tendencies to want to conceal their illness from those in local communities;
- even immediate family members and friends could sometimes lack understanding and be judgmental about the effects of mental illness (see Box 2.2);
- few agencies or individuals *other than children* could offer flexible domestic and emotional support to parents and had sufficient insight into the nature of their illnesses.

Furthermore, it would also seem that when adults with mental illness are *lone* parents, their opportunities for informal domestic and emotional support are even more limited. Parents in these contexts can therefore become increasingly reliant on their children for care. Even when a partner is available to lend support (in two parent families), children sometimes offer different or even more effective care and assistance. In the following case study, one respondent, Carol (43, with depression), said that her partner did not understand or want to talk about her illness, and that he was often unavailable to care immediately because he worked away much of the time and for long hours. Although she had the support of the community mental health team and friends from church, it was to her son that she turned for flexible domestic *and* emotional support:

> "[My son] will come home from school and he's really quite bright because he can tell if I'm, you know, if I'm down and he'll say 'Aren't you very well today mum?' Or 'Haven't you had a good day?' And I'll say 'No', and he'll say 'Oh, shall I make you a drink?' And he'll make a drink and say, 'So, I'll not go out tonight until my dad comes home'. And he'll stop in and he'll say, 'Have you been to the shop today, do you want anything?' I'll say 'Well

I haven't been'. He'll either go himself or he'll say, 'Do you want to walk with me?' Yeah he just stops, you know he gives me what I need."

Family concerns

"I was frightened [of contacting young carers project], you know, because I imagined them taking me kids off me for the way I was and things like that. Because I thought "Well, if I'm not well and this is the way I am the social services are going to be taking me kids off me for the way I am". So instead of bringing help in I was pushing them all away because I was too frightened of it. I think that's what's wrong with a lot of people because they don't … it took me time to understand, but people say because I can't do this and I can't do that you know they're going to take my kids off me." (Pauline, 36, with depression)

As Pauline's testimony illustrates, an overriding concern of parents (and children) can be fear of family separation as a result of the onset and chronicity of parental mental illness. These concerns can escalate when symptoms endure and when enduring factors themselves continue to be influential both in terms of the illness itself and in relation to more general family difficulties. The fear of separation or familial disjunction can also be heightened when parents experience periods of hospitalisation. Only six of our parent respondents had been hospitalised once during the course of their illness, whereas 26 parents had been hospitalised on more than one occasion (sometimes ten occasions or more). Eight respondents said they had forgotten how many times they had been admitted to hospital. Furthermore, 12 parents had been sectioned on more than one occasion (in total, five had been sectioned once, 11 had never been sectioned and 12 did not know or did not answer).

In the ten months between our two interview rounds, ten parents had been hospitalised again (in three cases, more than once) and one other had been sectioned. During these periods of hospitalisation children were mostly cared for by the well parent (nine cases) or other relatives, including older siblings and grandparents (15 cases). Some children had experienced periods in foster care or in the care of the local authority (six and four cases, respectively). In other cases, children either looked after themselves or stayed with friends (one child was cared for by a young carers link family; see Chapter Four of this volume).

Parental hospitalisation can represent uncertain and worrying times for parents and children since length of stay is often unpredictable and families can be fearful that separations might be permanent. Furthermore, children's worries about parents can be heightened by parents' *repeated* hospital admissions. As two young carers said, "I'm worried mum might go into hospital again", and, "whenever I hear an ambulance I think it might be for mum". Our evidence showed that the most significant factor underlining and sustaining both parents' and children's fears about family separations due to parental hospitalisation was loss of contact between children and parents during these times. Considering how many parents had been hospitalised, and how often, few children had had contact with their parent during these times through visiting (eight cases). Visiting sessions were often difficult or did not take place because parents felt that psychiatric wards were not suitable places for their children (parents were generally reluctant to talk about their hospital experiences) and some children's experiences here had proved distressing for them. As one 14 year-old young carer commented:

"I went once [to visit mum] and she was in this, in this like, it looked like a wacko room. It was all mats and everywhere and I thought that was quite good because I could do forward rolls, but that wasn't the point. Personally I don't think it was best suited to her you know. It had a door that could be locked from the outside you know what I'm saying? It looked depressing and I mean I know she was in a stage where she was going about, you know going all funny but the way they pin 'em down, pin 'em down onto the floor. You know I was in there once and they pinned somebody down and really hurt them you know, I think the staff should be trained a bit more to understand their feelings that they can't control it sometimes you know. They need help, they don't need to be locked away."

However, in some cases both parents and children felt there should be better facilities for families to be together once parents' symptoms were under control. An 18 year-old young carer said:

"We went to visit the hospital quite a few times. There was like people walking round with no clothes on and like the youngest of us was like me sister and she was only 11. And not being explained or nothing, from like the start, not growing up with like you know what I mean like sex education or what girls have and what boys have type of thing, it was just, you know what I mean all there for her to see which was like quite bad at the time. Nowhere at all [to visit in private]. But since I've been like 16 and that and I've looked back and I've reflected on what's happened and that, and how like bad I felt the hospitals were, a group of us have been saying, you know what I mean, maybe you should set up a family room and, you know what I mean, do all this."

In this respect, loss of contact between parents and children during parents' hospitalisation only seemed to exacerbate existing, or enduring, family concerns.

'Testing' the significance of enduring factors

Our study enabled us to gain further insight into the significance of enduring factors in the perpetuation of mental ill health among parents. Using two-phase interview methods (with a ten-month gap between the rounds of fieldwork), we were able to ascertain that the nature of illnesses (and their effects), family concerns, and financial or economic factors, were principles that endured over time, and would contribute therefore to parents' ongoing health problems.

Data from the 28 parents who participated in second-round interviews revealed that the significant changes that had occurred in the ten months between interviews related essentially to the nature and effects of mental illness and its treatment. Other enduring factors, such as employment and economic status, environmental factors and family concerns, remained virtually unchanged. For example, just one of the lone parents had a new partner; none of the respondents had obtained paid work; and, despite often cramped housing conditions only two families were in the process of being rehoused. Two parents were applying for an upgrade in their Disability Living Allowance; all lone parent respondents were subsisting on benefits. Families also experienced ongoing discrimination and remained concerned about family separations.

Only three respondents described improvements in their mental state during this time, whereas *ten had been hospitalised due to mental health crises and 13 had developed new physical health problems* (see Box 2.3). However, the only significant changes in terms of different or new (that is, flexible) treatments and support to accommodate the changing mental health needs of parents were changes in medication (and some other treatments). Support from formal agencies and professionals was rarely flexible enough to meet parents' changing needs in this respect. Indeed, formal support was more often *inconsistent* or *discontinuous* (see Chapter Four of this volume). One parent said that, while she often required

---

Box 2.3: Illness-related changes over 10 months as described by parent respondents

- Changes in medication (20 cases)
- New physical health problems (13 cases, including one new wheelchair user)
- Illness and symptoms worsened over time (11 cases)
- Hospitalisations (ten cases, three of these more than once)
- Had become more dependent on alcohol (five cases)
- New symptoms occurred (four cases)
- Cycles of 'good' and 'bad' periods continued (three cases)
- Improvement in symptoms (no overdosing or self harming as much) (three cases)
- Suicide attempts (two cases)
- New treatments (art therapy, advisory service for drinking) (two cases)
- Sectioned (one case)

---

increased support inputs due to the frequency of illness-related crises, flexible support at these times was often unavailable:

> "Well it's the [lack of frequency of contact with services] as well. Because it's affected the children and that and they think, 'Oh mum isn't going to see anyone for help for about a month, what's going to happen next week?'"

Furthermore, the enduring nature of mental illnesses and other contributory factors can be reflected in parents' negative experiences over time. Looking at Box 2.4, few parents experienced positive changes in the ten-month period between interviews, which could have had more long-term positive consequences for themselves and their families. The overriding impression from parents' 'best' and 'worst' times is that negative experiences far outweigh positive ones, and can have greater influence on the enduring nature of parents' mental health and wellbeing. Here, the short-term benefits of parents' experiences of "seeing the dog have puppies", for example, or having "only one hospital admission" must be weighed against the adverse consequences (for parents and families) of parents' deteriorating mental and physical health, the onset of new symptoms alongside housing, financial and relationship problems, and so on.

The nature of parent–child relationships

We have seen how genetic susceptibility, expeditious factors, and enduring factors can influence the onset and chronicity of mental illness among affected adults. What was also clear from our study was that these factors can also compromise parenting function among mentally ill adults and can precipitate parents' reliance on their children for care. In this respect, it is necessary to look more closely at the nature of parent–child relationships when parents have mental illness (and when children help to provide care) by considering both risk associations (for children) and parents' protective functioning.

Risk associations for children when parents have mental ill health

Statistically, we know that parental depression has been linked to children's abuse and neglect. Furthermore, the risk to children of serious mental or physical abuse increases when two parents are ill or when parents have psychotic illnesses (see Chapter One of this volume; also Falkov, 1998). Co-morbidity also increases the likelihood that children's development and physical or emotional safety may be threatened.

However, it seems that where children become particularly vulnerable to developmental and other risk associations is when parents experience long-term incapacity or loss of parenting function due to their illness. It is at these times in particular that parents can lack reflexivity about their children's needs, and it is here that children can become more vulnerable to neglect or adverse

Box 2.4: 'Best' and 'worst' experiences as described by parents over 10 months

Best

- Nothing (six cases)
- New college course (two cases)
- Early support services leading to a quicker recovery
- Lost weight
- Only one hospital admission and no self-harming
- Getting transport to drop in centre
- Getting Dialectical Behaviour Therapy (two cases)
- Family staying together
- A holiday
- Better budgeting and better attitude to life
- Seeing grandchildren (two cases)
- Seeing dog have puppies (two cases)
- Going back to the day centre
- More financial security and acceptance of disability
- Improved relationship with child
- New grandchild (two cases)
- Finding the courage to challenge the illness

Worst

- Deteriorating mental health
- Deteriorating physical health (three cases)
- Too many changes of doctors
- Deteriorating relationship with daughter
- Car accident (which brought on panic attacks and made depression worse)
- Worsening symptoms (five cases)
- New symptoms
- Moving house
- Taking more overdoses (two cases)
- Wanting to die more
- Self-harming
- Money problems
- Housing problems
- Lack of support
- Hospitalisation (five cases)
- Argument with neighbours
- Was doing well but self-harmed with Stanley knife and needed stitches to stomach
- The thought that this might go on forever
- Being alone and feeling lonely
- Miserable tests and waiting for results
- Discovered boyfriend was a paedophile
- Trying to come off sleeping tablets
- Coping daily with illness (three cases)
- Episode of breakdown lasted a few months
- Attempted to sever arm, needed surgery
- Leaving family home

experiences of childhood and care. Significantly, it is often at these times when children's caring responsibilities increase. The children in our study were providing higher levels of emotional and domestic care during those times when parents were incapacitated by their mental health problems, particularly when they became bedridden, for example.

The nature of parents' mental illness and its effects, the relatively high rate of co-morbidity among the parents represented in our sample, alongside other enduring factors – which can also contribute significantly to the chronicity of illnesses and therefore the circuitous (cause and effect) and negative consequences of mental ill health for all family members – undoubtedly placed the children and young carers in our study at increased risk of developmental delay and even maltreatment or neglect (see also Pound, 1996).

Our evidence also suggests that episodic deterioration in parents' mental health can and does lead to parental emotional 'absence'. However, we did not find that children were necessarily at increased risk of *physical* harm or maltreatment during these times. Indeed, it would seem that children's role adaptations in terms of their caring activities can sometimes help cement parent–child relationships rather than adversely affect them necessarily (providing that caring responsibilities do not endure over time).

However, what was clear from our findings was that episodic parenting as a consequence of parental mental illness was the main influence in terms of professional perceptions of children's *overall* risk of harm and neglect (see Chapter Four of this volume). However, episodic or intermittent loss of parenting function here is not necessarily indicative of harm to children generally although adverse outcomes can undoubtedly be influenced by the age of children. Cleaver et al (1999) have suggested that the effects on children of parental mental illness (domestic violence and alcohol and drug use) may be similar across childhood. In other words, the effects on children may be the same irrespective of age. However, it also seems that potential protective factors can be more prevalent when children reach school age and their social and educational networks begin to widen (see Falkov, 1998). Furthermore, episodic or intermittent parenting is likely to be more confusing for children who are younger (babies and toddlers), have little experience of parental illness per se, who cannot help or lend assistance to parents, and who need a great deal of practical and emotional nurturing and care themselves (that is, of the kind that is crucial for their survival – when children are babies and toddlers).

Falkov has argued:

> Effects will depend on the age and developmental stage of the child when the parent becomes mentally ill, together with the child's associated developmental needs. In general older children will be better equipped to cope with their parents' mental illness. (1998, p 57)

In this respect it would seem that the young carers who participated in our study were less likely than younger children to suffer adverse consequences of parental mental illness and loss of parenting function since all the parents had been ill for at least eight years and very young children or toddlers were not involved in care provision (the average age of the young carers in our study was 14). Indeed, our evidence shows that age was often a determining factor in the selection and time of onset of care among children (see Chapter Three of this volume). Furthermore, young carers' experiences of services (of being heard and listened to) also improved as they got older. (Children's resilience to harmful effects through normalisation, age and caring is discussed in Chapter Three of this volume.)

However, it is easy to see how observing or identifying children in family contexts where parents have mental illness will inevitably raise questions, particularly among child welfare professionals, about children's safety and development. Considering that children in these situations are known to be at increased risk of genetic inheritance of mental illness – and statistically *are* at greater risk of neglect or harm *because* their parents are mentally ill – it is easy to see how professionals are more likely to question parents' ability to parent effectively in these contexts (see Horwath, 2000). Therefore, when adults with mental illness are also parents, the only family type interventions they may encounter would be when professionals assess parents' capacity to adequately meet the needs of their children. Assessments here may relate to parents' ability to offer safe physical, and secure emotional, environments, appropriate role-modelling and behaviour, and secure and effective parent–child relationships.

Our evidence suggests that when parents experience mental illness, the predisposing, expeditious and enduring factors that can contribute to its onset and chronicity also serve to undermine some or all of these aspects of parenting and children's needs. In such instances, it becomes necessary to look beyond statistical risk associations and consider more carefully contextual evidence of parents' protective functioning, and effective parent–child relationships. We must *consult* with parents and children/young carers themselves and *observe* their relationships in a *family setting*. (Our evidence tells us that few professionals adopt a family perspective in this respect; see Chapter Four of this volume.) Only by doing this will professionals be able to understand:

- that parents with mental illness do not consistently neglect or physically harm their children simply as a consequence of mental illness itself;
- parental mental illness may result in episodic or intermittent parenting which may require more flexible interventions to accommodate these fluctuations in parenting;
- other individuals (including second parents and others) can provide appropriate role-modelling and behaviour for children;
- parent–child relationships can be strong and effective even when parents experience mental ill health;
- caring can sometimes help alleviate the worries children have in respect of their parents' wellbeing.

Parents' protective functioning

Parents with mental illness can often have strong and effective relationships with their children, and these relationships can endure within families even when other difficulties persist. Of the 40 parents interviewed in the first round of our fieldwork, 24 said they had 'good' or 'strong' relationships with their children; eight parents said their relationships here were 'reasonable'; two said 'neither good nor bad'; and six did not comment. Seven parents from the second-round interviews said their relationships with their children had improved, 14 parents described continuing close relationships, while five described some deterioration.

One parent, suffering from depression, commented about her relationship with her daughter (young carer):

> "We get on great. I mean we have our ups and downs and things like that but I mean we laugh at the slightest thing you know. It [caring] has changed our relationship, I feel more for her. If I had anything she wanted I'd give it to her for being there for me type of thing you know."

Another mother (with borderline personality disorder, depression and a range of other physical health problems) said:

> "It's very difficult as a parent because you think, you think that 'Oh this [mental illness] must be damaging'. In fact both of [my children] are very mature, very responsible and very caring individuals. And I think that possibly happened as a result of the situation. You wouldn't wish them to have had to deal with my difficulties but that's how life is."

From talking with parents and children we were able to identify factors that indicated parents' protective functioning in respect of their relationships with their children when they cared. These factors specifically related to parents' abilities to shield their children from some of the more negative consequences of mental illness even when parents relied on children for care during difficult times. As a consequence of parents' protective functioning, children could often be unaware of the full extent of their 'caring' responsibilities. In this respect, children's caring duties can not only be conducted within the confines of family life, and evidence of it often concealed from 'outsiders', but the extent of what children 'do' in these contexts can also be hidden from children themselves. Our evidence revealed that children's presence in the house (co-residency) and emotional support during difficult times for parents sometimes prevented self harming episodes and even suicide, although the children themselves were not aware of the importance of their roles here. The following examples illustrate this point:

"He [son/young carer] just stops with me, you know he gives me what I need …. I don't like being on my own … he's saved me quite a few times." (43 year-old mother with depression)

"It's also unsafe for them to know about my emotions because my emotions are so damn horrible at times that it's not safe for anybody to know." (41 year-old father with paranoid schizophrenia)

"I'm a person who's quite happy to be on my own. But in terms of maladapted behaviour it left me more … perhaps vulnerable to myself. For instance, some of my behaviours I would, however much I wanted to, I would never do if the children were in the house." (41 year-old lone mother, co-morbid as well as a range of physical health problems)

Of course, there are times when the need for parents to rely on their children for care can conflict with their need to protect their children. Therefore, we also noted that parents sometimes felt unable to successfully balance parenting and protective functioning with the overriding effects of their illness:

"And when you've got children dependent on you it's very difficult to answer their needs because you're so wrapped up in your own. I don't want to be, I want to put them first, but I haven't been able to do that. [At the moment] I'm not much of a role model for them." (36 year-old lone parent with borderline personality disorder, depression and a range of physical health problems)

However, while an increase in children's caring responsibilities can often be indicative of a corresponding loss of parenting function among adults with mental illness (for example, parents become physically incapacitated by their mental health problems), conversely, parents can also demonstrate during these times some concurring protective capacities in respect of their children's welfare. Some of the parents in our study, for example, were able to define the parameters of their children's caring responsibilities even during difficult times. As one parent commented:

"She [daughter] has to do a lot round the house if I can't do it like because we had the Home Help taken from us. Yeah because it's something about just all personal care now, but we're really getting to grips with it because we're going to fight it, because she's 11 and she shouldn't be doing what she's doing. Well she has to do housework, she has to do the dishes, if I'm not feeling too good, you know what I mean it's just, the only thing I won't let her touch is an iron so the ironing is just piling and piling and piling up." (45 year-old lone parent with depression and a range of physical health problems)

In many respects, evidence of parents' protective functioning, during difficult times of their illness, challenges the idea that children caring for their sick or disabled parents is indicative of the 'parentification' of children; that is, the inversion of parent–child roles. (Role reversal is discussed in Chapter Three of this volume.) However, if parentification reflects role dysfunction or reversal among children, and thus becomes an 'attachment disorder' (see Bowlby, 1977, 1980), how do we explain the fact that, despite parents' incapacity and periodic loss of parenting function when they have mental illness, they can often maintain some protective functioning at the same time, as well as build strong and effective relationships with their children?

The point is that the risks to children of parental mental illness in terms of neglect, inappropriate or missing role-modelling is rarely deliberate, long-term or irreparable. Our evidence tells us clearly that once parents' mental health improves and they are able to reflect on their own lack of functioning, they often try to compensate their children for the 'bad' times in this respect and parenting functioning can be restored. Many of the parents in our study, particularly those with unipolar and bipolar disorders, were able to identify times when their parenting functioning had been compromised by their illness (and other enduring factors) and that their children were not cared for as effectively as they would like during these times.

Perhaps a more appropriate view of young caring in the context of parental mental illness would be one that recognised the reciprocal and equanimous nature of parent–child relationships. Furthermore, that it is only when children's role adaptations become *disproportionate* and *endure over time* that parent–child relationships (and children's development) are more likely to be seriously undermined. We have suggested that periodic loss of parenting function is often neither intentional among parents, nor are its effects on children necessarily irreparable or long-term. Furthermore, parents' reliance on their children for care is not always intentional nor are children necessarily harmed by their role adaptations in the short-term. What our evidence does suggest, however, is that parents worry about having to rely on their children for care and recognise that, despite the reasons for this (inadequate services, low income, lack of close-by support, parents' isolation, a sudden downturn in their condition, and so on), it is sometimes the *only* choice they feel is available when needs arise quickly and at difficult times. Of the 40 parents interviewed, 14 said they worried most about the effects of their illness on their children, including the nature of their *caring* responsibilities. Only one parent said she was worried about the effects of illness and caring on her *relationship* with her daughter.

One parent (45 years-old with depression and a range of physical health problems) describes her feelings about having to rely on her daughter for care when the symptoms of mental illness become difficult to manage. This example also demonstrates the reciprocity of parent–child relationships:

> "I don't want her [daughter/young carer] to feel the guilt, I want her to go
> and have a life of her own. I don't want her being tied down. I think as [my

son] gets older, like you know, because he'll realise that there is a responsibility. I mean if I'm all right I look after them. So it goes like the other way around, that's the way I put it to them you know. 'I'm always here for you, you're here for me', type of thing. But otherwise if I'm all right, but I wouldn't want anything to stand in [my daughter's] way. I mean, as I said, I'd sooner go and shove meself in a home or something than stop her career from going ahead."

Parents can also recognise that role adaptations when children care are not always advantageous to children:

"[My son] washes up for me, he does loads he does. He's great, I'd be lost without him. In a way I feel like I'm tying him down, how can you put this, he feels, he's, I look at him as my son but he feels sometimes as my partner.... He's only a 16 year-old lad, he's got his own life. And I hope to God that, I keep thinking now that I hope to God that I've not affected his future.... I hope to God that he's going to be normal." (44 year-old lone parent with manic depression and arthritis)

"[My children/young carers] are very protective of me, both of them.... But they're very good to me, and I try very hard not to let my state of mind affect them, I try very hard with that. And at times, that is very difficult. I wonder about the impact on them, I wonder if it's damaged them. I think my biggest fear of, of having children, was damaging them emotionally." (41 year-old lone parent, co-morbid and other physical health problems)

Our evidence suggests that parents with mental illness can have good or effective relationships with their children/young carers and shows us the contexts in which these relationships develop and are maintained. Children, particularly when they care, often play an important role in the interdependent nature of parent–child relationships when parents have mental illness. This is because children are often the only family members who have personal insight into the nature of their parents' illness (through caring) and who are *also available to care* (through co-residency). More significantly, perhaps, the reciprocal and interdependent nature of parent–child relationships is also valued highly by parents and children alike because of the difficulty in maintaining relationships with others. Our evidence indicates that parents often have poor relationships with others, particularly partners, and for a number of reasons:

1. *Past traumatic life experiences.* These can precipitate the onset of mental illness, as well as compromise parents' abilities to develop and sustain relationships with partners. This might be particularly true where women have suffered sexual abuse in the past which has not been addressed in any therapeutic context, and which can make personal and intimate relationships difficult to secure and maintain. Out of the 23 parents who related their illness to abuse of some kind, 14 were lone mothers and 11 of these had few or no other

significant relationships (including friends or family) other than with their child(ren). One respondent (a 34 year-old mother of six children; initially diagnosed with post-natal depression followed by long-term depression and psychotic episodes) who said that past experiences of sexual abuse had caused problems in her current relationship commented:

> "How the hell do you tell somebody your father has used you for sex so that you could feed your brothers and sisters? Because my father, when my mum would be in hospital having babies and my father used to lock us in the bedroom and the only way you'd get money for food out of him is when he'd done what he wanted with you."

2. *The associated increase in responsibility placed on male partners*, when women in particular become ill, as well as the *(sometimes temporary and intermittent) loss of the mothering role*, can create marital discord and even breakdown. This, in turn, can foster closer filial and caring relationships between mothers and their (caring) daughters in particular. Some of the partners of the female respondents in our study had left home during difficult times when their partner's illness was perhaps at its worst, or families were in crisis. One woman commented, "[My partner] left when my illness got bad when my oldest daughter was seven and he ran off with my best friend". Therefore it seems that mutual relationships, where parents are jointly responsible for child-rearing, but where women more often undertake nurturing and mothering roles, can become strained with the onset (and perpetuation) of mental illness in the mother in particular, because 'accepted' role function here has been compromised. One mother (33 years-of-age with depression, anxiety and physical health problems) commented:

> "My [husband] knew everything that happened, I mean he saw what happened when I had [my son], with the womb getting infected and everything, he knew why I became ill, yet he stood by me for all those years, and all of a sudden, decided he couldn't take anymore. August '99 he walked out. I had a custody battle because of my illness. He didn't think I was capable of looking after the children."

3. *Relationships with ex-husbands or partners can be difficult, disruptive or mutually unsupportive.* For example, only one of those 25 lone parents in our study who were still in contact with ex-partners said their ex-partner was supportive and understanding about their illness. Other parents described a range of problems. One female respondent's ex-husband had an injunction served against him preventing him from coming to the house (because of past violent behaviour). Another mother had two ex-partners, "one doesn't want to know and the other's in prison". Some women said their ex-partners only "made things worse", while another said she could not communicate with her ex-husband because of the severity of his substance dependency.

4. Relationship difficulties can often contribute to the chronicity of mental illness. Many parents themselves have recognised this. In these contexts, then, we can perhaps understand how and why parents' relationships with their children can often be positive and effective, especially when compared with other relationships and when children provide the type of emotional and practical care that is missing elsewhere. (Children's views about their relationships with their parents are discussed in Chapter Three of this volume.)

Conclusion

The issues surrounding the impacts of parental mental illness on children and young carers are far from straightforward. Early in our study it became clear that we were seeking the views not just of parents with mental illness (and their children) but individuals *whose lives were also affected by a range of other expeditious and enduring factors.* The following example demonstrates this point:

> "I had depression as a teenager and then I was okay once, once I got to about 19 I was okay. And then when I had [the middle child] I got post-natal depression which turned into clinical depression and all the old problems came back and so, er, you know I've been dealing with that really. I took an overdose when I was at school, at 13. But you know I'd had a pretty bad childhood. My dad was an alcoholic and I'd gone to mainstream school from a special school, which was horrible because the kids were horrible. I couldn't tell my mum about it because she'd just left dad and so you know it was a really difficult time. I mean at the time I was being sexually abused and that only came out about five years ago, whereas maybe if I'd owned up to it then you know when it was actually going on you know things would have been better." (38 year-old mother of three children, diagnosed with depression, and also has cerebral palsy)

Our evidence has revealed that expeditious factors, such as the ones described in this testimony, as well as other life events such as past trauma or abuse, childbirth, bereavement, can have profound consequences for parents' mental wellbeing. Over time, these and other predisposing and enduring influences can help generate, maintain and perpetuate the symptoms of a range of mental illnesses. Furthermore, it is clear that mental illness and other contributory influences can compromise parenting function and increase the likelihood that parents have to rely on their children for care.

However, it is important to recognise that parental mental illness does not necessarily cause long-term loss of parenting function. Nor should it be assumed that parents in these contexts have poor or even damaging relationships with their children. As Falkov has said:

> The fact that a parent experiences a mental illness does not automatically imply a negative impact on the parent–child relationship, nor does it suggest inevitable inability to parent and to adequately meet a child's needs. (1998, p 27)

Our evidence has shown quite clearly that perceptions about the effects of parental mental illness on children, and its impact on parent–child caring and filial relationships, should be guided by a more equitable understanding about the conditions in which mental illness can arise and perpetuate. Perhaps there is also a need to move away from generalising about the effects of mental illness in isolation. That is, clearer distinctions should perhaps be drawn between different types of mental illness and how they affect individuals (particularly when they are parents) and, more significantly, how outcomes influence children's experiences of childhood, caring and family life. There is a need to more clearly define impacts in terms of the influence of other factors, and on a case-by-case basis (through mapping procedures, for example; see Chapter Five of this volume) in order to avoid assumptions that all children are at increased and interchangeable risk when their parents are mentally ill. To perceive the effects on children of, for example, living with and caring for a lone parent with paranoid schizophrenia to be the same as the effects on a child whose second parent has unipolar disorder would be misguided. No doubt as misguided as Anthony's (1970) early medical conclusions that children's experiences of parental disorder were the same whether parents were mentally or physically ill (see Chapter One of this volume).

Understanding parental mental illness from a *family* perspective – that is, by looking at the needs of parents and their children/young carers – would undoubtedly address some of the anomalies in current intervention procedures (including the *perceptions* of professionals about the impacts on children of parental mental illness). Currently, these procedures seem either to be patient-oriented or based on principles of safeguarding children. Both medical and social work literature is far from conclusive about the effects of mental illness on parents and children, no doubt since the polarity of views here rarely converge to consider the needs of *families*. If they did, there would perhaps be greater understanding about the reciprocal and interdependent nature of parent–child relationships when parents have mental health problems and when children help to provide care (see also Appendix B: 1995 (ii), 1996 (iv), 1999 (ii), 2000 (i) for further analysis of this family-oriented approach).

While it is true that the onset of mental illness among parents can generate its own set of problems, vulnerabilities and exclusions for those affected and for their families, it is also the case that mental illness causes symptomatic outcomes that are difficult for parents to control by themselves, as well as with medication and other treatments. In such instances symptoms can perpetuate despite parents' best efforts.

Mental illness can also result in parental 'absence', lack of reflexivity and loss of parenting function. This means that children often have to fulfil parent-like roles, especially when others (such as partners, other adult family members, health and welfare professionals) are unavailable to lend assistance in this respect. However, it is also important to recognise that caring can sometimes help cement parent–child relationships. Furthermore, problems other than parental illness can adversely affect children's experiences of childhood and family relationships, and 'well' parents can also be 'absent' parents for a number of reasons.

In the following chapter we examine the nature of children's experiences within families and their relationships with parents with mental illness.

THREE

Children's experiences of caring for parents with severe and enduring mental illness

Representing young carers

> On the video, two teenagers discuss their mother's illness. "We were blamed
> for everything", says one girl. "To this day she believes we are making her
> ill". Her sister adds, "For a while, we thought it was us", recounting how
> the pair scrubbed the home until their hands bled ... the girls also experience
> violent and frightening incidents including being soaked in turpentine and
> chased with a match. (Kendra Inman in *The Guardian*, Society Supplement,
> 2 January 2002)

This excerpt from an article in *The Guardian* newspaper reports on a video
produced by a young carers project about children who care for parents with
mental illness. Perhaps more than anything, however, the above excerpt
exemplifies the representation – or, rather, *mis*representation – of young carers
by the media more generally (see also Chapter One of this volume).
Furthermore, the article as a whole also reflects the failure to consider the
contexts in which mental illness and young caring occurs, an oversight which
is often reflected in public and professional attitudes towards adults with mental
illness. The personal, social, and other external factors that can influence the
onset and progression of illnesses, as well as the onset of care by children, are
often overlooked in these cases. Significantly, the details about, and perspectives
of, significant others – not least the nature of the mother's illness and her views
– are also neglected.

In addition, the interventions of professionals are referred to only in relation
to the further delineation of the two young carers' additional 'burdens'. The
article goes on:

> With coaxing from professionals the girls can reflect on painful times. But
> talking about their problems goes against the grain when they have been
> conditioned to bottle it up.

Later, the report refers to the "stigma which accompanies mental illness".

We have used this example to illustrate a significant theme that has emerged from our work: that in both public and professional domains, adult mental illness and young caring, as well as the needs of children and families in these contexts, are rarely considered *interdependently*. In Chapter Four we discuss the tendency of professionals, for example, to listen to just "one voice" (Gorell Barnes, 1996, p 98). Yet our evidence suggests that, more than anything, the experiences of children and parents in these contexts must be viewed concurrently, and their relationships and needs seen as inter-dynamic.

While we can perhaps understand how the perspectives of medicine and social work tend only to consider the patient's or client's viewpoint in isolation (see Chapter Four of this volume), it seems that when children care they become the victims of the duality of their (competent, adult-like) roles as carers, and their position in society as children (and therefore in need of nurture and support). However, we would suggest that it is not simply a matter of deciding whether or not young carers are children first and carers second, and as such in need of adult-type interventions. Rather, it is a matter of recognising the duality of their lives when they care as an important first step in addressing their needs both as children and carers. Only by understanding the diversity of their experiences and circumstances does this become possible.

Our study shows that ignoring or excluding the views of parents (and their children) when parents are ill only serves to misrepresent the settings in which young caring occurs and may further compromise or undermine children's experiences of care in this respect. The earlier excerpt from *The Guardian* illustrates this point. However, if we contrast this with an example from one of the young carers in our study we can perhaps see where and how young caring becomes more than just about the risk consequences for children living with a parent who has mental illness.

Julia is 15 years-of-age and has a twin sister. Both help to care for their mother who has manic depression. They also help to care for their younger brothers (aged seven and nine) when their mother is unable to. Their mother is a lone parent and is unable to work because of her illness. She has been hospitalised on several occasions, leaving the daughters to take sole responsibility for the care of the two boys. Julia described her tasks and relationships as follows:

"I would always have to mind the boys and tidy you know the whole house like. In a way it prepared us for later on, we learnt to cook and we're all tidy you know.... Because most girls our age – you know I mean we're only 15 – but a lot of girls do go clubbing and sneak out clubbing but like we don't. And I don't really feel like that, you know I don't feel I have to go clubbing but I would like to go out a bit more you know just with mates. A lot of people just don't understand about [mental illness] and we don't go round telling people 'yeah our mum is depressed', but it's because of incidents me mum's had where the police have had to come out and people have sat on the walls and literally watched ... and that's when they've said she's mental.

But they don't, they don't know that she's not mental, she's just you know depressed ... but we know that she's not really like that because she's very patient when she's well you know."

We would suggest that it is not simply that society and professionals do not "always understand the potential impact of parental illness on children's development and welfare" (Göpfert et al, 1996, p 3), and thus may not respond to needs 'appropriately'. Rather, it is that so little is understood about children's direct experiences of care when their parents have mental health problems. Our evidence has revealed the dominance of an adult-centred view of mental illness over a children's perspective, and that recognising young caring and the contexts in which it occurs is rarely understood in any systemic or holistic sense (see Chapter Five of this volume). Göpfert et al have argued that service interventions also seem to reflect these divisions:

> Services are thought sometimes to attend to the needs of one family member at the expense of another's. Families see adult mental health services as concentrating on the needs of their patient and forgetting that the patient is also a parent. Children's services, where they are involved, are seen to be mainly about child protection and the assessment of parents as being fit. (1999, p 4)

It is to these and other issues that we turn our attention in this chapter. We also want to improve our understanding of children's individual, caring, and family relationships when parents are affected by severe and enduring mental health problems. It seems from our evidence that professionals (and other adults) often perceive these relationships to be mainly disadvantageous and damaging to children. And yet few studies have considered the impacts of parental mental illness from the point of view of the children and young people themselves who help to provide care in these contexts. As we have shown, the medical and social (and child protection) literature that describe the range of potential outcomes for children when their parents have mental illness rarely include the views of children, and even more rarely the perspectives of young carers. This is because children are not consulted directly, and, as a direct consequence, their experiences are rarely understood beyond the assumption that they are at increased risk of serious developmental delay and harm *because* their parents are mentally ill.

However, it is not our intention to further examine the impacts of mental illness on children purely as a childhood development issue, nor to look simply at the effects on families in general when parents experience mental ill health. Rather, it is our intention to consider the nature of parent–child relationships, children's role adaptations and their positive and adverse experiences of living with and caring for a parent with mental illness. We also want to understand if and how children's caring responsibilities are affected by the chronicity of the mental illness as well as other external dynamics.

While it was never our intention to try to assess, or 'measure', from a psychiatric standpoint the degree or nature of risk to children when their parents experience mental health problems according to scientific health or wellbeing criteria, we were able to compare some of our evidence with that of medicine or psychiatry. In other words, we were able to understand young caring and adult mental health from the point of view of children and parents – considering what they had to *say* – and were then able to compare it with the information and evidence so far provided by researchers, clinicians and psychiatrists (see Chapter One of this volume).

Young carers – who, what and why?

First, we turn our attention to the 40 young carers who were involved in our study and look at their profiles and caring biographies. We will then look in closer detail at the nature of their caring tasks and the factors that mediate the onset and continuation of care. Table 3.1 sets out the age range, gender and family composition of the 40 (first-round) and 28 (second-round) young carers involved in our survey (the rate of attrition in our sample, between first- and second-phase interviews is explained in Appendix A of this volume).

We must also consider what it is that young carers 'do' in terms of the caring

Table 3.1: Profiles of young carers from first- and second-round interviews

	First round	Second round
Age (range)	10-19	10-19
Average age	14	15
Median age	14	15
Female	27	17
Male	13	11
Caring for mother	35	25
Caring for father	5	3
Female young carers		
caring for mother	24	15
caring for father	3	2
with older co-resident siblings	2 (1 twin)	1 twin
with younger co-resident siblings	15	9
with no co-resident siblings	9[a]	7
Male young carers		
caring for mother	11	10
caring for father	2	1
with older co-resident siblings	3	3
with younger co-resident siblings	4	4
with no co-resident siblings	6	4
Total number of young carers	40	28

[a] Missing data = one case ages of co-resident siblings unknown.

tasks they undertake for their parents who have mental health problems. Previous research has uncovered a wide and diverse range of activities and responsibilities that young carers undertake when their parents are ill (Meredith, 1991; Bilsborrow, 1992; Aldridge and Becker, 1993a, 1994; Becker et al, 1998; Dearden and Becker, 1998; see also Chapter One of this volume). However, from talking to the children in our study it soon became clear that it was less appropriate here to try and delineate children's caring tasks in any strategic form by compiling lists or tables of responsibilities. The young carers themselves sometimes seemed to find it difficult to define the *exact* or distinct nature of their caring roles and responsibilities. This was mainly because of the difficulties involved in differentiating between the pervasive impacts of their parent's illness, the influences of a range of other social problems, and their caring duties. It is also important to note that one third of the young carers in our study were caring for parents who had a mental illness *in addition to other mental and physical health conditions*. Clearly this combination of influences can also help to determine the nature and extent of children's caring duties.

The majority of our sample of young carers were caring for parents with depression or manic depression (35 cases) and, as we have said, who also had combinative illnesses (see Chapter Two of this volume). Many of these illnesses caused rapid cyclical changes in both symptoms and behaviour. It followed then that the nature of children's caring responsibilities changed in accordance with their parent's condition or state of health at any given time. One voluntary worker talked about a young carer who had "adapted his life according to the nature of his mother's illness".

Therefore, trying to define broadly the nature of children's caring duties is made more complex by the fact that the responsibilities of each young carer are more often than not determined by their particular individual circumstances. The nature of our qualitative study lent itself well to uncovering individual 'pictures' of what children 'do' in this respect, and emphasised the need for mapping or monitoring their experiences on a case-by-case basis according to the nature and severity of their parents' illness. (This is discussed in more detail in Chapter Five of this volume.)

As we have said, it was not our intention to present children's caring responsibilities in a list-type format, but base our discussion about their tasks and duties on what they told us more broadly about what it was they did for, and on behalf of, their parents. Interestingly, all of the young carers in our study said they were undertaking what we might consider to be 'emotional' caring tasks (although the children often found these hard to categorise as such). These included 'just being there' for the parent, talking to parents when they were upset, 'trying to cheer them up', and so on. The following examples help to illustrate the diversity of young carers' responsibilities in these contexts:

"There's, if you're helping her [mum] and that, say she's emotionally like, erm, ill, I like make her laugh and that, and she'll start laughing, we'll have a laugh and a joke and that. She'll forget all about it, and then I know I've helped. Or when she's struggling, I know I can help her and then, it's just a sense of achievement." (Marc, 14)

"I don't really have a very big social life anyway. But erm, I usually, I usually, like, watch her [mum] a bit more when she's feeling depressed. Half the time I don't realise I'm doing it, but I do." (Sam, 13)

"Sometimes it's a bit of both [practical and emotional caring], you know what I mean, just, er I come home from like my placement and like something will have happened or she'll be in a mood or I mean she'll go from all right to like a completely different person so it's just having to deal with it at whatever time it comes around type of thing." (Karl, 14)

Often the type of caring tasks and duties involved were less easy to define because the children themselves were unaware of the full extent of care and support they offered to parents. In the previous chapter, for example, we showed how the nature and extent of children's caring roles and responsibilities are often not fully understood by children themselves because of the parents' protective functioning, even when children care at more difficult times (such as when parents' mental health deteriorates).

What was also significant from the findings was that all the young carers in our study undertook practical, domestic duties at some time, to a lesser or greater degree, depending on the condition of their parent at the time. Therefore, the need to undertake more household chores arose when parents became incapacitated by their illness (having become bedridden, for example). These tasks ranged from cleaning, cooking and feeding pets, to looking after younger siblings (19 of the young carers in our study had younger siblings and had had to take care of them at some time) and household management. One young carer likened her work in this respect to "all the stuff that parents do".

Some children had also taken on nursing tasks such as administering injections and other medication. Two young carers were helping their parents learn to read and write and one spent time "encouraging mum to eat". In many respects when children care for parents who have severe mental illness, the symptomatic outcomes and behaviours here can mean that children often care for a parent who is not only mentally ill, but who is also physically incapacitated. The following example of a young carer whose mother has psychotic depression illustrates this point:

"I put the washing in and, er, then I take it out and I put it on the clothes horse. And I do my room as well, but I don't have time most of the time because I have to look after my mum because I have to give her medication. And like if she gets, I have to give her her medication morning and night and … I have to do the washing up and sometimes I do the cooking and sometimes my mum does. I go with my mum to do the shopping. I do the housework. The weekends – she can't bath herself you see properly – so at

weekends when the carer doesn't come ... I bath my mum yeah and I wash her hair as well sometimes if I remember to wash it at the weekend. But in the weekdays somebody comes to bath my mum so I don't need to bath my mum. But they've only just come about a month ago .... I don't like [helping to bath mum] neither, I don't like doing that. But I feel that I have to help my mum because if I didn't do it then who else, because if I didn't do it, then my mum would end up being unclean and I wouldn't want that."
(Helen, 16)

The type and extent of children's caring duties are influenced initially by the nature of the illness itself and therefore vary and are unpredictable in terms of the level of demand required. While such task and demand inconstancy may be what differentiates children's duties in these contexts from those who care for parents who are physically ill or disabled, it is difficult to determine whether the unpredictable nature of children's responsibilities here have different or more intangible outcomes for the children themselves. What we can say is that the need for children to care on what might be seen to be such a capricious basis, and to varying degrees, means their own needs as children and as carers are perhaps less 'stable' and constant. Consequently, they are less easy to predict and provide for. Once again, this points to the need for flexible support services that can accommodate children's changing requirements on an individual basis (see Chapter Five of this volume).

Perversely, evidence from our second-round fieldwork would suggest that the flux and change in the demands on children to provide care at varying levels is one of the few *consistent* features of their caring experiences. Data from our second round of fieldwork included information from 28 of the 40 families in our original sample. All of the young carers interviewed here described continuing fluctuating levels of care demand. Ten young carers said their parents' health had improved since the first round of fieldwork, and two of these described a corresponding increase in services. However, 11 young carers said their parents' mental health had deteriorated (two of these noted a corresponding decrease in services). Therefore, the need for them to provide higher levels of care also increased (only one of the young carers who said their parent's health had worsened said that services had increased accordingly).

The demands on children to provide care are often determined by the state of health of parents over time, as well as any changes (increases or reductions) in services received. While many of the children in our study were encouraged by improvements in their parents' conditions, they also recognised that this could change quite rapidly:

"So when she goes out I don't worry about her and when she comes in I don't worry as much. But things are going well now, you don't know how things will be in a couple of months so they might dip. But I like things how they are because she's happy." (Gordon, 16)

"And I think that's one of the things that you know sometimes worries me, if sometimes she changes something and it all goes wrong again. You know, because we're on the right road and it's like with smoking, she's dropped smoking and after two weeks she goes back and there we are back to square one. And that's just one thing that worries me if something, just one little thing goes wrong then it causes everything to go wrong." (Leilah, 11).

Age as a task determinant

The nature and extent of children's caring responsibilities can also be influenced by their age. Talking about her experiences as a former young carer, Marlowe has said, "As I got older my domestic chores increased and I became mum's main carer, dad being more the provider" (1996, p 100). The significance of age as a determining factor in the type and degree of caring responsibility children undertake is also illustrated in the following example from one of the young carers in our study:

"I was still, when my dad died, I was still little. And then my mum didn't like want to put all of that onto me when I was that age and like I could see, at 13 I could see my mum was upset so I just like talked to her about it and then we started talking to each other. So it [caring] started when I was 13. But it wasn't as much as like what's put onto me now because like I don't think my mum wanted to put too much onto me then like emotionally and helping her." (Gordon, 16)

The nine young carers in our study who were aged 16–18 and had been caring for longer, while not necessarily more informed about the nature of their parents' illness, seemed to be more cognizant of diagnostic and prognostic indicators. More significantly, these young people seemed to have become more accustomed to their unpredictable caring routines and responsibilities, as well as their parents' symptomatic behaviours and how to cope with them. It was clear that for these young people, caring for and coping with parents with mental illness, even on an unpredictable basis, had become accepted and routine over time, and often also seemed to suggest that they were more competent as carers.

Furthermore, such 'routinisation' also meant that some children developed effective predictive skills in respect of their parents' illness and how it manifested itself symptomatically, and thereby learnt to predict times of increased demands on them in terms of the care and tasks they had to undertake. In this way, young carers learn as far as possible how to mitigate their changing circumstances. In addition, children who had been caring for longer, and were older (for example, those on the threshold of adulthood) were able to recognise when their experiences changed from childhood ones (excluded) to adult-type experiences where others listened more seriously to what they had to say:

"It felt like a constant battle. Right up until recently, the past two years is really when they'll actually start taking you seriously you know and listening to actually what I say and think that perhaps 'well maybe she does know what she's talking about'. But for years, I mean I was told by consultants and people you know 'you're only a little girl, what do you know?' Sort of at the age of 15 I was told this you know it is so frustrating when you're trying to say 'I live with my mother, I see it'." (Ruth, 18 years)

Factors mediating the onset of care by children

Just as the impacts of adult mental illness can be both cumulative and mediated by other factors, the same is true for young caring. We argue in Chapter Five that identifying and meeting the needs of young carers and their families relies on the recognition of parental mental illness as a potential trigger for caring. However, it is clear that other factors, in addition to the presence of parental illness, will also be important in determining the *continuation* of care by children and whether they are given opportunities to choose, or decline, their caring roles. Factors such as family composition, the age of children, children's availability through co-residency, as well as a family's socioeconomic status are also important considerations.

In this respect, young caring becomes influenced by both inter- and extra-familial dynamics. We know from previous research that one of the reasons children take on care responsibilities for their parents when they are ill is that support systems are either inadequate or ineffective (see Becker et al, 1998). We also know that family circumstances, such as parents' ability to take on paid work, their level of income and the availability of informal support, can also be influential here. Co-residency is also key and, alongside issues of public and professional discrimination, becomes particularly apposite when considering the reasons children care in the context of parental mental ill health.

Age of young carers, family composition and income

Looking more closely at our sample, 15 of the young carers were from two parent families and 25 were from lone parent families. Of the 15 two parent families, 11 of the ill parents were mothers and four were fathers. Clearly, in two parent families, when a well parent is available to care or provide support then the onus on children also to care will be less than in the case of an ill lone parent. However, ten of the affected parents from two parent families had additional mental or physical illnesses. Therefore, sometimes children are also required to care in these circumstances because illnesses often coincide with other physical health and social problems or external demands such as employment, that mean it can be difficult for (well) parents to care alone.

Age is an important factor in respect of how individual children are drawn into, and sustain, caring roles, as is the availability of other children to provide care or participate in some caring activity. Where there are a number of children available to care in families, age can be a determining factor in the young carer 'selection' process. Of the 25 young carers in our study who had siblings, 20 were the eldest child (with one or more younger brothers and sisters). Of these 20, 14 were female (six male young carers had either no younger sisters or had very young, toddler-age sisters). In this respect, age and gender coincide to become significant indicators in care role selection or adoption. Of the remaining five young carers whose older siblings were available to care, these brothers and sisters were aged 16-18 and appeared to have 'transferred' care responsibility to their younger sibling.

Fifteen of our sample of 40 young carers did not have any siblings; therefore, there was no available pool of children to lend assistance. Where these children were also from lone parent families (nine cases), this also meant that the pressures on individual young carers was even greater.

It is also important to note that, where mothers from two parent families are unwell, well fathers in these contexts can often become 'providers' rather than 'carers' (see Marlowe, 1996). In the cases where the fathers from two parent families were in paid work, children often undertook care duties when fathers were working or away from home (that is, when children came home from school, and sometimes in the evenings and at weekends). It is also clear from our evidence that the nature of parent–child/young carer relationships can sometimes be exclusive in that fathers in particular can either be 'left out', or 'opt out' of the caring equation, and therefore mainly undertake 'provider' roles. Of our 15 two parent families, two fathers who were unwell said that their partners were their main carers whereas only four of the 11 mothers in our sample said that their partners were their main carers. Seven mothers said that their mental illness had caused strain in their relationships with their partners (see Chapter Two of this volume).

Of our sample of 15 two parent families, none of the parents who had mental illness was in paid work although eight had partners who were in paid work. However, 31 out of the 40 families received no income other than from welfare benefits and were therefore unable to pay for alternative care services.

Co-residency and consistency

As we have already indicated, it would seem that a significant factor mediating the onset and continuation of care by children when parents are mentally ill is the fact of children's availability through co-residency. This is particularly pertinent given that most of the parents in our study described their experiences of Care Programme Approach (CPA) support and services as satisfactory (see Chapter Four of this volume). Yet parents continued to rely on their children for care (Appendix B: 1991 (i), 1999 (ii), 1999 (iii) for the CPA). This might suggest that parents either have low expectations of services, or understand that resource limitations mean they must accept the services that are available at the time (as opposed to those that are really needed). However, we would suggest that parents' reliance on their children for care in these contexts is more indicative of a fundamental problem facing adult mental health services. That is, the need to provide *consistent* and *continuous* support (see Chapter Four of this volume). Perhaps more than anything our evidence has shown us that children's availability to care, through co-residency, as well as the fact that caring relationships can enhance bonds between children and parents, means that from a parent's perspective children often become invaluable providers of *cohesive* and *sustained* assistance.

Furthermore, given the often unpredictable nature of mental illnesses and their symptomatic outcomes, which can mean inconstant and changing levels of care requirements, children are also ideally placed in this respect to meet transitional demands. In addition, children are often drawn into care because parents who have mental ill health in particular may be less likely to call on other individuals who, because of their proximity, could offer support similar to the type that children provide – as and when needed. Our evidence suggests that mentally ill adults' relationships with their neighbours – in particular, those close enough residentially to lend support during times of crisis – are often problematic because parents fear (and experience) discriminatory responses from others. As one parent commented:

> "I'm quite a private person and I think they [children], I think they shielded and protected me as they were growing up you know. 'We know what Mummy does, but no one else is to know, kind of thing'." (Lone parent, with depression and borderline personality disorder).

We found that children often collude in the silence and secrecy surrounding their family circumstances and caring responsibilities, particularly when parents have mental illness. Therefore, children's responsibilities and indispensability as providers of continuous and flexible care is perpetuated. Although co-residency is a key mediating factor in the onset and continuation of care by children, we are not suggesting that children are merely unwilling providers of 'rapid response'-type care services. Rather, it is in these contexts (co-residency, lack of formal and *consistent* avenues of support for parents, secrecy, and so on) that the interdependent relationship between parents and their children develops and is maintained.

Factors influencing children's experiences of living with and caring for parents with mental illness

The consequences for children, and families, of parental mental illness have been documented widely in medical research and elsewhere (see Göpfert et al, 1999; Chapter One of this volume). It is not our intention to further examine the effects on children in terms of their behavioural and cognitive development. However, it is our aim to consider the effects of parental mental illness from two key perspectives: firstly that of *children*, and secondly that of children as *carers*. We will then be able to compare these views with those of their parents (see Chapter Two), and the professionals who participated in our study (discussed further in Chapter Four).

Our evidence tells us that there is some divergence between parents' notions about how their illness affects their children when they care, and children's experiences in this respect. When asked direct questions about what they understood to be the consequences for them of (parental) mental illness, 11 of the 40 young carers in our study said the effects were negative (another 14 said they did not know). These ranged from limited social opportunities and fear of discrimination, to fear for parents' health and wellbeing. However, when asked the same question, 22 parents perceived their illness to have only negative outcomes for children and the family (six parents suggested both positive and negative outcomes; three said neither positive nor negative; seven did not comment, and two suggested only positive outcomes). For the children these ranged from poor educational performance and loss of childhood to assimilation or learned behaviour among children. It was clear then that parents seemed to worry more about the effects of their illness on their children than the children themselves. Significantly, 15 of the young carers who were asked to comment about the effects of parental mental illness for themselves *only* expressed concern for their parents' wellbeing. As one young carer said:

> "I'm worried in case she goes back to the way she was again. She was really bad. She used to cut herself.... She don't now. She used to either cut herself or take tablets ... few years ago now. She's been all right for a few years. [It was] horrible." (Gary, 17)

Another young carer commented:

> "Well, my mum she like reached a low point. I think it was a combination of things, children was being naughty because they were getting a bit on top and like she wasn't getting on well with her boyfriend at the time so she reached a low point and she just needed a break so she went to hospital to have that break. She did, she did do, she, I think she took some tablets or whatever and she had a bit of drink so that showed to me that she was really upset and she needed a bit of time to herself." (Gordon, 16)

While parents – more so than their children (and professionals, more than any others) – may perceive the impacts of parental mental illness on children to be detrimental, even harmful, it seems that children themselves often do not perceive or define their childhood experiences in wholly negative ways. The need to look at the broader picture – outside adult, patient-oriented perspectives – and to consider other factors and influences is paramount. By doing this it becomes possible to perceive how other issues (such as children's exclusion from support services and interventions, and the lack of family approaches) can compromise children's experiences of co-residency and caring in the context of parental mental ill health. A number of other factors are also influential in this respect. We found that children's experiences of parental mental ill health and caring can vitiate when:

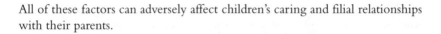

- mental illness concurs with other physical illnesses, addictions and other social problems;
- significant others (professionals, members of the public) and children themselves compare their experiences with normative standards of family life and childhood experiences;
- perceptions of risk to children in these contexts creates fear of family separations (and when temporary separations, for example, through hospitalisation, exacerbate these fears);
- children (and parents) experience public and professional discrimination.

All of these factors can adversely affect children's caring and filial relationships with their parents.

Co-morbidity, combinative mental and physical illnesses and social factors

The effects of parental mental illness on children will to some extent be determined by the nature of those illnesses in a diagnostic sense. Depression, schizophrenia, personality disorder and so on, will have different symptomatic outcomes for those parents affected and, as a consequence, children's (and families') experiences will be influenced accordingly. Certainly our evidence would suggest that the (often rapid) fluctuations between the 'good times' and 'bad times' of family life as described by children often directly relate to the nature of parents' episodic illnesses in particular (depression and manic depression, for example). However, it would seem that the effects of parental mental illness on children when they care can escalate when illnesses and social problems concur, or, as Cleaver et al have suggested, "When the [mental] illness coincides with the onset of additional problems" (1999, p 40). Furthermore, they argue:

> Children do not necessarily experience behavioural or emotional problems when parents suffer an illness, problem drinking or drug use, or domestic violence. However, when these parental problems co-exist the risk to children increases considerably. (1999, p 40)

It is also the case that the risks to children of harm or neglect could be greater when parents are affected by personality disorders (when children can become drawn into parents' delusional systems). However, we did not find particular evidence of this in our study, but the numbers of parents affected by personality disorder were not sufficient to draw any firm conclusions (although this would be an interesting area for further investigation).

Of the 40 families in our study, eight parents experienced co-morbidity (had more than one diagnosed mental illness); ten had a mental illness plus a physical illness or disability, and 12 parents experienced co-morbidity plus a physical illness or disability. (Therefore, only a quarter of the sample had only one diagnosed mental health condition – see Tables 2.5 and 2.6.) Furthermore, if we add to this the fact that, of those parents with more than one mental illness, or who had combined mental and physical health problems, 21 were lone parents and were also unemployed, then the situation and outlook for these families seems considerably worse. (Statistically, the children in these families are at increased risk of harm or neglect themselves – this is discussed in greater detail later in this chapter.) It is also important to emphasise that few of these families were in receipt of effective *family* support services and thus their problems were rarely seen in any holistic or systemic context.

We must also consider that more than half of the female care recipients (22 cases) had experienced domestic violence, physical or emotional abuse at some time in their lives, and 19 of these women considered these factors to be the major trigger for their illness. It is in these contexts that we can perhaps understand how the effects of mental illness per se cannot be viewed in isolation as determinants for poor childhood (and family) development. Indeed, outcomes for children here must be seen to be influenced by a range of other complex, and interrelated factors (poverty, isolation, exclusion, discrimination, violence, or abuse of parents during their own childhood).

The following example from a young carer whose father has schizophrenia illustrates how mental illness and other social and family problems can concur to create further difficulties for well parents and for children when they care:

> "When my mum and dad are arguing, when we've got to like stay upstairs, Mum says 'go away', and we don't know what's happening .... Say we were doing something, like, a job for them like, anything we're doing for them, and they're arguing. We can't do our job, and we really hate doing the jobs because when we have to do the jobs, and they're arguing we can't get on with our job, because we don't know what's going on in the next room. I've been, I've had to ring the police a couple of times, but, the worst bit was, is when my mum and dad were really, really arguing. My mum decided to, erm, stab my dad, well they were arguing, and, I didn't know what she had, and she lent like that, and then she stabbed him in the arm. She was, it was that bad at one point. And then so my dad screamed, and I went screaming down the road, got this first aider that somebody just lives down the road from us, and then she came. And then I had to go to school that day, I just couldn't think of anything but my dad 'is he okay?" (Kate, 13)

It would be easy and perhaps appropriate to assume that such experiences can be threatening or harmful to children, since there are undoubtedly times when child protection procedures are required. However, it is also important to understand that children are more likely to be at risk from harm when parents have combinative illnesses as well as other problems, and particularly where children are drawn into their parents' delusional systems (see Cleaver et al, 1999). Our evidence supports the significance of co-morbidity, combinative illness and other problems among parents in terms of the risk to children of harm or neglect. The few examples we found of children who had been physically hurt or frightened by parents' behaviours were those whose parents had experienced other problems alongside their mental illness, particularly drug or alcohol addictions. One young carer described how her mother had punched her sister in the face when the mother had been drinking while depressed. Another commented:

> "Mummy likes to drink a lot and it doesn't mix with her medicine and her medicine don't mix with the, what she drinks and she'll forget what she's doing when she drinks and she like, she starts talking a lot and the next minute you know she's just like speaking into another world and that's what gets me really confused when I don't understand what she's talking about. She'll start asking funny questions. She'll be sleeping on the floor, weeing, going to the toilet in the wrong place." (Leilah, 11)

Normative standards of family life

It is clear from the examples given in the previous section that children will sometimes require interventions that protect them from harm when crises arise, and other support inputs that address the range of social and other problems that can adversely affect family life. However, many children's experiences of living with and caring for a parent with mental illness are neither harmful nor *necessarily* detrimental to their development or childhood experiences.

It is more appropriate to look at individual cases when children care (see Chapter Five of this volume) and to recognise that children often adapt reasonably well to their home circumstances, and may do so more effectively when given opportunities for *inclusive* and dedicated support interventions. Furthermore, we must acknowledge that children often value and cherish their family life and their caring experiences even if, to the outsider, these may seem irregular or inappropriate to their age and status as children. Therefore, it is important that the perspectives of professionals and others outside the confines of family life do not assume children's experiences of living with and caring for parents with mental health problems are necessarily 'inferior'. Our evidence suggests that it would be inappropriate, perhaps even offensive to children, to suggest their family and childhood experiences were 'abnormal' or mediocre compared with other children's experiences whose parents are well.

Zetlin et al (1985) have argued that, when comparisons are made between families where parents are well and where parents have mental illness, normative 'middle-class standards' are often used. Evidence from our study suggests that children often understand and recognise their family's 'difference' in this respect but accept the idiosyncrasies that set them apart. Children also develop diverse ways of reconciling family 'deviation':

> "I mean I had no help whatsoever, but [when I was younger] I still didn't think anything of it. You know, that was just the way our family was. I thought other families were strange." (Ruth, 18)

> "[Mum] is very different from my friends' mothers. Sometimes I think about it and say 'Well, that's it, that's their mum, my mum's very different. And that's just it'." (Kerry, 10)

Fear of separation and discrimination

Our evidence indicates that children's recognition of the difference of their childhood and family experiences when they care, and when parents have mental illness, should be acknowledged by professional interventions that help children understand further their idiosyncratic experiences. However, children's abilities to reconcile and understand their experiences of family life and their parents' mental health conditions can be compromised by the perceptions of others – people in local communities, professionals, and so on – especially when, in these contexts, these perceptions are underscored by notions of risk to children. It is here that public and professional misconceptions and misunderstandings about the impacts of parental mental illness for families and children can create further anxieties for children when they care.

Children's and parents' fears of familial separations caused by the onset or chronicity of parental ill health are widely documented in the literature on young carers (see Becker et al, 1998). These outcomes are reinforced by statistics that tell us that parental illness is the third most common reason for children being taken into care (DH, 2001). When children care for parents with *mental illness*, these fears may be amplified by the stigma associated with adult mental illness and with caring. Falkov has argued that this can also affect family relationships:

> The fear of children being removed from their families continues to affect the quality of child, parent and practitioner relationships. There is evidence that some parents who are severely mentally ill are at greater risk of their children being removed from their care but child maltreatment is not inevitably linked to parental mental illness. (1998, p 16)

Of the 40 parents and children interviewed for our study, 25 parents said they had experienced discrimination from local communities or from relatives (see also Chapter Two of this volume). Another eight parents said they tried to hide the fact of their illness because they were fearful of discrimination. Twelve of the young carers in our sample said they had also experienced stigma by association with their mentally ill parents, in school, among their friends and in local communities. (Other children purposefully kept quiet about their parents' illness, or felt they had no one to talk to who they could trust.) One young carer commented:

> "I used to get picked on over the road there because I used to lose my temper when people used to start calling me names I used to start getting really angry ... and this day I just got really fed up of it and then I just ran home from school. They were picking on me because they just thought, I think they thought that I was different and that's it. Sometimes like they start saying 'Look at your mum she's got bad problems and she ...', stuff I can't repeat, it gets me really upset. They kept on saying that she was a tramp." (Leilah, 11)

Children can experience peer discrimination because their parents are mentally ill but also because they help to provide care for their parents:

> "They [local youths] used to bully, they used to bully us. Well they used to bully me. And hit, and punch me and everything, when, when my dad was watching, and, and he couldn't really do anything, cos like they're all faster ... and their mum used to come up and start shouting at us.... Well, like [they would say] 'You look after your mum and dad, ha, ha', all that. And they go 'At least I haven't got a mental dad' or something." (Kate, 13).

Data from our second-round interviews with families indicated that these discriminatory experiences were common and ongoing. This was equally true of parents' and children's experiences of professional interventions, particularly from those untrained in mental health issues (this is discussed in Chapter Four of this volume). Therefore, it becomes clear that children's experiences of living with and caring for parents who have mental health problems can be adversely affected, not just by the presence or chronicity of parental mental illness itself, but by the perceived impacts of mental illness of those *outside* of family life. Children's experiences are determined not simply by their relationship with the parent who is ill but by the reaction and attitudes of others. We found that children face discrimination by *association* with their mentally ill parent, by the fact that they have to provide *care* as well as by professional perceptions and assumptions that children are at risk in these circumstances simply on the basis of a parents' diagnosis (see Chapter Four of this volume).

Perhaps then we can understand why and in what contexts children (and parents) purposefully try to conceal from their peers, and others, both the presence of parental mental illness and the fact that children often have to provide care in these situations. Twelve out of the 40 young carers in our study said they tried to conceal the fact of their parents' illness from others outside the family. One young carer explained:

"My friends know about [mum's] asthma and stuff but they don't really know about the health problem, the mental health stuff. Just because I'd rather other people not know. Someone will just like try and crack a joke or something ... but it's not [mum's] fault or anything. It's just like, it's just it's not exactly something you talk about a lot, what's up with your mum and stuff." (Gary, 17)

In this respect the purposeful obfuscation of caring can create further obstacles to effective professional interventions that recognise children's roles and needs as carers. In this way, children's isolation and exclusion from dedicated interventions and care plans can be further perpetuated. Unless children can be encouraged to talk more openly about their feelings and about their parents' illness, as well as how caring affects their lives, their extra-familial experiences will no doubt continue to be negative ones. However, children need also to feel reassured that the consequences of talking more openly about their experiences and needs will not inevitably lead to further discrimination and family separations.

The nature of parent–child relationships

Comparisons with normative standards of family life, children's actual experiences and fear of discrimination, as well as the fear of family separations: all of these factors can influence the nature of children's caring and filial relationships with their parents. Once again, professionals often perceive these relationships to be compromised by the onset or presence of parental mental illness in families (see Chapter Four of this volume). And yet, evidence from our work with young carers and their families has demonstrated the need for children to *maintain* their relationships with their parents, especially when they are ill.

We would not underestimate the effects on children of worrying about their parents or of sublimating their personal concerns for those of their parents when they are ill. However, our evidence seems to support the notion that, whatever affects their parents – be it physical or mental illness – the relationship children share with their parents is of paramount importance to both parties.

In terms of trying to understand the nature of children's caring and filial relationships with their parents when they have mental illness, it is useful to refer to indicators from other disciplines, particularly in this case from psychiatry. Göpfert et al (1996) have suggested that four factors need to be considered when looking at the impacts on children of their parents' mental illness:

- the ability of parents to understand and respond to the needs of the child;
- the ability of parents to transmit the values of society;
- the quality of the attachment relationship;
- the continuity of relationships.

Our evidence has shown us that the only way to 'test' the interplay of these factors is to listen to what children and parents have to say about the nature of their relationships with one another. It is equally important that interventions are based, in part, on observing how these relationships manifest themselves in a family context. In Chapter Two we demonstrated how parents' abilities to respond to children's needs change according to the nature and chronicity of the mental health condition itself as well as the efficacy of treatments and other interventions (this demonstration continues in Chapter Four of this volume). However, it is clear that the ability of mentally ill parents to 'transmit the values of society' can be undermined by external dynamics over which parents often have little control, for example, combinative illnesses, domestic violence, poverty, exclusion, knowing what society's values are, and so on. Furthermore, the onset or continuation of mental illness can also amplify the effects of these influences. Significantly, it may be more difficult for parents to 'transmit the values of society' when such 'values' become distorted by the impingement of the negative and discriminatory perceptions of a largely misinformed society.

In light of these issues, we must try to understand the *quality* and *continuity* of parent–child relationships and attachments when parents have mental health problems. In this respect, our evidence shows clearly that, despite the adverse consequences of a range of other extra-familial influences, the caring and filial relationships children have with their parents in these contexts are generally good and positive ones.

Half of the 40 young carers interviewed for our study described positive *caring* experiences (although 16 described negative experiences). These positive outcomes ranged broadly from filial closeness and increased maturity to enhanced friendship experiences and better understanding and empathy for other vulnerable people. However, parents were once again less optimistic about the effects of caring on their children (only a quarter of the 40 parents interviewed said they thought caring had positive consequences for their children, such as increased maturity and understanding).

More significantly, when asked specifically about the nature and 'quality' of their *relationships* with their parents (the care recipients), 23 of the 40 children interviewed described 'good' or 'strong' relationships (12 described them as 'reasonable', two said 'neither good nor bad' and two did not comment; one said their relationship was 'poor'). Parents' perceptions of the quality of the relationships they shared with their children were broadly similar (see Chapter Two of this volume). However, it was clear that parents were more likely than their children to see caring itself as having negative consequences for children.

These figures, as well as the accounts of the children and parents themselves, contrasted significantly with the perceptions of the professionals in our study about the nature and quality of parent–child relationships when parents are affected by mental illness (see Chapter Four of this volume). While we would not suggest that children do not suffer any adverse consequences of living with and caring for a parent with mental illness, the evidence tells us that effects are not wholly negative or necessarily detrimental to children's wellbeing. Neither are the consequences for children in this respect necessarily damaging in terms of the nature of parent–child relationships, nor does it seem to be the case that poor or negative relationships are determined simply by the onset or presence of parental mental illness.

Furthermore, our evidence would point to the fact that *caring* may serve to offset some of the negative consequences of other, external dynamics and may indeed strengthen parent–child relationships. Göpfert et al have also argued:

> It may be easy to lose sight of the fact that any child will at times worry about his/her parents. In the case of mentally ill parents it is the right of children to deal with such worries by caring for their parent. (1996, p 282)

In order to 'test' the strength or enduring nature of parent–child relationships, it is helpful to consider the changes to those relationships that occur over time. This also helps us to understand further the significance of *continuity* in such relationships. Evidence from our second-round interview data suggests that, despite the influence of other factors (for example, loss of or changes in key workers and other support services), as well as the fact that children continued to be excluded from statutory intervention strategies and care plans, enduring parent–child relationships were often the one constant in the lives of these families. Of the 28 young carers interviewed in our second round of fieldwork, 16 said that their relationship with their parent (care recipient) was 'good' or 'strong'. Ten young carers described *improved* relationships and only one young carer said their relationship had deteriorated (one did not answer). Talking about the relationship they had with their mothers during the second round of fieldwork, two young carers commented:

> "We are still the best of friends. We do really have a strong relationship and also I feel that I've matured a lot quicker which to me I think is a good thing because I've got a different outlook to a lot of other girls that are my age, you know people are still in school and I think 'My god ...'." (Ruth, 18)

> "I think it's made us more caring, and understanding that if your mum can't be normal, a lot of people have got problems, and everything." (Julia, 15)

Our evidence tells us that children's relationships with their parents can be intermittently compromised by illness and caring. We have said that the need for children to provide care changes according to the nature – improvement or deterioration – of the parental condition over time. In Chapter Two we explained how mental illnesses can affect parents' ability to respond to their children's needs depending on how they are feeling at a given time and also that parents often try to compensate their children for the 'bad times'. These symptomatic fluctuations are also often reflected in children's descriptions of their relationships with their parents who are ill:

"She is just so funny, you know, when she's well, she is just the best mum ever. She's just funny and everything you know, has a laugh with you. She's not like a normal mum, you can tell her about anything, you know, boys or anything like that ... she'll understand. And she'll tell us about her past and everything, and, you know, she always just makes my little brothers laugh, you know, just get on dead well, when she's well. Brilliant. And then when she's not well, then, we still get on with her, because even though she's nasty to us, I haven't got the heart to be nasty to her back. Because I still love her, and it's not her fault." (Julia, 15)

What is clear from our findings, and what these two examples illustrate, is that children do not necessarily look for *consistency of parental health* or care, but hope for *continuity in their relationships* with their parents, through co-residency and family unity. In these circumstances, many children (and parents) resist family separations by any means, including concealing the nature of their parents' illness and the fact that parents rely on them to provide care. We have already said that fear of family separation has been a dominant feature of the literature on young caring. Falkov, as we read earlier, has also argued that this fear continues to affect "the quality of child, parent and practitioner relationships" (1998, p 16).

It is important to emphasise also that relationships with significant others can be beneficial to children and help to sustain secure attachments:

An absolute pre-requisite for optimal psycho-social development of any child
is secure attachment to a primary carer, usually, but not always the mother.
(Göpfert et al, 1996, p 279)

Fifteen of the 40 young carers in our study were from two parent families and of these, 12 described 'good' or satisfactory relationships with the parent who was well. Furthermore, 20 children said they had good or effective relationships with other non co-resident family members (grandmothers, aunts, uncles, and so on) even though these relatives were often unavailable to lend practical, caring support. Therefore, in looking at the context of *family* life, it is often the case that children can and do form important attachments with other family members and carers that can augment their own feelings of security and wellbeing. Some of the young carers in our study had also formed important relationships with young carers project workers who they often saw on a regular basis (weekly or fortnightly).

Parentification and parent–child attachments

It has been suggested that the quality and continuity of parent–child relationships can be seriously undermined by role disorder, or role reversal, among children:

> The task of parenting in the context of the nuclear family is a difficult one, and the balance between discipline and care is a complex one.... Problems occur when the relationship becomes too symmetrical or even reversed. (Göpfert et al, 1996, p 279)

In this respect, children's 'role reversals' or transformations are seen by the medical practice to occur as a consequence of parental illness and have been described in the literature as "precocious competence" (O'Neill, 1985), "false maturity" (Arnaud, 1959), a "doing defense" or "care taking" (Sturges, 1978). These have more recently been described in psychiatry as attachment or role disorders, in short, as evidence of "parentification" (see West and Keller, 1991; Barnett and Parker, 1998; Chase, 1999):

> Parentified children, in effect, are parents to their parents and fulfil this role at the expense of their own developmentally appropriate needs and pursuits. (Chase, 1999, p x)

In sociological terms we might describe children's roles here as young caring. However, conversely, we would not argue that young caring is necessarily evidence of parentification. Perhaps it is more the task of the psychiatrist to gauge whether young caring provides direct evidence of parentification and what this then means for children in terms of their development. However, our work with young carers and their mentally ill parents presented us with the first opportunity to look at young caring in terms of children's ('parentified') roles. While, from a social scientific perspective, role reversal is difficult to gauge or 'test' in any exact way, our evidence would point to the fact that generally young caring seems to be less about role *reversal* or attachment *disorder*, and more about role *adaptation*. It appears that children do not simply become the 'parent of the parent' when they care, but they do take on *parent-like roles* intermittently, particularly, as we have seen, when parents have mental illness. We can also assert that, although on many occasions children and parents alike may experience some sense of role transposition when children care, this often only relates to one aspect of parent–child relationships.

We asked children and parents to describe their relationships with each other in terms of the different or changing roles they often undertook. Only four of the young carers in our study described their caring responsibilities in terms of role reversal. One young carer commented, "You have to like be her [mum's] parent as well, looking after her" (Karl, 14). Nine of the parents specifically talked about role reversal in relation to their children's caring activities, although some parents described their experiences of care relationships not in terms of parentification, but as inversions of *other* adult roles:

> "He [my son] does everything a husband should do, which in some ways, I feel is as embarrassing for me, as what it is for him." (47 year-old lone parent, with depression and a range of physical health problems)

> "He [my son] washes up for me, he does loads he does, he's great, I'd be lost without him. In a way I feel like I'm tying him down, how can you put this, he feels, he's, I look at him as my son but he feels sometimes as my partner." (44 year-old lone parent of five, with manic depression and arthritis)

Our evidence further suggests that children in particular can differentiate between the adult-type nature of their caring *tasks* and the filial relationship they have with their parents even when parents are ill. Göpfert et al (1996) argue that parenting is about the balance between 'discipline and care', and although it seems clear that different role adaptations do occur when children care, children continue to perceive their parents as mainly fulfilling loving parental and disciplinary roles. It seems that children can also recognise that there are times when parents are unable to fulfil their parenting roles as effectively as they would wish, and that role adaptations become episodic depending on the state of their parents' health at any given time.

However, it would seem that, regardless of the nature or degree of role adaptation undertaken when children care, children (and parents) are still able to recognise the distinction between caring *roles* and filial *relationships*:

> "I still know that me mum's me mum and I get in trouble all the time. I get told off you know for having a messy bedroom." (Ruth, 18)

One parent said:

> "I like him [my son] being there, he's my son first and I'm his mother. I, well, it's right like that. We're fine together."

Another young carer commented:

> "She's still, yeah, she's still around to be like a mum like." (Karl, 14)

It seemed that most of the children in our study were able to recognise that their parents retained the status, if not always the task effectiveness, of parents. Parents, on the other hand, were more likely to equate their lack of practical (parent-type task) function with loss of power or nurturing capacity. This may be due to the fact that, despite the duality of children's roles when they care (they are both children *and* carers), children need secure attachments or parental role models. They continue, therefore, to see their parents as 'parents' despite what they might 'do' for their parents when they are ill.

For parents on the other hand, the fact of their illness, as well as the need to rely on their children for care, seems to emphasise for them their loss of parenting function. The parents in our study who talked about changing roles seemed to equate young caring with their own (parenting) role surrender, rather than the adaptation of new or different roles by their children. In this context, parents are perhaps more likely than their children to describe their *cared for* experiences in terms of role reversal. This is how one young carer described her mother's reaction to being cared for:

> "When she [my mother] come back out of hospital and I was doing everything and I had the three kids as well and she went, what was it, she said something to me like 'Have we swapped roles?' I went, 'What do you mean?' and she went 'Well I'm not like the mum anymore, you are'. I went, 'Well, what do you mean?' She went 'Well, look at all the things you're doing, I'm meant to be doing all them'. And then she'd get angry with herself and then she'd get frustrated because she couldn't do all the things that like you know what I mean, an ordinary house mum would do." (Debbie, 18)

Chase argues that:

> Parentification describes behaviours transmitted across generations and involving assumptions of what children and parents are obliged to give and receive from each other. (1999, p xi)

Our evidence tells us that where parents have mental illness these 'obligations' are often unclear, or are subject to regular but unpredictable changes. However, children can recognise that parents affected in this way cannot always parent *consistently*. Therefore, children provide care (for parents and also for themselves) when parents are unable, or less able, to care themselves. This is not necessarily because children feel obliged to care, but often because they want to help or contribute in this way.

The effects of caring on children and their needs

Perhaps it is more relevant to ask not if young caring provides direct evidence of parentification, but whether children's role adaptations are damaging either to themselves or to the relationships they share with their parents. In this respect, we must also consider the extent of risk to children of living with and caring for a parent with mental illness.

We suggest that there are two ways of understanding or perceiving risk associations for children in this respect. The first relates to the increased genetic risk to children when their parents are affected by mental illness and the associated (expeditious and enduring) factors that help to perpetuate symptoms and further personal and socioeconomic difficulties (see Chapter Two of this volume). The second relates to inter-familial and interpersonal factors (children's relationships with their parents, the importance of caring for parents, and so on) that can often become guiding protective principles for children in these circumstances.

From talking with the parents, children and key professionals in our study, we found no evidence of actual physical harm to children in these families.

Earlier we drew attention to the case of one young carer who related an experience of past physical abuse involving a sibling and that this was during a time when their mentally ill parent was also misusing alcohol. We know that in these circumstances (where parents have co-morbidity and other combinative physical health and addiction problems) the risks to children of physical harm or neglect increase.

However, among the parents who self-harmed or attempted suicide we found no evidence of corresponding harm to children. Indeed, it seems clear that parents' symptomatic behaviours should not be conflated with a threat to children's safety. Of the 40 parents in our study, 17 self-harmed during 'bad' periods of their illness and 27 had attempted suicide (the majority by overdoses). However, according to parents *and* their children, none of the parents who self-harmed, for example, had attempted to physically harm their children. As one of the parents commented:

> "In terms of maladapted behaviour [being on my own] left me more ... perhaps vulnerable to myself. For instance, some of my behaviours I would, however much I wanted to I would never [self-harm] if the children were in the house and I would *never* hurt them at all." (41 year-old lone parent, with BPD, depression and memory loss)

However, 'testing' or gauging the psychological (risk) consequences for children of co-residing with parents who have mental health problems and who regularly self-harm or attempt suicide is less easy. Cleaver et al have stated that "to witness parental distress and suffering can have an adverse psychological impact on children" (1999, p 45). However, they have also said that many children do not experience long-term behavioural or emotional disorder when parents have mental health problems, but that they would "benefit from services" (1999, p 46). The apparent conflict represented in these two statements is reflected in problems of measuring or gauging the impacts on children of living with and caring for a parent with mental illness. We argue that in these circumstances it is necessary to weigh children's risk of physical harm or neglect with their resilience and the extent of parents' protective capacities. We have already seen where and how parents can protect children from damaging childhood experiences, even when parents experience downturns in their mental health (see Chapter Two of this volume). We would further propose that children can be more resilient to harmful effects when:

- they are older (we have said that younger children, particularly babies and toddlers, will be at increased risk of neglect, particularly where parents have psychotic illness);
- they have been caring for, and co-residing with parents for longer;
- they feel included in their parents' treatment and care.

All of the young carers involved in our study had been caring for and living with parents who had been mentally ill for more than eight years, and to some extent children had adapted to the 'difference' of family life. Furthermore, the children often described positive and effective relationships with their parents that were important to both parties. As one young carer commented:

> "But the best thing about [mum] being like that is because we always thought, like I just say to her, oh what is it, 'God gives people, you know, an illness so that, you know, he knows that they can cope with it really don't they?' And she's like I say to her since she's had this depression it's brought her out to be a better person because you know me and [sister] and mum are like that, we tell each other everything you know we're dead close and have our own little laughs all the time, we're just really close...." (Julia, 15, whose mother suffers from manic depression and alcohol problems)

However, we know from a wider literature on the experiences and needs of young carers more generally that caring in and of itself can have detrimental effects on children (Meredith, 1991; Bilsborrow, 1992, Aldridge and Becker, 1993a, 1994; Becker et al, 1998; Hill, 1999; see also Chapter One of this volume). It seems also to be the case that when parents experience co-morbidity and combinative illnesses and other social problems including poverty, exclusion and ineffective support, children's caring experiences and relationships can be compromised. Undoubtedly these factors can adversely affect children's educational, psycho-social and emotional development, as well as their transitions into adulthood (see Dearden and Becker, 2000a).

Our evidence further confirms *some* of these consequences for children when they care for parents who have mental health problems. For example, 18 of the 40 young carers in our study said they had missed some school as a result of caring (although this was not necessarily reflected in poor educational performance or attainment). The same number of children and young people said they felt they had limited social opportunities as a result of caring. However, children's lack of school attendance here was associated less with the need for children to stay at home and carry out physical caring *tasks* than the anxiety children experienced while away from home and their parent. Although *regular* school absenteeism was not high, almost half of the young carers in our study (19 cases) said that they were anxious about their parents most of the time they were in school. Consequently, they found it difficult to concentrate on school work.

It seemed that children were particularly concerned that parents' behaviours might result in serious outcomes (for example, hospitalisation) while children were at school:

> "I find it worse when like I come home from school and like I'll get a phone call from grandma or someone. Like when I come in. Well most of

the time I come in like and nobody will know [mum's] done it [cut her wrists]." (Ian, 15)

Without adequate support for themselves and recognition of their concerns – as well as their caring contributions (see Marlowe, 1996) – children's worries about their parents' illness in a prognostic and personal sense can become detrimental to their own wellbeing and development. Children's unchecked anxieties in this respect can also make them feel that they are to blame for their parents' illness:

"Sometimes it is [scary] yeah because you think what is really happening in her head? And you know, is it my fault that this is, that she is like this you know, have I done something bad? You know, because like I am 11, I am going through periods when I'm growing up so I am naughty obviously, I won't deny that. But sometimes we're all friends again eventually but sometimes I think have I done something really, really bad so that she can get to this stage you know, have I just topped the limit?" (Leilah, 11)

Children's lack of social opportunities are not necessarily only influenced by the need to eschew friendships in order to be available physically to care for their parents at home. The need for children to be with parents can sometimes translate as a desire for reassurance for both. We found that children were also often fearful of ridicule or discriminatory responses from their peers, and often did not easily make or trust friends. However, in other more familiar contexts, young carers can form important friendships, particularly among children who also attend young carers project sessions, and even with project workers themselves because these are likely to present opportunities where their experiences can be *shared*:

"When we thought my mum was the only one, we did all that [caring] you know we was really, really depressed and everything and then we went to Barnardos [young carers project] and, you know, [caring is] very common isn't it?" (Julia, 15)

"Oh yeah it did make a difference meeting others who'd had the same experiences because at first I didn't really want anyone to know at first. I actually thought that we were all going to get taken into care ... but in going to young carers [project] oh it was definitely [good] because I felt like I weren't, I weren't the only one this was happening to you know what I mean, it weren't something that just got wished upon me type of thing." (Debbie, 18)

A fundamental difficulty facing children whose parents have mental illness is that the effects of living with (and caring for) an affected parent can be all-pervasive. Effects can influence their life at school, their social lives, as well as their personal and emotional wellbeing. And yet, because parental mental illness and young caring are largely hidden within families, the psychological impacts on children can be even more difficult to define or address in any formal or practical sense. It is clear that the *effects* of parental mental illness (for parents and for children) are not as 'obvious' as *outcomes* among family members where parents are affected by physical illnesses or disabilities. One young carer described her mother's mental illness as "there all the time", and that it was not obvious "like a cut or a bruise".

What we can say is that, where parents have mental illness, the consequences for children of caring and co-residency are inextricably linked. Children in these contexts often experience increased levels of anxiety because of the unpredictable nature of their parents' mental ill health (and associated expeditious and enduring factors). However, it is not necessarily the case that outcomes for children are difficult to anticipate, address or provide for, as long as we – as adults – do not assume the consequences of parental mental illness to be inevitably damaging to children. Nor should it be assumed that children do not want to live with or care for parents who have mental illness *without first consulting children and their families*. We argue that assessing the risk to children, as well as the nature and level of their needs, should be done on a case-by-case basis using effective mapping and monitoring procedures (see Chapter Five of this volume).

Considering the effects of parental mental illness and caring on children and listening to what they have to say in these contexts would lead us inevitably to a deeper understanding of children's needs. This is particularly important given that the children in our study, as we have said, often seemed to find it difficult to define the specific nature of their own requirements, no doubt because they were rarely consulted formally about their own requirements in this respect (see Chapter Four of this volume).

From talking with the young carers (and their parents) in our study, we were able to identify their key requirements:

• *Children should be encouraged to identify the nature and extent of their own childhood and caring requirements more, since they can often subjugate their own needs in favour of the needs of their parents.*

Among the children and young people in our study, the most frequently identified need was for parents to be well or to recover completely (12 cases). (Six young carers said they needed financial support; five described specific types of support for parents – 'new trainers', 'home help', for example; four young carers said they needed practical support, such as home care, help with shopping, and so on.) This suggests that children need reassurance about their parents' condition and wellbeing and that, as carers, children need to feel included in parents' formal treatment or care plans.

- *Caring can help children feel involved and needed, and professionals need to recognise the caring contributions children make.*

Most of the young carers in our study said that, although they thought the services their parents received were good and effective, they themselves often had better insight into the nature of parents' illnesses and their requirements.

> "[Mum's], I can't think of any other way to put it but she's sometimes easy to read in the way that I can ... tell if she's about to burst into tears or if she's just, well both sad and annoyed really with things that have gone wrong. So that way I can, I know whether to, well support her or just leave her alone to get over it." (David, 12)

In this respect children, as carers, should be consulted about their experiences and understanding of their parents' illnesses.

- *Professionals need to reconcile children's fear of professional interventions with their need for formal support.*

We know children, and particularly young carers, fear formal interventions that might result in their family being separated. Once this fear is addressed, children may feel more able to talk openly about their experiences and needs.

- *Children need to talk to someone they can trust and who understands their needs – as children and as carers – but who is also understanding about mental health issues.*

Evidence from a wider literature on young carers has consistently pointed to children's need to talk to somebody they can trust about their circumstances and experiences (see Becker et al, 1998). Sturges (1978) has also argued that talking to someone can help in the successful regeneration of families where parents are ill or disabled. In many respects the work of young carers projects has been crucial in addressing a range of children's caring and other needs, including their need to talk to someone about their experiences (many projects offer befriending, counselling, one-to-one support and group work). However, children (and parents) often do not have access to any one individual who understands the needs of both themselves and their parents (see also Göpfert et al, 1996).

- *Children need age-appropriate and reliable information about a range of mental health problems and how these can affect parents, children and families.*

Children's need for information has also emerged as a consistent finding in work on young carers (see Becker et al, 1998). Our evidence also points to children being 'information poor'. It seems that children whose parents have mental health problems have the same (if not a greater) need for information, particularly about mental health conditions. Half of the young carers in our study had obtained information about their parents' illness from the parent themselves. (Eight young carers said they had received no formal information but had learned 'on the job'; five said they received information from formal sources such as printed literature, young carers projects, and so on; two obtained information from their other parent; and five did not know where the information had come from.)

While parents might prove to be a useful and sometimes the only source of information for children about mental illnesses, it can also be the case that parents provide too much (anxiety-provoking) information. Falkov has argued that if family members are unable to provide information to their children, "then a professional will have to address this need" (1998, p 281). We suggest that other family members and parents are not always the best sources of information for children, particularly when this involves parents relaying details about their own illnesses. Therefore, it becomes the responsibility of professionals to provide age-appropriate information that adequately addresses children's need to understand and be more knowledgeable about the mental health conditions which affect both their parents, and they themselves through co-residency and care. Without this information, children's experiences of care can be confusing and undermining:

> People tend to protect children and young people. For me this translated into ignoring my need to be informed and involved. My life was affected anyway and if I had had guidance it might have made the experience more positive. I needed good, age-specific information about my mother's condition and its consequences. And I needed someone to talk to who would listen in confidence and help me to express and explore the complex feelings and situations I was dealing with. (Marlowe, 1996, p 101)

Considering the important role young carers projects play in young carers' lives (see Chapter Four of this volume), they may be ideally placed to provide health and other information to children. However, our evidence suggests that young carers project workers may not always be sufficiently trained or proficient in providing age appropriate information about psychiatric conditions they sometimes know little about (we discuss this further in Chapter Four). However, it is imperative that training and resources are made available to professionals (from both statutory and voluntary sectors) to enable them to address information deficits. In this way, it should be possible to prevent young carers from being mistaken as "problem children" as opposed to "problemed" children in need of "information and support" (Marlowe, 1996, p 105).

- *Where parents have mental illness, professionals need to be aware of the contexts in which children are at increased risk, as well as to the impact of other factors that can perpetuate symptoms and difficult family circumstances.*

Our evidence shows that the damaging effects for children of caring for and living with parents with mental health problems are not determined by mental illness in and of itself, but by a range of other factors, including isolation and exclusion (from care plans, service interventions, approaches from family and professionals, and community misunderstanding and discrimination) in particular, as well as by other social determinants (including low income, poverty, and so on). It is important, therefore, that professionals understand the wider context of children's lives when they care for parents with mental health problems.

Conclusion

It has been suggested that a significant proportion of children living with a mentally ill parent will develop psychological problems or disorders (see Falkov, 1998). However, others have said that many children show no *long-term* behavioural or emotional disorder when parents have mental illness. However, children do need formal support if and when problems occur (see Cleaver et al, 1999).

Caring may be one way that children can address (and try to alleviate) some of the concerns they may have about their parents and their filial relationships. We have shown that, rather than being wholly negative experiences, children's *caring* relationships can in fact help cement secure attachments with their parents (who are ill), and help to allay some of the fears associated with mental illness. In this respect the need for some children to care, out of choice, should be acknowledged, and flexible, sensitive interventions should be made (we discuss this further in Chapter Five of this volume). Providing proper age-appropriate information about mental illness, for example, would benefit children, and it may also help to alleviate their anxieties while they are in school or away from home.

From our work with the young carers in this study we have seen that, despite their often difficult and 'different' lives, as well as the negative consequences of other combinative factors, young carers often have positive relationships with their parents. In many cases they want to continue living as a family unit. Certainly we did not find any evidence of 'blackmailing', 'eating disorders', 'inability to relate to peers', for example, or observe children demonstrating 'learned behaviours' from their parents, as some of the professionals would have us believe are the outcomes for children of caring in these contexts (see Chapter Four of this volume). Furthermore, if the chronicity of illnesses or the long-term nature of 'role reversal' among children when they care are indicators of developmental problems in children, then the effects of caring and mental illness themselves were rarely consistently negative in our survey.

However, it is undoubtedly the case that children's *secure* relationships with parents when they are ill – and especially when they have severe and enduring mental health problems – can be undermined by the symptomatic outcomes and behaviours of parents. Our evidence tells us that this is more likely to be the case when:

- parents are inadequately or ineffectively treated or supported;
- continuity of parent–child relationships is compromised (for example, by hospital admissions, child protection procedures, family separations);
- parents and children fear discriminatory professional interventions;
- parents have a range of physical and mental health problems coupled with social problems such as poverty, low income and social exclusion.

In many respects, the dilemma facing professionals is distinguishing between situations where children develop "task oriented competencies which can be a strength in their lives", and those where children have "too many responsibilities because they are forced early to take care of their sick parent and miss out on their social development" (Göpfert et al, 1996, p 282). Professionals have long struggled to make decisions based on these apparently opposite outcomes. However, our evidence suggests that it is only by listening to what children (and parents) have to say in these contexts on a case-by-case basis – which means understanding the 'good' and the 'bad' of caring – that decisions will become appropriate and beneficial to children *and* parents.

Our evidence also tells us that, while children need to be recognised, monitored and supported when they care in a systemic sense, it is also important to consider their role adaptations as a combination of both positive and adverse experiences. From a broader perspective, but in the same way, the phase of childhood also represents diversity of experience for all children:

> It is probably true to say that for most people childhood is a mixed experience where periods of sadness and loss are balanced with moments of happiness and achievement. Such complexity, however, is rarely represented in the literature of childhood. (Cleaver et al, 1999, preface)

It would be easy to assume from medical practice and social work that children whose parents are mentally ill only experience this diversity as detrimental to their development and wellbeing.

FOUR

The role and responsibilities of professionals: services and support for young carers and parents with mental illness

Young carers – seen but not heard

Early evidence from research on young caring in general pointed to the neglect of such children by welfare professionals from both children's and adult services (see Bilsborrow, 1992; Aldridge and Becker, 1993a, 1993b; Becker et al, 1998). At the time, such inattention could be accounted for by the contemporary nature of young caring as a welfare issue, as well as by the lack of formal legislative procedures that could accommodate and address young carers' experiences and needs (see Appendix B of this volume). We can then also more readily comprehend why some professionals, while overlooking children's needs as carers, seemed at the same time to be condoning their caring duties by including them in the informal 'package' of care for their ill or disabled parents. Children were rarely consulted about the nature and consequences of their caring activities, but services were sometimes withdrawn or withheld because children were considered capable of care management (see Aldridge and Becker, 1993a). At that time it seemed that young carers were quite literally children who were seen but not heard.

Although we know from research more generally that young carers have been overlooked in service delivery plans, key policy and legislative changes have since occurred to address these oversights (see Appendix B: 1995 (i), 1999 (i), 1999 (ii), 2000 (ii)).

What research on young caring *and* on the impacts of parental mental ill health on families and children does not tell us, however, is the nature of professional interventions where children are caring for parents who have mental illnesses. And yet research in this area is important for a number of reasons. First, what little evidence there is on this subgroup of children has emphasised more the impacts of the *parental conditions themselves* on young carers (see Elliott, 1992; Landells and Pritlove, 1994) than the ways in which professionals respond to young carers whose parents are thus affected.

Second, it is important to ascertain whether young carers whose parents have mental health problems have distinct and particular needs which may be different from those young carers whose parents have physical illnesses, disabilities or other conditions.

Third, as service users both young carers and parents with mental illness require inputs from children's services and adult mental health services. Therefore, it is important to consider the nature and extent of any service division and integration here. In order to do this, it is essential to seek the views and perspectives of a triumvirate sample. In our study this involved talking to the parents, young carers and the professionals who support them. Social research often fails to address this three-way perspective, and yet in order to fully understand the nature and extent of professional intervention assessments, how services are delivered and how they are received, it is essential to obtain the views of each subject group. Furthermore, children's views are too often overlooked in this respect. As Alderson has argued:

> Adult-centered research is conducted about the public world of the environment, politics, economics and other social affairs with little reference to children. (1995, p 40)

Our evidence suggests that, without the views of young carers, the picture we have of how and in what ways professional interventions occur would be very different. Professional accounts of how they respond to young carers' needs at times contrast with how young carers themselves describe the ways they are approached or included. The picture we have here in relation to young carers is one of exclusion rather than inclusion in service plans and delivery. Moreover, it is important to seek the perspectives of parents, whose views of services and professional interventions add another key dimension to our understanding.

Fourth, given the assumptions researchers and professionals tend to make about the effects of parental mental ill health on families and children (see Chapter One of this volume), it is important to establish whether the risk associations suggested by medical and some social work – which has had an influence in terms of informing public perceptions of mental illness – is at all inculcated in current professional attitudes and approaches to parents with mental illness, and their children who contribute to their care. It is also important to examine and identify models of best practice where professionals make constructive and sensitive approaches to these families.

Professionals from both medical and social welfare agencies, especially those in direct contact with families, such as the 'street-level bureaucrats' (see Chapter Five of this volume), are key. And they are no more so than in those families where parents are experiencing hardships through long-term illness or disability, and associated socioeconomic factors (such as poverty, low income, social exclusion), and are often having to rely on their children for care. Until recently, young carers in these contexts were overlooked, especially in formal needs assessment procedures. We can account for such oversight in a number of ways: the confusion among professionals about appropriate policy procedures; the fear among families of professional interventions that can mean some families resist support inputs; and the lack of recognition among professionals ab young caring as a welfare issue, as well as parental illness or disability as potential trigger for young caring. (These issues are discussed further in Chapter Five of this volume.)

Professionals who are directly and practically involved with families at the 'front line' of service delivery are ideally placed to assess children's needs, both as children and as carers, and to acknowledge their right to formal support (see Becker et al, 1998). Given that young caring can often be purposely concealed by families from professionals and their agencies due to a fear of familial separation and discrimination, it is the professionals who have direct contact with families where trigger factors might occur (that is, where parents are ill or disabled in some way). These professionals are also more likely to uncover young caring, more so perhaps than, say, teachers or family doctors who often do not 'see' how domestic and caring roles are organised in a family context. In this respect it has become the responsibility of these front-line professionals to assess children's and young carers' needs according to the criteria set out in the new framework for the assessment of children in need and their families (DH, 2000; Horwath, 2000). Therefore, professionals should consider young carers' developmental needs, their parents' capacity to parent effectively and family and environmental needs (see also Appendix B: 2000 (i)). While these assessment domains may or may not be appropriate in respect of the diversity of young carers' experiences and requirements (an issue we discuss later in this chapter), we can at least propose that any needs assessment procedures in this respect can only be implemented effectively by *direct consultation and involvement with families themselves*.

We found little evidence of any strategic or formal assessments being made in terms of the domains set out in the new framework (although this is hardly surprising given that the framework was not published until 2000). However, we did uncover its thematic relevance in terms of the *informal* judgements professionals made in relation to these families. A number of professionals made assumptions or judgements about mentally ill adults' efficacy as parents, and about the impacts of parental mental illness on children, which were perceived as mainly negative or detrimental in nature. Therefore, while the framework was not pertinent to our findings in any formal or obvious sense, theoretically at least some of the issues contained therein – especially in relation to parental capacity and young carers' developmental experiences – were reflected in professional attitudes and responses.

Seeking the perspectives of the three respondent groups enabled us to better understand the aggregate and often complex picture of support and service provision aimed at these families. Returning to these families for second-round data collection also enabled us to quantify and understand better the nature and effects of professional changes and replacements. Some of our findings mirrored those from other studies. The divisions between adult and children's services that are so often referred to in social work studies, as well as in psychiatry and mental health debates (see Göpfert et al, 1996; Falkov, 1998;

), were also evident in our work with young carers and
l illness.

also uncovered a range of further omissions and disparities.
statutory and voluntary-based service providers was marked,
factors (such as the boundaries between adult and children's
arlier), but also by the level of professional understanding
_____ mental ill health and young caring. Our evidence also
suggests that statutory mental health professionals rarely extend their approaches
to children or young carers. While support for young carers from voluntary
agencies such as young carers projects seems able to cross service boundaries
more readily, we also found evidence of a lack of awareness among young
carers project workers about the symptomatic outcomes of mental illness for
affected parents. This absence of understanding not only seems to be reflected
in the service divisions commonly described in social work but also presents
distinct challenges to family-oriented or holistic professional interventions.
Untrained or insensitive professional responses can also impede effective
interventions for young carers and their mentally ill parents.

The role and responsibility of professionals: the parents' perspective

Most of our parent respondents (38 cases) were on enhanced levels of support
on the Care Programme Approach (CPA) because of the severity and enduring
nature of their mental health problems (see Appendix B: 1991 (i), 1999 (ii),
1999 (iii) for discussion of the CPA). As such, they had access to a psychiatrist
as a Responsible Medical Officer and a range of other professionals as part of
the Multi-Disciplinary Team. A CPA coordinator was responsible for
systematising the whole package of care.

A number of issues emerged from our findings relating specifically to the
organisation and delivery of services through the CPA. The first was that few
of the respondents recognised or described any formal structure of support
(that is, through the CPA) and did not necessarily identify their CPA coordinator
as their key worker (that is, the professional to be included in our sample). The
second was that the nature of the particular parental condition, combined with
other familial and domestic influences (such as poverty, lone parenthood, poor
housing conditions, and so on) could also determine how parents with mental
illness experienced CPA and other service delivery. Third, the efficacy of an
individual CPA professional (not necessarily the designated key worker) could
play a key role in helping parents maintain personal and family stability.
Appropriate interventions here could also help offset the deleterious impacts
of other social and family dynamics (poverty, lone parenthood, and so on).

However, ineffective professional interventions (even from an individual
worker) could serve equally to undermine parental and family equilibrium.
Therefore, although the CPA gives adults with mental illness access to a
multidisciplinary team of professionals, we found that the effectiveness of a

multi-agency approach can be compromised by a *single* agent. A further significant influence on how mentally ill adults experience CPA service delivery, and equally how young carers experience professional interventions, relates to the stigma associated with mental illness. Professional perceptions of the impacts on families, and on young carers, of parental mental illness were important factors in terms of the appropriateness and sensitivity of the approaches professionals made to these families.

The type, range and quality of support received by parents on the CPA

Although our study focused on the experiences and needs of *young carers* whose parents were affected by mental ill health, understanding the nature of professional interventions for affected parents was fundamental to our inquiry. This was essential in order to understand where and how young carers were included in, or excluded from, both *family* and *child-focused or dedicated* support networks.

Table 4.1 describes the type of CPA and other regular support the parent respondents in our study received. As we have said, most of these parents received enhanced levels of support on the CPA. This accounts for the numbers of Community Psychiatric Nurses (CPN) or Community Mental Health Nurses (CMHN) involved. Each of the parent respondents received multi-agency support and almost half received more than four support services. However, some parents had only two or three professionals involved in their care at the time of interviews, while others had had services withdrawn or were undergoing changes in care provision (see also Appendix A of this volume).

Although the type of support available to parents here represents and includes a diverse range of CPA and other professionals, it is important to understand how parents perceive the *quality* of these support services. While diversity and quantity may be beneficial, adults in receipt of CPA and other mental health services may not always describe satisfactory or constructive experiences of service delivery. Indeed, it has been argued elsewhere that multi-agency support can sometimes be counterproductive or counter-therapeutic for patients (Schuff and Asen, 1996).

Ten of the 40 parent respondents in our study described the range of CPA and other support services as 'good' (three described all support as 'average'; one all 'poor'; five said some services were 'good', some 'poor'; and three did not know or could not comment). However, 18 of the 40 respondents recognised and identified *only one professional* as effective and who played a key role in their lives and the lives of their families. Although when asking service users about the quality of services received, a range of 'good', 'average' and 'poor' responses is to be expected, the relatively high number of respondents who emphasised only one professional among a multidisciplinary team of workers is significant. Furthermore, as we have said, these identified professionals were not always their designated CPA coordinator, but were interviewed in the triumvirate sample as the key professional in their lives. In trying to account

Table 4.1: The type and range of support received regularly by parents on the CPA

Type of support received	Parents/care recipients
Mental health statutory	
CPN/CMHN	24
Psychiatrist	23
Social worker	9
Day centre	9
Counsellor	4
Support worker	4
Drop-in centre	3
SSD unspecified	2
Intensive support team	2
Community support team	2
Crisis team	2
Other statutory	
GP	9
Homecare	8
Nurse (HV/DN)	4
Respite	3
Social worker (child/family)	2
Voluntary support	
Young carers Project	1
Victim support	1
Samaritans	1
General other	14[a]
Total number of parents	40

[a] Individual cases included family therapy, art therapy, private cleaner, and resource centre.

for this professional primacy we must look at types of identified professionals here and the nature and extent of support offered. Table 4.2 shows the key professionals identified by families in our study.

Although more than half the identified professionals here were from the statutory mental health services (delivered through the CPA), the relatively high number of young carers project workers identified is significant. Perhaps more than anything this signifies the value of young carers projects, not only for the dedicated support they offer to young carers, but also to the wider family, including parents. Nine of the 11 young carers project workers identified by families said they were offering support to other family members as well as young carers themselves.

Indeed, the type of support offered by young carers project workers in this respect is closer to the definition of key worker, or to what Cleaver et al have described as "not only a pivot for the family but also as a link between the different agencies involved" (1999, p 100). Significantly, all of the young carers projects identified had involved and coordinated other agencies and services. Therefore, young carers projects were instrumental in offering both dedicated

Table 4.2: Key professionals identified by families

Professional	Number
Young carers project worker	11
CPN/CMHN	9
Mental health support worker	4
Mental health social worker	4
GP	2
Day centre officer	3
Child and family social worker	2
Psychiatrist	2
Clinical nurse specialist	1
Community occupational therapist	1
Family support	1
Total number of key professionals identified	40

and needs-led support to young carers, as well as in recognising the wider needs of the family and liaising with other agencies. The following account from a young carers project worker illustrates this point:

> "I mean I do try and get round to lots of people, you know other professionals ... the head teacher ... the health visitor and the CPN ... mental health worker ... and the social worker. I felt that from [the mother] she did want me, you know, that [the mother] needed support and I think often, especially with mental health I do try to get involved with whole families because I think you can't, my view is you can't support the one without the other and that it was important. So I saw [the mother] and I arranged to take [the daughter/young carer] out at half term because [the mother] felt she never laughed."

Voluntary-aided young carers projects – on shifting financial sands

Research tells us that young carers projects are valued highly by young carers and their families as well as by statutory welfare professionals (see SSI, 1996; Aldridge and Becker, 1998; Becker et al, 1998). Indeed, the work of young carers projects can be seen as invaluable in offering dedicated young carers support services, help for families in general where parents have illnesses or disabilities and in providing a resource for children who might otherwise be referred to the public child care system. However, although there are now more than 120 young carers projects across the UK, they are in the main voluntary-aided organisations, often with uncertain funding futures. Sometimes projects can be developed in only a matter of months but then disappear as quickly because of the 'shifting sand' nature of their subsidy. In that time, children's expectations can be raised and dashed with no other agency or professional able to pick up the pieces. Furthermore, the informal ways in which some projects operate have been challenged: some are very small organisations with few staff and run on a very ad hoc or informal basis. Further debates have focused on whether it is the case that young carers projects are a means by which statutory agencies can circumvent their responsibilities to these children (see Howell, 1998).

However, evidence from our research here and previously (SSI, 1996; Becker et al, 1998) confirms that the work of young carers project workers is important and valued by families affected by parental illness or disability. From our work with young carers and parents with mental illness it seems that parents also look to individual young carers project workers for a kind of support that might not be available elsewhere, even from their community mental health teams. One of our parent respondents, who identified the young carers project worker as her key worker did so even though she had access to a range of formal (and informal) support for herself via the CPA. She said that this was "because they're the only ones who really care".

Some young carers project workers offered advocacy for families as well as dedicated support for young carers. Many of these workers were instrumental in involving other agencies and professionals, such as family doctors, housing officers, social workers and even sometimes the police. In these ways, project workers were pivotal both in addressing young carers' needs and in helping to maintain family relationships and stability. Project workers also played a key role at times in preventing the onset of crises. Equally, at critical times, parents often called on young carers project workers rather than other (statutory) professionals from community mental health teams. One parent described calling the young carers project during a violent incident with her ex partner.

> "Well, maybe I shouldn't have you know [called young carers project worker] like I said to her I do apologise ringing her and saying 'This has just happened you know'.... And I didn't know what the hell to do and she, she did come, I mean I don't know if she was supposed to have done that, she came round here though."

Consistency and continuity of care and support

The fact that a relatively high number of parents in our study, all of whom were receiving support from a multidisciplinary team of professionals, 'championed' one professional who was not necessarily their designated key worker perhaps underlines the need mentally ill adults have for consistency and continuity of care. This is also reflected in our findings in terms of the length of time professionals had been involved in their patients' care. Although the shortest involvement from an identified statutory professional was 18 months, the longest was 12+ years. Looking at the median figure, the length of involvement among both statutory and voluntary professionals was four years. Therefore, we can see that perhaps one of the reasons parents (and young carers) identified the professionals that they did (their professional 'champion') was because these workers had been more consistently and continuously involved in their care. Göpfert et al have argued, "children and parents exposed to traumatic discontinuities through illness and adversely experienced life events need *continuity of care*" (1996, p 299, emphasis added). Furthermore, they suggest that treatment or support "should be offered by the same person".

However, we noted that in the ten months between interview rounds, many parents had lost their key worker or a number of staff changes had occurred (staff changes are discussed later in this chapter). It is in this increasingly transitional support environment that parents come to rely on their children for immediate, flexible and continuous support.

Poole has suggested that it is likely to be the psychiatrist who "sees the outline of the person beyond the mental illness" (1996, p 6). Data from our research would refute this. Indeed, evidence from all three respondent groups pointed to a more narrow view: the patient was often treated (by psychiatrists in particular) in isolation from the rest of the family. Therefore, although parents may recognise and 'champion' the interventions of one key professional for themselves, often these professionals (especially when they are from the statutory services) generally are not offering support outside their client base, that is, to children and the wider family. The exceptions are the young carers project workers, most of whom offer a wider, family focus, but whose funding base within the voluntary sector is often precarious.

We have seen how the ecology of illnesses, the context in which they arise and progress is perhaps as important as the immediate symptomatic outcomes for affected individuals, as well as for other family members (see Chapters Two and Three of this volume). In this respect, not only do professionals need to offer consistency and continuity of support for their patients or clients, but also adopt a wider, more holistic or ecological perspective in relation to service users, their families and the environment in which illnesses first occur. While a professional 'champion' may be valued and relied upon for their consistency and long-term involvement with service users, particularly for parents when they have mental illness, evidence from our two-phase approach suggests that even valued professionals could be lost and continuity of care disrupted, and that few of these professionals were addressing the needs of *families*, particularly children and young carers. Without this wider perspective, it is clear how and why young carers continue to be overlooked, especially in assessment procedures (these issues are discussed further later in this chapter).

Obstacles to consistent and effective support

Our evidence suggests a number of reasons why professional interventions and responses are not always effective. There can be adverse consequences for parents and families in general of an ineffective *individual* professional response (the obverse of the parents' 'champion'), particularly when such responses are inconsistent or discontinuous. Lack of choice in terms of service users' support needs as well as the counterproductive nature of multi-agency support can also impede successful intervention procedures. Furthermore, misconceptions, even discrimination, among professional and local communities towards adults with mental illnesses must also be considered as contributory factors.

The problems that parents highlighted in terms of professional interventions were not only specific to inputs from statutory mental health workers. Regardless of the nature of service provision, effective support for mentally ill parents and their families could be impeded by the actions or *inaction* of just one professional (from either the statutory or voluntary sectors). We found that a negative or unsympathetic response from any of these professionals could leave parents feeling frustrated and could also exacerbate symptoms. Göpfert et al (1996) have also argued that the *personalities* of professionals can be influential in terms of agency collaboration and cooperation. A number of the parent respondents in our study described poor relationships with individual professionals who they either did not like or could not get on with. While this is not particularly surprising given the range and diversity of professionals involved in the care of a parent (patient), some of these professionals could be key or pivotal in influencing a parent's diagnosis and their progression through a range of treatments and service interventions.

Some of the parents in our study had waited a considerable length of time (in some cases several years) for a diagnosis to be confirmed. Given the difficulties in the 'legal' definition of mental illness (see Appendix B: 1959 (i), 1983 (Box B.1)), never mind the clinical considerations, it is perhaps not surprising that making a diagnosis can be both a complex, difficult and protracted process. In the period of waiting for diagnoses and treatments, parents can be forced into an increasingly dependent relationship with their children and sometimes must further rely on them for care and support. Children's caring roles can then become more firmly established and 'institutionalised' within the family. Professionals' indecision or inability to confirm a diagnosis can have profound impacts on affected individuals and the wider family. Although we can understand why a family doctor, for example, may be unable to decide about a patient's diagnosis given that presenting symptoms can sometimes be ambiguous and resourcing issues can be a factor, waiting for treatment can exacerbate a patient's symptoms and create further crises. In this respect a professional who does not respond well, quickly and in the ways in which a parent (or child) would wish can aggravate symptoms and create crises for families as a whole. The following case study illustrates this point.

Robert is a 41 year-old father of three. He has had 'various diagnoses' in the past, but his symptoms include hearing voices, which he says become unbearable at times and have led to several suicide attempts. In the past he has received cognitive therapy and psychotherapy and a range of medication. He has recently moved house to a new area. Previously he was on the CPA and had positive experiences of mental health service delivery. Since moving and being assigned a new GP he says his life has been made more difficult by the GP's indecision about his diagnosis. Previous diagnoses have suggested either schizophrenia or paranoid schizophrenia. His current GP disagrees with both diagnoses and will not confirm either. In the meantime Robert says the voices he hears have driven him to a further suicide attempt and he has been sectioned, resulting in a crisis for the whole family. He believes a firm diagnosis is the only response that will help him now. He relates a recent experience with his GP: "I saw the doctor and he just said 'What do you want us to do, there's absolutely nothing we're prepared to do for you. You know, you've got to stop doing this game' [referring to Robert's suicide attempts] and I thought to myself I ain't playing a game ... but I thought if they send me away with no help I'm not living any more. I can't carry on living the way I was."

It was only through talking with Robert's identified professional (a mental health social worker from his previous community mental health team) that we were able to ascertain that Robert's difficulties were less to do with diagnostic factors and more about funding issues. His mental health social worker explained:

> "I put a request that he, you know, be allocated to someone because there was a few things outstanding but at that time and we were extremely short-staffed and there was a severe budgeting crisis at county hall so they literally went to the most severe, because our criteria is for severe and enduring mental illness and they were literally going as local authorities do when there's bad funding literally stripping to the most severely needy."

This case illustrates clearly the importance of the roles professionals undertake. Robert was reliant on his family doctor in order to access services through the community mental health team. Funding problems aside, an effective professional response here would be one that offered support through advocacy and 'acquaintanceship' with both the patient and his family. In these contexts it becomes the responsibility of professionals to try and overcome obstacles to effective treatment and support strategies that might be based on funding limitations or discontinuity of other professional interventions.

Discontinuity of support and change

Consistent professional responses and continuity of care can be compromised by staff turnover and changes in approaches in adult mental health service delivery. Where staff changes do and must occur (and given the range of professionals involved in CPA support through a multidisciplinary team, for example, such changes are inevitable), the importance of the smooth exchange of information and efficient transfer of cases are further underlined. Our evidence suggests that parents and young carers look for avenues of consistency in their lives, which are often made inconsistent by the nature of parents' mental illnesses themselves, as well as wider social and economic influences that affect family life. Changes in staff or levels of care provision from the welfare services can lead to further disruptions among these families. Some of the parents in our study described situations where, for example, "the whole set-up at the hospital has changed recently". Or, "Most of the time, unless it's something really serious, you see the house officer, and, at the moment, the house officers are changed left, right and centre". Furthermore, as we have said, valued professional support from an individual worker could often be subject to discontinuity.

Notably, young carers' experiences were also influenced by changes in formal care provision. For example, some young carers were placed with foster carers when parents were hospitalised (see Chapter Three of this volume). One young carer told us:

> "The first family I went with, went to I was with them for about a year. And then I went to another person and then I was with them for a year, then I went to another, and then another. So, I think I've been to about four, since I was about ten."

Such disruptions in formal care provision can compromise family security as well as foster further dependency on a valued individual professional. One parent commented:

> "It is still far easier for me to do something [self-harm], so that takes a lot of courage on my part and I feel very ashamed of it. I shouldn't be feeling like this, and I shouldn't need to go to them for help. But it, it seems to work quite well, but then you get, 'She's out of the office. Is there somebody else you'd like to talk to?' 'No'. And, this is understandable, you know, they, they're working out, I can perfectly understand it. But I have to be really desperate before I actually ring, so it's, it's sometimes a bit of a, well, I did what I was supposed to do, and there's no response. So I go and do what I want to do [self-harm]."

Data from the second-round interviews with parents and young carers showed that even in a relatively short period of time (ten months), families – and parents in particular – experienced many changes in terms of professional inputs. Out of the 28 parents interviewed in the second round, 13 had experienced changes in support from professionals other than their key worker. A further ten parents had had services withdrawn completely. Furthermore, of the 28 families included in the second-round interviews, only 12 professionals were also interviewed that were the same key workers as identified by families in the first round. Of the remaining 16 second-round key professionals identified by families, 12 could not be interviewed because they were new or different key workers (from the first round); two refused to participate, one was on long-term sick leave and one was on secondment. As we have said, these revisions in staff inputs can and do have profound impacts on families. While staff changes are unavoidable, replacement staff can present new or additional difficulties for parents and for families, as the following examples from two parents demonstrate:

> "What I did have a problem with, at first, when he [new key worker] first came here he wanted the full details of me and that did get a little painful for a couple of weeks because I'd sort of put it all back, on the back burner and by talking, it all brought it right to the head again, you know."

> "You see a different one [mental health professional] nearly every time, they say 'How do you feel?' You say, 'Well, I still feel the same. I want to die'. 'Oh all right then'. And they will write you out a prescription and say 'Off you go'. And you see them again in another three months and that's it. So it's no help whatsoever."

Choice and the effects of multi-agency support

Although most of the parents in our study were *generally* satisfied with the mental health services they received, some described limitations. Changes in staff and services may perhaps have had less impact if parents felt they had some choice in professional inputs and service delivery. For example, some parents said that, despite the amount of support on offer, this was not always what was requested but was what they were told was available at the time. Consequently, some parents felt that the services they received were not necessarily addressing their particular *individual* needs. Lack of choice in this respect had led a number of parents in our study to set up their own mental health groups in order to address the gaps in service provision. One parent said:

> "Services are bad, mainly social services, but then health are equally as bad, the reason I set the group up is that most of what is out there is latter-day basket weaving. It's just offensive.... It does actually make the level of illness worse.... Nothing is tailored to needs, it's all resource-led."

Our findings also indicated that multi-agency support is not always seen by parents to be necessarily beneficial or advantageous. While it may seem contradictory that a diverse range of services and professional interventions could be in and of themselves disadvantageous to parents with mental illnesses and their families, our evidence suggests that mentally ill parents can find the nature of multi-agency support confusing. This, in turn, can sometimes make it difficult for parents to identify a key worker responsible for coordinating the system of care. In this respect we can see how some families can be made "helpless by being helped" (see Göpfert et al, 1996). Schuff and Asen also found:

> The more problems the disturbed family presents, the more professionals get recruited to provide 'help'. Frequently such 'help' further enhances the parents' sense of failure – thus requiring more help which, in turn, leads to an even more helpless posture of the parents. (1996, p 137)

The inability of some of our parent respondents to identify their CPA coordinator (or other mental health professional) as their key worker perhaps reflects the counter-therapeutic potential of multi-agency interventions. The fact that a multidisciplinary team of professionals is more susceptible to staff changes and inconsistent or discontinuous professional inputs may also account for why some parents were unable to identify a key worker from their community mental health teams. This may also account for a relatively high number of young carers project workers being identified as key workers among the parents in our study. In this respect, parents were perhaps more able to recognise consistency by association – that is, through their children's (voluntary sector) service interventions (all of the young carers in our study mainly received support through the young carers projects – see Table 4.3) – especially when such professional consistency was missing from their own community mental health teams.

The counterproductive (or counter-therapeutic) nature of multi-agency support can also be exacerbated when co-morbidity and combinative mental and physical illnesses occur, and therefore where service inputs and interventions further increase and diversify. The following case study illustrates this point:

Caroline is 31 years-old, a lone parent and has two daughters aged 12 and eight years. She has depression and a serious, potentially life-threatening physical health condition. She cannot work because of her illnesses and is often confined to bed. She has spent long periods in hospital because of her physical health problems. Her mental health problems also mean she spends intermittent periods confined to bed. She is often very emotional, cries a lot in front of her daughters, and is suicidal at times. She has a GP, home care support, district nurse, community mental health nurse, child and family social worker, social worker, welfare rights officer and foster carers for her daughters. One daughter also receives the support of the local young carers project. At the time of interview, homecare support had been increased because Caroline had recently returned home from hospital and was bedridden. The district nurse and various GPs were also visiting regularly. The homecare workers changed on a regular basis and Caroline said she did not get on with some of them. She is on a wide range of tablets for both her physical and mental health conditions. The treatment for her physical health condition has exacerbated her depression and has caused serious weight gain. Her mental illness was, she says, triggered in childhood, when she was physically abused by her mother. She has since experienced further physical abuse from a violent partner who has had an injunction served against him that prevents him from coming to the house. Caroline's daughters have received counselling in the past relating to the possibility of their mother's death. Caroline was unable to identify a key professional for interview. She said: "I did have a support worker but she's just left not long ago to have a baby so they're arranging to have a different support worker come. But I can't have a support worker you see until I'm well. [The 'home help'] is only temporary at the moment till the other one comes back. She's off ill at the moment. Before I went in hospital this time the person who runs ['home help' services] came out to see me and she said that she were going to get more help for me to do a bit of housework once a fortnight, er, ironing once a week and, er, to like do the pots, breakfast pots in a morning when they've had their breakfast and things like that and this one doesn't do any of it.... But I thought, 'Well she's only temporary', so I thought 'she'll probably be gone soon'."

Given the range of interventions here from the community mental health team, health, social and children's services, perhaps we can understand why Caroline was unable to identify one professional for interview in our study. Furthermore, in light of the diversity of inputs and staff changes it is also clear why she was unable to form a relationship of trust and consistency with any one professional. Although generally her medical needs were being met, psychologically she felt anxious and disappointed by the lack of support from someone who would talk to her about other (stress) factors, which she felt were also exacerbating her depression. (These, in turn could also have been contributing to the deterioration in her physical health condition.) Therefore, among the range of service inputs no one professional seemed either to be coordinating her support, listening to her problems, or looking at the needs of the whole family and wider issues (for example, family and environmental factors; see Horwath, 2000). Indeed, the one person who was offering both emotional and practical support in this respect was Caroline's eldest daughter, the young carer in our sample.

While we found no evidence of families such as Poole (1996) describes, who received 20 or more professional interventions, we did find that, despite the range of support offered to mentally ill parents through the CPA and other services, few professionals were looking at the needs of *families* and the relationships therein (see also Göpfert et al, 1996). A narrower, more patient-oriented perspective was more commonly the case in terms of the professional interventions in our study.

The discriminatory effects of a mental health diagnosis

Our evidence suggests that when parents experience mental illness they (and their families, and children by association) have to contend with a crossfire of discrimination and misunderstanding. Community prejudice and misconceptions among professionals outside mental health services can compound assumptions that question the adequacy of the parenting capabilities of mentally ill adults. These in turn can help perpetuate the notion that to be mentally ill *and* a parent results in parental incompetence. Falkov has argued:

> Polarised perceptions about the parenting capabilities of those who are mentally ill simply serve to perpetuate unhelpful myths and stigma – for example, the view that mental illness precludes being able to be a good parent. (1998, p 16).

Therefore, families as a whole can become stigmatised by the presence of parental mental illness. We have also seen (in Chapter Three of this volume) how and where children can experience discrimination from their peers and others when children are living with and caring for an affected parent. However, the parents in our study described inequitable responses from professionals outside mental health services as well as from those who worked within them whenever their roles as *parents* became the subject of professional scrutiny and appraisal.

Although many mental health professionals demonstrated symptomatic awareness and understanding about their patients' *conditions* and made constructive approaches in this respect, professional responses in terms of the wider implications of mental illness when these patients were also *parents* were less constructive. It became clear that adults with mental illness face ongoing judgements both about their competency as individuals in the community (public discrimination) and about their efficacy as parents from welfare and legal professionals (professional discrimination). And yet these very issues, encountering and challenging community prejudice and fighting to retain their rights as parents to raise their children themselves, can also exacerbate the effects of mental illness on parents and the wider family. Göpfert et al argue:

> If a child is taken into care, a parent will be grieving which, on top of a mental illness, may be particularly difficult to recognise and treat. (1996, p 300)

This point is illustrated in this example:

> "[The CPN] turned up with the social, childcare social worker. And they said they'd had a meeting and they'd decided that the children needed more stability so they were going to take them into care with a view to applying later on for a long-term Care Order which made me very upset. [The CPN] said I should go into hospital for a few weeks. So they stayed, the children stayed with me that night and we slept all together in my bed and then we ... they went to school the next day, I went into hospital and they went into care. I speak to them every day on the phone but it's not the same."

It was clear from our work with parents and young carers that judgements made by legal professionals, for example, about what it means for parents to be mentally ill (see Appendix B: 1983, Box B.1) and, more importantly, how this affects children, are rarely based on any firm medical evidence (see also Poole, 1996). On the basis of these assumptions, legal professionals can and do make childcare decisions which can have profound implications for parents and families. One of the parents in our study, for example, lost custody of her child following the parent's mental health breakdown because she was not considered competent as a parent:

> "The judge in the case said that had I been normal he would've given her custody to me ... those were his exact words."

Poole (1996) describes similar cases, and one in particular where, despite evidence from a psychiatrist about his patient's ability to parent, the judge heard the words 'manic depression' and custody of a child was lost. Poole said the judge in the case had suggested that "it would not be safe to leave a child in the care of a 'maniac'" (sic) (1996, p 5).

Young carers and professional interventions

We have said that it is important to explore and understand the experiences of parents and the perspectives and nature of interventions from professionals in order to more fully understand the experiences and needs of children when they care. In this respect, understanding young carers' experiences of professional approaches becomes equally, if not more, important. However, our work with young carers suggests an imbalance of evidence relating to their encounters with statutory professionals in particular, simply because they have so few experiences to report. Despite the thrust of recent policy initiatives that underline the need for more holistic, family approaches, and the need to include young carers in children's services and other care plans (see Dearden and Becker, 2000b), the picture that emerges from our evidence is one of exclusion rather than inclusion. Apart from services from young carers projects it seems that young carers have access to few alternative support networks.

Previous research has suggested that, despite key policy changes, statutory professionals in particular continue to overlook young carers' needs, especially when implementing formal needs assessment procedures (Dearden and Becker, 1998, 2000b). Evidence from our triumvirate sample suggests that such professional oversight continues, despite the participation of statutory (and voluntary) professionals in the research process. (Their involvement in our study, which was specifically about young carers' experiences of support and services, had, it seems – from evidence from our second round of fieldwork – little impact in terms of any further attempts professionals made to include young carers.) We have seen that the boundaries between adult mental health and children's services are rarely crossed, and that statutory professionals from mental health teams in particular tend to adopt narrower, more patient-oriented perspectives. Furthermore, it seems that in the main young carers project workers are more willing and able to cross service boundaries when addressing the needs of young carers.

Table 4.3 describes the range of support received by the 40 young carers in our study. While it is not surprising that so many young carers were supported by a young carers project (given most of the sample was selected from the projects themselves), what is significant is that so many (25) had *only* the support of a young carers project at the time of first-round interviews. (It is important to note that the professionals who were offering support to the young carers – mainly young carers project workers – were not necessarily the key professionals who were interviewed as part of our study.) By the time of second-round interviews, five young carers no longer had any form of support or services. Therefore, while the parents in our study received a range of interventions through the CPA and other services, their children/young carers were 'support poor' (certainly in terms of inputs from statutory professionals) by comparison.

It is clear from our evidence and other research that statutory professionals, particularly from adult mental health services, rarely include or consult children and sometimes are not even aware their patients are also parents. Göpfert et al have also recognised this in their work with mentally ill adults:

Table 4.3: The type and range of support received by young carers at first- and second-round interviews

First-round interview		Second-round interview	
Type of support received	**Young carers**	**Type of support received**	**Young carers**
Mental health statutory		*Other statutory*	
Counsellor	Past: 3	Social worker	2
Other statutory		Family support worker	1
Respite	Past: 1 Current: 2	*Voluntary support*	
Family support worker	2	Young carers project	17
Family centre	1	None	5
Family therapy	1	Not known	3
School nurse	1		
Social worker (child/family)	9		
Voluntary support			
Young carers project	34[a]		
General other	3		
None	4		
Not known	1		
Total	40	Total	28

[a] Twenty-five young carers had *only* the support of a young carers project at time of first-round interview; six had two support services; two had three support services; two had four or more support services.

> It is a common experience that adult psychiatrists and mental health workers
> often do not know whether or not their patients have any children. (1996,
> p 273)

It was evident, from talking with the young carers project workers in our study
that they were more able to cross service boundaries and liaise with a range of
statutory and other agencies, and coordinate alternative support services. Indeed,
all of the identified young carers project workers interviewed in the first round
of fieldwork said they had coordinated or liaised with other agencies as part of
their work with young carers. As only six (first round) young carer respondents
were not receiving support from projects, it is likely that the 14 young carers
who also received support from other professional agencies had been given
access to these via the projects themselves.

However, it should not be supposed that young carers necessarily require
multi-agency support from different voluntary and statutory teams of workers.
Often young carers project support itself can represent diversity of services (see
Aldridge and Becker, 1998). This can mean that, despite the lack of statutory
inputs, young carers can in one sense become 'support rich' through the range
of services offered through regular contact with a young carers project. However,
this is not to suggest that the responsibilities of statutory professionals to include
children as carers in support strategies, and in assessment procedures in particular,
become redundant or unnecessary. More holistic, family-oriented approaches
and needs assessments are still required for children when they care (see Chapter
Five of this volume).

A significant finding from our study points to the primacy of an adult-
oriented medical model which focuses on medical pathology and the mentally
ill adult as patient. Therefore, adult-based statutory professionals, particularly
psychiatrists, doctors and other health workers, consistently overlooked children,
their needs and the needs of their families and demonstrated a lack of awareness
about the prevalence and consequences of young caring and a lack of
understanding of a 'social model' of illness. And yet the potential for recognising
and formally identifying young carers – using mapping procedures, for example
(see Chapter Five of this volume) – via interventions aimed at adult service
users is high. Given the range of professionals involved in CPA provision, it
would seem natural to assume that the chances and opportunities for recognition
of young caring in domestic settings would be considerably increased. While
our evidence suggests that this is often not the case, there is an opportunity for
this to change. For example, from April 2002 young carers were included in
CPA care plans (see Appendix B:1999 (ii)).

The recognition and identification of young carers by professionals in practice
is complicated by a number of factors:

1. Young caring can often be purposively concealed within families, as well as
   obscured without;

2. Parents and children are often reluctant to reveal both the incidence and nature of parental illness in families, as well as the nature and extent of children's caring roles, for fear of oppressive or discriminatory professional interventions;

3. The prevalence and extent of young caring in families is often intentionally obscured by parents' need to prevent children understanding the full extent of their caring duties (the double, hidden nature of caring; see Chapter Two of this volume);

4. It could be argued that mentally ill parents' fear of children's admission into local authority care are further amplified when children occupy what might be seen to be essentially parent-like roles;

5. The onset or prevalence of parental mental ill health can also often obscure evidence of young caring when it occurs in families because of the narrow, patient-oriented medical perspectives of adult-based professionals.

Therefore, we can see and understand more clearly the contexts in which professional assessments of children's needs as carers continue to be omitted from intervention strategies. We can also comprehend the underlying reasons for this in terms of the obfuscation of young caring both as a welfare issue and in respect of cases in practice. The dominance of a medical model (that puts the adult patient centre stage and children only as 'casualties' of their parents' illness) over other social and family perspectives means children are further obscured and overlooked as non-competent (seen but not heard) individuals. In this context we can understand why the adoption and continuation of caring roles among children generates confusion among adult-oriented statutory professionals about whose responsibility – medicine, adult or children's social services – young carers really are. (This is an issue we return to in Chapter Five of this volume.)

Consultation

These issues were reflected in young carers' perceptions of the quality of services they received and the extent to which they were included in professional interventions. Only five of the 40 young carers interviewed in the first round of fieldwork said they had been included in formal discussions with statutory professionals. Furthermore, two of these five children said that there had been no practical outcomes as a result of their inclusion; another said that, although they had been included, their needs, and what they had to say, had been ignored:

> "Social services are horrible because they like, they change, they're making all these decisions about your life and then they keep you in the dark and not telling you about it.... Once we had a review with the man out the house and it was for us to say things what we thought. Everything we said he disagreed with and they just of course went with the adult, they don't care what we say.... We had one [review].... No they did not listen to any of

us.... They said like if any of you have any questions you want to ask us out of the whole thing just say it. I did that even though it was [sister's] turn and they just told me to shut up."

Perhaps more significantly, only two of the children interviewed in the first round of fieldwork said that they had received a formal assessment of their needs. However, neither of them knew or understood which type of assessment they had received or the outcomes here. Ten months later, as we have said, few new interventions had taken place. One young carer had been assessed for a new respite placement, one had received a social services assessment and another had been involved in a care-planning meeting, but did not know the outcome.

Our evidence also indicated that sometimes even those professionals who were visiting the family home on a regular basis to treat their patients or clients (the parent respondents in our study) also neglected to consider children's roles and needs. One young carer, who was undertaking care duties for her sister as well as her bedridden mother, described the response from her mother's visiting GP:

"She only really stopped five minutes. She just come and had a look, told me mum that she'd got to start coming off antibiotics a bit and just went again."

Our data confirm evidence from other research that has underlined the ongoing exclusion of young carers from statutory interventions, particularly assessment procedures. We may ask why, in light of key policy changes and developments (see Appendix B of this volume), young carers continue to be overlooked in this way. And we must look once again to the divergence and exclusivity of different (medical and social) paradigms that somehow allow the needs of children as carers to be circumvented. (We discuss this issue further in Chapter Five of this volume.)

The value of young carers project interventions

Research on young carers suggests that what these children need most in terms of professional interventions is increased access to services, the ability to make decisions about (whether or not to continue) caring, and access to someone they can talk to about their experiences (see Aldridge and Becker, 1993a; Becker et al, 1998). More often than not, young carers projects are meeting all of these needs combined, and our evidence suggests that young carers rely on the contact they have with other children socially at projects, as well as on individual workers, many of whom young carers come to view as friends. Often the inputs from young carers project workers extend beyond simply helping young carers make choices about caring, accessing other support networks and making social contacts. They are also instrumental in helping to build young carers' confidence and self-esteem by *listening* to what they have to say. The following case study illustrates this point.

> Hannah is 17 years-old. She helps to care for her mother who has severe depression, is often suicidal, and cannot be left in the house on her own. Hannah has low self-esteem, has experienced prolonged bullying at school, and discrimination from neighbours and others in the local community partly because of her mother's illness. Hannah attends a local FE college where she is doing a Performing Arts course. She was inspired to do the course by her desire to be a pop star. Her ambitions have been encouraged by staff at the young carers project, particularly during a residential weekend break organised by the project. Prior to this weekend, Hannah had worked closely with the young carers project worker who had tried to encourage Hannah in her poetry writing and in talking more openly about her feelings. Here, Hannah describes her time with the project and during the residential weekend:"It's helped me a lot and it gets me out, away from home, it gives me something to look forward to. I went there [weekend trip] on the first day and I was really, really dreading it and I wanted to come home, I was scared.... Once I got the first night over and done with and I woke up on Saturday morning I felt a lot better. And I had a bit of a laugh it was really, really nerve-wracking, but as soon as that party was up on the evening and they got me up to do my poem, I actually felt a lot more confident. I did a creative poetry workshop ... it gets me emotions out, it gets me feelings out and it tends to help me a lot. It's kind of therapeutic."

Considering young carers projects often represent the only access to dedicated support children have as carers, it is important not to underestimate the value and significance of the type and degree of support these projects offer. However, as we mentioned earlier, project funding is precarious and can lead to raised expectations among young carers that can be quickly dashed. This can be confusing and deflating for young carers who often learn to rely on individual young carers project workers for both practical and emotional support. One parent commented:

> "One particular worker who's left now, she were really nice and she used to come out once a week to them and they got really close to her and when she left it really upset her [daughter/young carer] and she hasn't really got close to anybody at the project since."

However, significantly, we found that most of the young carers project workers in our study were unable to offer specific support to young carers in relation to their parents' mental health conditions. This was often because generic project workers had received little or no training in mental health issues. While young carers project workers could sometimes provide information to young carers about illnesses, including mental health conditions, project workers themselves did not always have sufficient understanding about symptomatic outcomes of mental illness among adults to help young carers effectively in this respect.

Figuring it out

Our evidence suggests that, as with parents, young carers need effective, *consistent* support. In this context, Marlowe has argued that "a sensitive worker can aid a child's development as a child and empower their caring role as part of that" (1996, p 105). However, outside young carers project work we found that young carers were often having to rely on forming opportune relationships with a diverse range of professionals who were propitiously understanding. Therefore, young carers' professional alliances were often based on serendipitous interventions from individual professionals who had somehow 'figured out' a child's caring responsibilities, as the following example from a young carer demonstrates:

> "It were about two years ago when I was in a bad state because I was getting bullied all the time going through school ... and there was a Personal and Social Education teacher and she was really, really nice and helped me through it. And she figured out that I was helping at home and I'd got to support the family at home and everything."

In this respect, like their parents, young carers are as likely to attach themselves to – and value – one 'good' or effective professional. When these professionals offer constructive, non-demeaning assistance, young carers' experiences of *statutory* service interventions, while scant and irregular, can also be meaningful ones. We found evidence of good practice, where referrals through young carers projects and coordination between these and other services (in this case, children's social services) had resulted in the introduction of link families for young carers. Two young carers in our study had access to a locally based link family. These families lived close by and were available for support when parents were hospitalised, or during times of crisis. Link families were recognised foster carers but had awareness of young caring issues and some of the problems young carers could face in these contexts. They would also have some insight into the nature of parental mental health conditions. This was clearly important to the young carers in our study. It is also where the young caring distinction becomes an important one as dedicated support in this respect, based on an assessment of young carers' specific needs, can lead to sensitive and constructive interventions.

Recognising young carers' contributions

Falkov suggests that "The term 'young carer' is a label. There are times when it may be perceived as stigmatising and unhelpful" (1998, p 123). Categorising children as young carers has also been challenged by some disability rights commentators who have suggested that the 'label' only serves to undermine the parenting roles of ill or disabled adults (see, for example, Keith and Morris, 1995).

However, we have argued that the 'young carer' classification is an important one as it underlines children's rights to recognition and offers a gateway to support as carers and as children. Our evidence further confirms this assertion. Data from both first- and second-round fieldwork clearly showed that children continue to care even when their parents are supported by a range of multi-disciplinary services, from community mental health teams and others, not least because of the consistency and continuity of support children offer through kinship and co-residency. Describing her own experiences as a former young carer, Marlowe has said:

> To think of myself as having been a young carer helped me to realise how much I had done to support my family. Previously this role had been unrecognised, taken for granted and undefined. (1996, p 103)

Where children are caring for parents with mental health problems, the need for recognition of children's role adaptations is perhaps even greater given the prevalence of assumption and misconception among professional and local communities about the effects of parental mental illness on children. Perhaps, then, classifying children as young carers in this context would avoid 'knee jerk'-type child protection responses that a children in need assessment on its own might point to initially. By promoting the formal recognition of young caring – as well as the triggers for its onset – through mapping procedures for example (see Chapter Five of this volume) means that the responses of statutory professionals would be based more often on recognition and inclusion rather than on exclusion and neglect. In this context the 'young carer' classification can become a mechanism by which young carers can access services and support by right as children and carers.

The nature of professional interventions – professional perspectives

In seeking the views of professionals about the nature of their approaches to young carers and parents affected by mental illness, we hoped to be able to provide examples of good practice, as well as establish the nature of the impediments to effective interventions. In addition, our triumvirate sample enabled us to compare the approaches of professionals with the responses of the parents and young carers in our study.

What was significant from our findings was that there were so few contradictions in terms of the responses from our three respondent groups. Data from professionals confirmed the evidence from the parents and young carers in our study. Therefore, we found evidence of service divisions within adult and children's sectors, individual professional responses that were sometimes constructive (depending on effective *individual* professional approaches) but more often seemed to be based on misconceptions or misunderstanding about the effects of parental mental illness on children and young carers. Furthermore, as well as an absence of holistic, family-centred approaches, particularly among statutory sector professionals, we found that young carers were rarely assessed or included in discussions with these professionals. Of the 29 statutory sector professionals identified as key workers by families (11 others were young carers project workers), 15 were cognizant of young carers' issues, and eight said they had included young carers in their discussions about parents' care plans. However, only one had made a formal needs assessment in respect of the child concerned. Furthermore, just three of these professionals said they thought a 'whole family' approach was important. In contrast, interventions from young carers project workers, while fundamentally aimed at the needs of children (as carers), were more likely to include *family* approaches.

Narrow professional perspectives and distancing

Our research findings reflected the divisions in adult and children's services, and more particularly between statutory adult support and children's services through young carers projects. All young carers projects were instrumental in involving or coordinating support for young carers and their families from other (statutory) agencies. Statutory professionals on the whole were not coordinating other services nor were they including young carers in discussions, and were even less likely to implement formal needs assessments for these children. However, what is interesting here is the difference between professionals' perception of the importance of young caring as a welfare issue and the absence of practical interventions for young carers. While most statutory professionals demonstrated awareness about issues of young caring as well as some cases in practice, few had involved young carers in discussions, implemented needs assessments, or referred them to other agencies.

The level of recognition of young caring as a welfare issue may, as we have said, be falsely elevated due to the nature of the study itself. Participation in initial interviews would have inevitably raised professional awareness of young caring among those involved. However, our second-round data revealed that *no new children's or young carers' needs assessments had been made by statutory sector professionals*. Where identified key workers were from statutory agencies (usually from community mental health teams), none of these reported any further family interventions or inputs specifically aimed at children or young carers during the second-round interviews. Most statutory-sector professionals either seemed satisfied that children's needs were being met entirely by support from young carers projects, or made decisions about children's abilities to cope with family circumstances based on suppositions that children had grown accustomed to their circumstances and roles. As one intensive support worker said: "I judged he [young carer] was coping well enough". Another (day care officer) professional said:

> "It's a close family, very loving and loved. The chaos of their daily lives is normal for them and they just get on with it."

What our evidence shows clearly is the division between statutory and voluntary service provision to families, and particularly children, and the narrow perspectives of some mental health professionals and others working in adult services. Our evidence disputes Poole's assertion, then, that because adult psychiatrists, for example, have such close contact with the families of mentally ill patients, they are "inescapably key professionals for the children of mentally disordered parents" (1996, p 3). In fact, our evidence supports a different notion that suggests few statutory professionals, including psychiatrists in adult services, are trained or effective in looking after the interests of adult patients *and* their children or the relationships between the two (see also Göpfert et al, 1996). Mental health professionals in these contexts may be ideally *placed* to address the needs of both parents and children, but it would seem that rarely do such joint *family* interventions actually take place.

In many cases the lack of more holistic, family-centred approaches seemed to be reflected in professional attitudes about their own personal responsibility (or indeed, absence of responsibility). Professionals from a range of backgrounds or services, while recognising the need for family interventions in theory, did not perceive these to be within the parameters of their own work practices. We found evidence of professional 'distancing' in this respect. In these contexts, while some adult mental health service professionals understood issues of young caring, and the changes that can occur in respect of children's roles when their parents are mentally ill, professionals often did not perceive the need to address these issues themselves. One psychiatric social worker from adult services said:

> "I think there's training in mental health to give some insight into the effect of the parent's mental health on the child. If not a childcare worker, a mental health worker [could support the child]."

Equally, most statutory professionals working outside the mental health services also seemed to distance themselves from mental health issues even when dealing with families where parents had mental illness.

Most mental health professionals, on the other hand, were uncertain about how to address the experiences and needs of their patients' children, especially when these children were helping to provide care. Sometimes professionals used the research interview process itself as a way of *figuring out* the best or most effective ways of responding to young carers' needs. As one GP commented:

> "Erm, well I'm sure whatever help they can get would be worthwhile really. I don't know what specifically I mean. Over fives now we've got what they call the zero to 16 team which is a place we refer primarily really which they have a mix of different skills really, social worker and god knows what else so we've got that."

This confirms evidence from other research that, despite more recent policy developments for young carers and their families (Appendix B), statutory-sector professionals in particular remain uncertain about which policy guidance and procedures are relevant in terms of meeting young carers' needs (see SSI, 1995, 1996; see also Chapter Five of this volume). Certainly it would seem that statutory professionals have few strategic opportunities to formally recognise or identify young carers' experiences and needs, which would no doubt increase young carers' opportunities to access dedicated support, alongside their parents.

Perhaps one of the reasons professionals 'distance' themselves from the responsibility of including young carers' and families' needs within their own professional sphere is that they perceive such intervention to be time consuming, or more onerous than their own work commitments would allow. However, it might be more appropriate and convenient for professionals simply to *recognise* that their patients', or clients', children may have a role to play in providing care and may require support for themselves. As Göpfert et al have argued:

> It might be more important to move just alongside a family and try to be helpful as a professional, rather than 'assess'. (1996, p 277)

The five-minute phone call

While not undermining the need for more needs assessments for young carers, our evidence suggests that what young carers often require most is recognition of their caring contributions alongside practical support as and when it is needed (Marlowe, 1996; Becker et al, 1998; Bibby and Becker, 2000). In this respect, the nature of young carers' needs are often much more straightforward than professionals outside children's services may suppose. Referrals to young carers projects and other agencies need not be time consuming or involve more commitment than can be given by (statutory) professionals. Furthermore, our evidence suggests that consistency and continuity of *care and support* can sometimes be more important to young carers (and their parents) than multidisciplinary inputs or elaborate professional interventions (see Chapter Three of this volume). Monitoring young carers' progress on a regular basis would ensure consistency of support and also ensure that these children's needs are not overlooked (mapping procedures are discussed in Chapter Five). In some instances, all that may be required of professionals is, as one young carers project worker said, "just a phone call ... that's all it takes, a five-minute phone call".

This could be equally true for parents, as the following (approved) social worker commented: "I mean, a five-minute phone call on a regular basis is the, I think is as good for [the parent] as me seeing her formally in an office for an hour once a week". The need for helpful and *consistent* aid to families in this respect is confirmed in the evidence from our three respondent groups, including professionals themselves.

The professional 'champion'

Evidence from the professionals in our study also confirmed the significance of what we have termed the professional 'champion'. We found examples of individual professional interventions that were efficacious and continuous. Some of these were also highly valued by parents and young carers alike for the holistic, 'whole family' approaches they made, and because one or two statutory professionals seemed to understand the needs of both, even when the patient (parent) was the professional's primary focus of responsibility. As one parent said of her community psychiatric nurse (CPN):

> "My old CPN who you should talk to could spot my illness even before [daughter/young carer] did. He just knew about my illness. He was always right."

In this case, the CPN was offering support to the mother (his patient) as well as to the daughter who was helping to provide care. During interviews with the CPN it was clear that he was also aware of the effects on families of different professional approaches from within adult psychiatric services:

> "Some CPNs will have their basic training, three years, mainly working in hospitals, some community experience, then gradually progress onto community.... Others will have gone on further ... looking at interventions with severe mental illness and that is about, a lot of that is about family intervention. My assessments were first about [family's] joint knowledge about the diagnosis.... I involved [the young carer] at that point because I said, 'How much information have you got about the medication, about the risk and pitfalls for [the mother] to avoid in managing her illness, what works and what doesn't?' So [the young carer] was involved from quite an early point."

Differences in professional approaches are not only reflected in the micro perspective – that is, in the *personalities* of professionals and their understanding of mental health issues and young caring for example – but also in the macro perspective, which relates to resource constraints and gaps in professional training. We found that, while many professionals were aware of their objective responsibilities, subjectively it seemed they often felt constrained by external, structural dynamics in relation to the effectiveness, and indeed the extent, of their interventions. One CPN commented:

> "A lot of the generic CPNs in this area have caseloads of upwards of 50 to 60 people, I've got a caseload of 12. And that's capped although I'm a key worker for 12, I see maybe four, five others but that is capped. So I can

spend far more time looking at all the aspects of the problems people have rather than just mental health problems."

We have already seen how resource problems can influence diagnostic outcomes and treatment on the CPA, for example. Successful or effective treatment and support can also vary depending on the area in which patients and their children live. One young carers project worker explained:

"I mean, for example, I am based in [area 1] and there's something called Family Friends which I think [the parent] is involved where they have people that befriend families where there are children under 8, take them out and do things, but there isn't anything as yet here [area 2].... I mean, I think the services of [area 2] are incredibly stretched in every respect ... but unfortunately [the parent] lives in [area 2] which is absolutely stretched in every way and I think she possibly gets a good deal."

The influences of geography in this respect apply equally to the level of support young carers receive, some of whom may be well served by efficient and well funded young carers projects while others may be less fortunate. Currently there are only around 120 young carers projects across the UK and some of these experience ongoing funding problems (see Aldridge and Becker, 1998).

Obstacles to a family approach

Although the thrust of recent policy and guidance has emphasised the importance of a family approach (Appendix B: 1995 (ii), 1996 Box B.3, 1999 (ii), 2000 (i)), both in terms of assessments for children in need and for young carers, the message of each policy does not seem to be reaching statutory professionals, in particular those on the front line of service delivery and interventions. Although young carers project workers were more likely to make family interventions, this was more often because of recognised gaps in adult mental health service provision than any strategic intention on the part of the project workers themselves, whose aims were, in the main, to serve the needs of children. While young carers project workers often assisted the mentally ill parents of their clients (young carers), project staff did not always recognise the need for formal, family-based interventions in any strategic sense. Some project workers said that they had been 'drawn into' lending assistance to parents in order to fully meet the needs of young carers, and, as we have said, because of identified gaps in adult mental health services. One project worker explained:

"I mean, we've always said we don't have a complicated referral system, we are one phone call away and we will react ... within 24 hours of that phone call.... I think the problem, I don't know if you hear it from other people but I mean but there are a lot of agencies that aren't prepared to stick by the families and I certainly feel you know you can't just say that's it."

Data from our research here enables us to identify the gaps and divisions in training and services (an issue discussed in Chapter Five of this volume). However, it is also clear that other factors often influence the ability of statutory service professionals to offer comprehensive and effective support services to *families*. For example, parents themselves can be instrumental in reinforcing the divisions in services because they fear the consequences of agency collaborations. However, such fears may not be unfounded. Poole has said:

> Multi-agency working brings together very different organisational, professional and ideological systems and demands, and in the UK at least there is no formal structure to coordinate these except for child protection issues. (1996, p 4; see also Appendix B:1999 (iv)).

Support to mentally ill parents through the CPA gives parents access to a multidisciplinary team of professionals for themselves, and generally these professionals understand the nature of their patients' illnesses and potential outcomes. However, they may be less understanding about the fact that as mentally ill *parents* they may sometimes have to rely on their children for care. Some social work professionals in our study recognised that families sometimes resisted support inputs because they feared social work interventions, in particular, that might lead to familial separations. One CPN described a parent's response to being offered social work support:

> "The difficulty is in having [parents] accept it because they feel very threatened, from my experience a lot of them feel very threatened by what they see as the, you know, professionals and authority stepping in and doing things with their children. You know, especially things like social services. That's the biggest reason given to me [fear of losing children] why they don't want people involved. You know, once that happens that's the thin end of the wedge basically.... They're not going to get their kids back. And I mean I have to say I don't blame them ... I can't blame them at all, I wouldn't want that you know if I did not know what I know I definitely wouldn't want that, have wanted that for my kids."

It is clear that, for family support to be fully effective and implemented by professionals involved in front-line service delivery, it is important not only to address the training needs of such professionals, but also the ways in which families' fears of more generic, social work interventions can be allayed.

Perceived impacts of parental mental illness on children and young carers

One of the intentions of this study was to establish whether professional responses were reinforcing the negative associations relating to parental mental illness and its effects on children, particularly when they care. We have already described the negative outcomes and misconceptions recorded in much of the early medical and more recent social work and child protection literatures on adult mental illness (see Chapter One of this volume). Furthermore, we know from other research evidence that professionals are often guilty of 'pathologising' mental illnesses (see Göpfert et al, 1996). By talking directly with professionals, our evidence has suggested that many misconceptions and assumptions about the impacts of parental mental illness on children and young carers are inculcated in current professional responses to these *families*.

These professional assumptions were demonstrated in a number of ways:

- in the level of professional understanding about the impacts of parental mental illness on children and young carers;
- in professionals' perceptions of the impacts of caring on children when parents are thus affected;
- in professional judgements about mentally ill adults' ability to *parent* effectively.

These factors also underlined the more general lack of understanding among professionals about wider family issues, particularly the nature of parent–child relationships when parents are mentally ill. As Gorell Barnes has argued:

It is as if professionals can only hear one voice at a time. (1996, p 98)

It seems that while mental health professionals often have a deep understanding about symptomatic outcomes and treatments among their patients, they rarely consider the nature of children's roles and responsibilities in the home, even when they have close contact with their patients' families. Similarly, although many young carers project workers involve parents and other family members in their support strategies, they often demonstrate little understanding about mental health issues. Significantly, our evidence revealed that most professionals were competent in describing a range of effects of adult mental illness both when these adults were patients and when they were parents. Furthermore, professionals felt equally confident in outlining some of the effects of parental mental illness on children, young carers and on parent–child relationships in these contexts. When we asked key workers to describe their perceptions of the impacts of parental mental illness on parents themselves, on parent–child relationships and on children's development, the majority (35 cases) outlined only negative consequences, particularly for children (see Box 4.1).

Only one of the professionals interviewed in our study said they felt unable to comment about the effects of parental mental health in terms of the categories presented in Box 4.1. A further (mental health) professional recognised both positive and negative outcomes for parents and children. Another mental health worker talked about the impacts of wider dynamics here such as community discrimination:

"I think, I don't think there should be sort of that stigma attached to mental health ... but society in general I think there is that stigma attached to adults."

Box 4.1: Effects of mental ill health as perceived by professionals

Consequences of mental health for parent	Consequences of mental health for parent–child relationships	Consequences of mental health for child/young carer
Behavioural	Breakdown in relationships	*Behavioural*
Dependency	No modelling – loss of mother role	Low self-esteem
Selfishness	Power imbalances	No confidence
"Mother behaves like a child"	Role reversal	Learned behaviour
Self-absorbed	No discipline	Worrying
Distant	Inconsistency	Lack of understanding
Lack of support	Mixed messages	Silence
Lack of understanding	Lack of nurturing	Embarrassment
Delusional	Over-protectiveness	Lack of discipline
Mood changes	No ability to parent	Immaturity
Emotional	Dysfunctional relationships	Responsibility
Emotional void	Lack of communication	*Emotional*
Distance	Fear of separation	Feeling unloved, unwanted
	Child unable to predict moods	Feelings of isolation and confusion
		Guilt
		Feelings of unhappiness
		Anxiety
		Educational
		Absenteeism
		Bullied at school
		Will not reach 'full potential'
		Social
		Cannot bring friends home
		Will not know how to play

What is significant is that, not only are professionals' perceptions about the effects of parental mental illness almost wholly negative, but that professionals across the range of disciplines felt able and competent to describe the effects on children, *despite the fact that so few adult services professionals had any direct contact with the children in these families.* Therefore, we must conclude that professional understanding about the effects of parental mental illness on children are, in the main, based on assumptions – as well as the messages from child protection work and joint working, within a legal framework (Appendix B) – rather than on any direct evidence through close contact with families. It also seems that professionals often consider the negative effects of parental mental illness on children and young carers to be determined simply by the presence of the mental illness itself, rather than by any extraneous influences that may affect the progression of illnesses or family stasis, or external considerations such as poverty, low income and poor housing.

Despite their lack of formal mental health training, many young carers project workers felt equally able to comment about the effects of parental mental illness on children and young carers, and particularly on parent–child relationships. As we have said, young carers project workers often involved other family members in their support strategies (albeit generally in a secondary fashion), especially where there were gaps in adult service provision. However, their lack of formal training and expertise in mental health issues could sometimes also mean young carers project workers were less understanding about symptomatic outcomes and behaviours among affected parents. Therefore, they made judgements about parent–child relations based on their limited 'observations' (most young carers project work takes place outside the family home at project bases and during outdoor activities) and on their general lack of expertise in mental health issues. The impacts of diagnostic and prognostic factors, treatments and wider social influences were also rarely acknowledged by young carers project workers.

What is also significant is that professionals outside mental health services made no distinctions in terms of the effects of the various types of mental illnesses involved. In this respect, all effects were viewed as the same (negative). And yet, while the numbers in our sample do not allow us to make comparisons between types of illness, some mental health conditions can be differentiated in terms of their outcomes for individuals. For example, some evidence would suggest outcomes for personality disordered parents and their children could be potentially more complex and damaging in the long term than the effects of depression (see Chapters One and Two of this volume). By the same token, many illnesses respond well to treatment. Perhaps it is unhelpful to perceive all mental illnesses as the same in terms of their negative outcomes for individuals and children, as well as in how individuals respond to the onset and treatment of these conditions.

Having said this, it is important to recognise that the impacts of parental mental illness on children and young carers *can be detrimental in some contexts,* especially when treatments and support are ineffective and when young caring becomes disproportionate, long-term and deleterious to children's emotional, social and educational development. However, it is equally important that professionals do not assume an inevitability of risk in this respect simply on the basis of a diagnosis. Göpfert et al have recognised that mentally ill parents can experience "huge problems over minor issues and trivialities" (1996, p 289), and that psychiatric and psychotic symptoms can "impair parental competence", but that these may also "respond to treatment" (1996, p 290) and that a patient's mental state "has no direct bearing on parenting" (1996, p 278). All of these issues are important when considering the impacts of parental mental illness on affected individuals and their families, particularly children.

Perceived effects of caring

Nine of the professionals interviewed in our study were unable to comment about the effects of caring on children whose parents were mentally ill. Eight of these were from the statutory services. This perhaps reflects a general lack of insight into the issues surrounding young caring as well as the fact that so few of the statutory professionals interviewed for our study *talked to children about their caring roles*. However, of the remaining 31 professionals who commented, only two described the effects of caring as positive. (One other professional described the effects as both positive and negative, and a further professional said that they could not differentiate between the effects of mental health and the effects of caring on children.) Box 4.2 describes the range of effects of caring as perceived by the professionals in our study.

Some of these effects are reflected in findings from other research studies on young caring, for example outcomes such as secrecy, impaired social development

Box 4.2: The impacts of caring on children as perceived by professionals

- Eating problems
- Disrupted sleep patterns
- Isolation
- Inappropriately mature
- Do not develop like other children
- Cannot relate to children their own age
- Resentment
- Covering up and secrecy
- Results in blackmailing parents
- Power imbalance
- Silence
- Unable to go out/socialise
- Scruffiness
- Will become future patients

and early maturity (see Bilsborrow, 1992; Aldridge and Becker, 1993a; Dearden and Becker, 2000a). However, none of the professionals in our study referred to other social and economic factors which might also result in similar outcomes for children (for example, lack of adequate support for parents, housing problems, poverty, exclusion, and so on).

What is also significant is that, once again, effects are described as mainly negative and seem to be based in most cases on professional assumptions about the effects of caring on children (and since so few statutory professionals, in particular, included children in their work). Of course it could be argued that as evidence from medicine, social work and child protection studies (as well as from professionals themselves) points absolutely to the mainly negative effects of parental mental illness on children and families, then perhaps there could be some truth in the notion that children are at risk of significant harm in these contexts. However, this is where our three-way sample proves invaluable, for it tells us that the risk to children of physical harm and neglect, as well as wholly negative outcomes in terms of children's future development, is not as prevalent or absolute as medical and social 'evidence' would suggest. The parents and children/young carers in our study, as we have seen, did not describe the effects of parental mental illness in purely negative ways, particularly when describing the nature of parent–child relationships (see Chapters Two and Three of this volume). Neither did any of the children, as we have said, seem to be at inevitable risk of significant harm.

Although most statutory professionals had little or no contact with the children and young carers in our study, the indicators for young caring would have been evident had these professionals looked beyond their patient-oriented and adult-focused perspectives. However, rather than being alerted to children's/ carers' needs by the indicators for 'need', which professionals themselves perceived to be wholly negative (such as a 'decline' in cleanliness or domestic order, children's 'scruffiness' and so on; see Boxes 4.1 and 4.2), most statutory professionals (from adult services in particular) seemed to make judgements about *parents'* lack of domestic competency in this respect. These judgements seemed to be based on middle-class assumptions about 'appropriate' standards of domesticity and hygiene (see also Zetlin et al, 1985), as the following example from a social worker in the adult services illustrates:

> "The actual sort of, erm, standard to which the house is kept is lower than one would like. Two years ago it got absolutely dreadful. She [mother] really got depressed, she was having problems with the neighbour, and the house completely went to pieces, it was, it was quite disgusting.... The new house has stayed reasonably, erm, within tolerable limits."

While covert evidence of young caring, or 'children in need', in domestic settings was often overlooked among statutory professionals, the onset or presence of parental illness and the tendency of parents to succumb to them were often seen as the root cause of a family's problems. In this respect, the mental illness itself becomes the invidious agent of family instability, domestic disorder and the need for parents to rely on their children for care. While professionals could often readily describe the effects of caring on children, the root cause of a families' problems, including the need for children to take on domestic and caring responsibilities, was often seen to be the illness itself. Caring by children in this context was also attributed to the absence or lack of 'appropriate' role modelling, especially when mothers – the 'lynchpin of domestic order and stability' (see Chapter One of this volume) – became ill:

> "She [mother], I mean the house was in quite a muddle, she had no routine for doing the washing or cleaning so I tried .... The other thing is that the children often take on some of the traits of their parent ... and they would mimic their parent's behaviour. You know if their parents are unhappy and staying in bed all day they would see no reason why they couldn't do the same." (Family support worker)

Professional responses in these contexts are not based on assessments of need but become judgements about parents' domestic (and parenting) competencies, with no reference to the role and importance of other adults in the home, including professionals, or indeed to what, as in this case, an organised cleaning 'routine' might be. Each of these testimonies was given by professionals outside the mental health services. This illustrates the point about how those professionals who are not trained in mental health issues can lack understanding and insight about both the effects of parental mental illness on affected individuals and their children, and, more significantly here, the triggers for young caring. In this respect we can see how professionals can be instrumental in perpetuating the negative associations of parental mental ill health and its effects on children and young carers.

Assessment of 'parenting capacity'

Göpfert et al have talked about the "negative effects of pathologising commonly associated with professional responses to serious mental health problems" (1996, p 2). Our evidence would suggest that at the very least professionals make assumptions about children's (compromised) development when parents are mentally ill. When children care, professionals may 'see' evidence of what they consider to be the effects of parental mental illness, such as children's untidy or 'scruffy' appearance (see Box 4.2), but rarely are interventions made that address children's needs as carers. In this respect, recognition of a need for additional services, such as homecare support, would reduce a young carer's domestic responsibilities and may even lead to 'improvements' in the child's appearance. Therefore, a more constructive professional response would have been to address the underlying cause for the child's so-called 'scruffiness' rather than question the parent's competency as a parent and domestic manager.

'Parenting capacity' remains a fundamental motif of current guidance on the assessment of children in need (Horwath, 2000). However, it is less easy in this respect to understand how questioning adult parenting capacity can be constructive for parents when they have *mental illness*. Göpfert et al have argued, for example, that an assessment of parenting capacity already and fundamentally "carries the message that the parents are not good enough" (1996, p 277). Add to this message the fact that parents have severe mental health problems and often have to rely on their children for care and it becomes clear that both mentally ill parents and their young carers have even less chance of benign, needs-led and sensitive professional interventions.

Furthermore, if, as Poole (1996) has argued, neither childcare professionals nor mental health workers can assess parenting capacity in any definitive or accurate sense, then we must wonder just who is 'expert enough' to make these appraisals. This is especially true when parents are mentally ill and when their children are helping to provide care. Inevitably this leads us to ask whether or not assessing a mentally ill adult's capacity to parent is the most appropriate method of addressing and meeting their needs. Perhaps assessing children's needs, as well as those of their parents, would be better accommodated in professional interventions that considered parents' and children's *expressed needs* (including adults' needs as parents and children's needs as carers). Perhaps also we need to consider or challenge terminology – such as 'parenting capacity' – that seems to assume parental deficit from the outset.

We have already said that professional interventions can lead to knee-jerk child protection decisions when evidence of young caring emerges, particularly when parents are mentally ill. A quarter of the young carers in our study had been placed in the care of local authorities at some time. Furthermore, other figures reveal that, of those children who started to be looked after in the year ending March 2000, 10% of cases were a direct result of parental ill health (DH, 2001). We also know that both young carers and their parents are fearful of professional interventions that may lead to family separations, especially when parents have mental illnesses (see Chapters Two and Three).

However, our evidence suggests that *when asked*, children often say they want to contribute to the care of their parents in some way. More recent medical evidence has also suggested that both parents and children make better progress if they are kept *together* as a family:

> Clinicians report that if a mentally ill parent and her/his child can be rehabilitated together ... the prognosis can be better for both in the long term, sometimes even if the parent is rather seriously ill at first. (Göpfert et al, 1996, p 276)

Effective *family* support through coordinated services, and wider recognition of children's caring roles when parents are mentally ill, will go some way towards ensuring family unity is maintained.

Conclusion

Poole has argued that many of the effects of parental mental illness for children and families "cannot be predicted either by the medical sciences or other means" (1996, p 5). If these effects can neither be predicted nor necessarily observed by professionals in a family context, then it is to be supposed – and our evidence confirms this – that the effects in these instances are being assumed. One of the dangers of such assumption is that misconceptions become normalised and are perpetuated among professional communities.

One of our main intentions in undertaking this study was, by talking to three different respondent groups, to understand the nature of professional interventions when parents are mentally ill and have to rely on their children for care. Considering the mainly pessimistic or negative outcomes for children in these contexts reported in the medical, social work and child protection literature (see Chapter One of this volume), we needed to understand whether this negativity of effect was being perpetuated or reinforced by current professional attitudes and responses. Our study revealed that professionals from both the statutory and voluntary services described only negative outcomes for children and young carers when parents have severe and enduring mental illnesses.

We also found that the divisions in services continue to present problems in terms of effective *family* interventions. One child and family social worker commented:

> "I think in childcare, because we're focused on the children, we're quite, we're not very kind to the parents if they've got mental health problems. Er, and we need to look at the family as a whole more."

Furthermore, given that the respondents in our study were on the CPA and therefore had access to multidisciplinary teams of professionals, we can only conclude that the onset or continuation of young caring in these families must highlight gaps in CPA training and service provision.

We have argued previously (Aldridge and Becker, 1996) that comprehensive support for ill or disabled parents will never provide a foolproof preventive measure for the onset and continuation of young caring. The reasons for this are reflected in the findings we have discussed here. Resource and budgeting constraints, the dominance of the medical model and adult-focused perspectives, the ineffectiveness of individual professional responses, the counterproductivity of multi-agency support, as well as the diverse range of needs of parents with mental illnesses, are all contributing factors. Therefore, we must accept that inter-agency collaboration and effective coordination between and across services will be essential elements of any strategic and inclusive support programme for young carers and their families. And that these services need to be of a high quality, consistent, and needs-led (and not geographically-led), goes without saying.

We have seen how inconsistent or arbitrary professional judgements and interventions undermine family stability and even exacerbate illnesses. Equally, consistent and continuous needs-led responses may serve to alleviate family problems and prevent crises, which can often lead to separations. We found evidence of constructive professional interventions for parents and for young carers (the introduction of link families, for example), but these were by no means consistent across local authorities. Differences can be accounted for in micro and macro perspectives; that is, in the nature of interventions where professional 'distancing' occurs and where the personalities of professionals become important, as well as in wider issues such as training and resource constraints.

Although gaps in training and service divisions were evident in our findings, it was also clear that professionals themselves often faced difficulties in terms of making effective individual and family approaches to young carers and their parents. Formal identification and monitoring strategies, as well as an absence of understanding about the triggers for young caring, were pertinent issues. Furthermore, current assessment guidance means professionals must understand children's (and young carers') needs based on assessments of their parents' ability to parent effectively (among other factors), when few professionals are sufficiently trained to make these judgements, especially when parents have mental illnesses (see also Göpfert et al, 1996). Finally, assumptions and misconceptions that have been 'handed down' from early medical research contributes little to further understanding among health and social welfare professionals about the effects of parental mental illness on children and young carers. Nor does it help to promote a wider view that considers the influence of other dynamics on the progression of illnesses and on family life, including structural (environmental) factors such as poverty, exclusion, poor housing, disadvantaged communities, social stigma and so on.

As a consequence of many of these issues, professionals may all too often resort to child protection decisions. Although such decisions may relieve their immediate professional concerns (especially when confronted with parental behaviour they do not always understand), ultimately they will not benefit families who continue to be anxious about the threat of family separations as well as having to cope with the presence of a mental illness. Indeed, some commentators have argued that professionals' decisions to implement child protection procedures are not necessarily addressing the needs of children or parents but may simply be "meeting the 'need' of professionals or institutions for containment of their anxiety" (Göpfert et al, 1996, p 287).

However, professionals are regularly made aware, through case histories, media representations, and so on (see Chapter One of this volume), of the consequences of *inaction* in respect of child protection decisions for children who *may* be at risk of serious harm. Schuff and Asen (1996) have recognised that professionals face ongoing dilemmas concerning the need to remove children from potentially harmful or neglectful family situations. How much more complex do these decisions become when untrained professionals are confronted with a parent demonstrating 'bizarre' behaviour and when their child, or children, are undertaking the care duties usually associated with adulthood?

These issues are addressed further in Chapter Five. There, we consider ways in which professional interventions can be more constructive and inclusive. Our data emphasise the need for professionals to be more understanding and empathic in their approaches to vulnerable *families,* and to try to overcome assumptions about the deleterious effects of parental mental illness on children and young carers. This is an important message for professionals if they are to avoid reinforcing the negative associations and 'pathologising' already affiliated to parents with mental illness by adding parental *in*competency to the 'risk list' simply on the basis of a diagnosis.

FIVE

Towards a systemic approach: ways forward and conclusions

The findings presented in this volume suggest that, where professionals engage in effective intervention procedures (recognising children's caring roles, acknowledging needs, making appropriate assessments and referrals), these can be crucial in preventing crises and allowing children (and parents) some degree of choice in undertaking informal care responsibilities. Furthermore, when professionals offer sensitive and non-demeaning assistance, this help is also highly valued by families. However, in most cases it seems that professionals fail to engage in these effective intervention procedures and to offer needs-led assistance. A notable exception to this, however, is the service and support provided by the many young carers projects. Our evidence suggests that these projects are more likely than statutory services to offer support to *families* when children are caring for parents with mental illness.

However, while young carers projects play a vital role in families where parents are affected by mental illness, in practice it seems that project workers and many statutory workers experience difficulties in implementing effective assessment and intervention procedures for young carers. There are a number of reasons for this. Firstly, there is a lack of available and consistent assessment tools, or 'local procedures' and guidance (see Dearden and Becker, 2000b). Secondly, we cannot discount the fact that the academic debate, which emerged in the mid 1990s and which considered whether or not children who care represented a valid welfare category, challenged fundamentally the direction of policy and practice developments. A disability rights perspective on young caring suggested that describing children as young carers was both unhelpful and unnecessary. Some disability authors promoted prevention as a key intervention strategy; that is, children would not have to provide 'care' if disabled parents were adequately supported practically and in their parenting roles (Keith and Morris, 1995; Morris, 1995; Parker and Olsen, 1995; Olsen, 1996). This debate has been muted to a large extent by the *recognition* in research and policy that children continue to provide informal care (and thus require strategic intervention), and often regardless of the nature and level of support offered to their mentally ill or disabled parents. Indeed, the evidence presented in this volume shows categorically that, despite the fact that all 40 parents in our sample were receiving services, and sometimes from multidisciplinary teams, parents still had to rely on their children for care.

The policy and legal framework

A third reason why professionals from both voluntary and statutory services face problems implementing effective assessment procedures for young carers is because of the plethora of policy guidance and the complex legal structure which many professionals find both confusing and difficult to interpret (SSI, 1996). While there are dozens of policies and a number of pieces of legislation that are relevant to young carers and parents with mental illness, many of the most pertinent policies generate from two years especially: 1999 and 2000 (see Appendix B of this volume). They are the *National service framework for mental health* (DH, 1999a), the *Framework for the assessment of children in need and their families* (DH, 2000), the National carers strategy (HM Government, 1999) and *Working together to safeguard children* (DH, HO and DfEE, 1999). As the chronology shows, they are among the most relevant to children caring for mentally ill parents, in that they define what should happen to and for children and parents in these circumstances, and why, and how, professionals should intervene (including assessment procedures as well as wider support and service provision to carers, children and parents with mental illness).

While policies create the framework for interventions and practice, laws provide the legal structure and authority for all services, and bestow 'rights' on certain groups. The 'rights' of children and their parents with mental health problems are enshrined in various pieces of child welfare and adult (mental health and community care) law, as well as in legislation referring specifically to carers. The 'rights' that any one young carer has in law will depend on a number of factors, including their age (under 16, over 16), whether they are defined as a 'child in need', whether their parents receive local authority services/assessments, and so on.

Therefore, various pieces of legislation are especially relevant to children caring for parents with mental illness, and each piece of law offers different opportunities (or limitations) and ways of meeting (or not meeting) children's and parents' needs, as the annotations to the chronology of Appendix B reveal. So, for example, while young carers of any age can be assessed under the 1995 Carers Act, many will go on to receive services as children in need under the 1989 Children Act (because the Carers Act does not bestow any rights to services other than an assessment). Young carers over the age of 16 can be assessed and receive services in their own right under the 2000 Carers and Disabled Children Act. On the other hand, young carers under 16 have no specific right to services (as carers) at all – they must be assessed under the 1995 Carers Act and receive services under the Children Act. In making any such assessments of young carers caring for mentally ill parents, local authority social services departments must also use the *Framework for the assessment of children in need and their families*, take account of the requirements of the *National service framework for mental health* (particularly Standard Six), and be mindful of their responsibilities for joint working with other professionals and agencies as contained in *Working together*. Therefore, the assessment of any young carer –

and the provision of services and support to them and their parents – are likely to be determined (and empowered or constrained) by a complex legal and policy framework which draws on different pieces of law and policy from child welfare, carers, community care and mental health fields.

Within these legal and policy fields it is possible to see points of convergence. So, for example, there is a growing emphasis in a range of policy documents, spanning community care, mental health, carers and child welfare, for better cooperation and coordination of services and professional responses – the promotion of 'seamless' or 'joined-up' services. Another point of convergence concerns the 'family approach' to assessing and meeting needs. Rather than a focus on service users or carers in isolation, or on children or parents in isolation, there has been a growing emphasis in policy documents on the need to consider the interrelated needs of all family members, and respond accordingly. This convergence has become increasingly apparent in recent years, and reflects in part New Labour's commitment to move towards 'joined-up' policy making, drawing on research evidence, and 'what works' to inform policy and practice developments.

While it is possible through a close reading of the chronology to identify these points of convergence, we must remember that there are still many conflicting and contradictory elements in policy and law as it relates to young carers and their mentally ill parents. In turn, this has led to difficulties for professionals in interpretation and implementation.

The science of 'muddling through'

A further reason for these difficulties in interpreting and implementing law and policy, and in particular assessment procedures, relates to the complexity of the legal and policy framework. Policy making for young carers with parents with mental illness combines both 'top-down', rationalist (Smith and May, 1980) and 'bottom-up', incremental elements (Lindblom, 1959, 1980; Lipsky, 1980). The key policy documents referred to in the previous section are 'top-down' documents, conceived by politicians and civil servants, as the agents of government, within a political and ideological framework rather than just an analytical and problem-solving one. Moreover, policies have developed through a process of debate, negotiation and adjustment. The development of a 'whole family' approach has been articulated in documents since the mid 1990s (the SSI reports of 1995 and 1996 being early examples), and this has been refined over the years to form the defining *paradigm* contained in many documents. The negotiated and incremental nature of policy is also a feature of the legal framework. For example, the 1995 Carers Act was the first piece of UK legislation to formally recognise carers (adult and young carers) and establish some (limited) rights, notably to an assessment of their needs (but only when the care receiver was being assessed or reassessed). As a 'new' piece of legislation it had distinct rationalist credentials, but at the same time it had been informed and influenced by other, 'bottom-up', factors, not least the carers lobby (advocating rights for carers) and the disability rights lobby (advocating rights for service users). The 'tie in' requiring carers' assessments to be linked to service users' assessments is just one of the compromises that arose from this type of negotiated process. The later 2000 Carers and Disabled Children Act extended the rights of those carers over the age of 16, making up for some of the deficiencies of the 1995 legislation. However, it also introduced new restrictions and limitations, particularly by excluding younger carers under the age of 16 to services in their own right. The average age of young carers in our study is 14. Thus, most of these children caring for parents with mental health problems have no rights to services under the 2000 Carers and Disabled Children Act.

While law and policy for young carers with mentally ill parents have rationalist, problem-solving purposes, they also invariably contain strong elements of incrementalism, or what has been referred to as 'a science of muddling through' (Lindblom, 1959; Gregory, 1989). The most relevant policies identified earlier would also not have been developed without the support of key ministers, the backing of the Treasury, the stewardship and commitment of key civil servants (especially within the Department of Health and Social Services Inspectorate), the pressure exerted by certain organisations, including (the then) Carers National Association and significant individuals, the contribution of the media, a sound research-base, and so on. Young carers themselves have also played an influential part in informing these policy and legislative developments. Many appeared before Members of Parliament and Department of Health officials at meetings convened by Carers National Association (now Carers UK) and other carers' or children's organisations throughout the mid to late 1990s.

Street level bureaucrats

Lipsky (1980) offers critical insights into how the implementation of policy actually works in practice. He focuses on the behaviour and actions of key implementers – what he refers to as 'street level bureaucrats', and their role in creating policy through their practice. As Hudson contends:

> If we wish to understand policy implementation, we must understand the street level bureaucrat. (1989, p 397).

Lipsky argues, "that the decisions of street level bureaucrats, the routines they establish and the devices they invent to cope with uncertainties and work pressures, effectively becomes the public policies they carry out" (1980, p xii). In other words, their day-to-day practice actually constructs policy. In response to organisational and workload pressures, street level bureaucrats (including social workers, young carers project workers, health workers, and so on) develop practices which maximise their use of discretion.

Discretion enables procedures to be adapted to the client or service user and the service user to be adapted to the procedures (Baldwin, 2000, p 83). According

to Lipsky, street level bureaucrats construct a version c
that is easiest for them to deal with among their workl
and this involves "client processing" (Lipsky, 1980, p 2
interface between those seeking services and the scarc
those services. They hold considerable power, ar
interpretation of policy guidelines and organisatic
who passes through the interface and who does no
what we term today 'gatekeeping', 'rationing' or 'selectivity'.

The professionals in our study correspond closely with Lipsky's 'street ie
bureaucrats'. They may often have good intentions as they attempt to do a
'good job' within their personal and professional sets of values. However, the
context of practice – resource shortfall, indeterminate objectives, a dearth in
controls on the use of discretion, and sometimes their personalities, abilities
and the ways in which they have been trained – undermine those good
intentions.

Identifying the triggers for young caring

In 1996 the Department of Health (SSI, 1996) recognised the lack of triggers
for young caring that might help professionals in all agencies recognise and
respond to family circumstances where young caring might occur. Indeed,
perhaps one of the fundamental reasons professionals face uncertainties about
how to implement effective intervention procedures for young carers is the
lack of consistent pointers for when young caring presents itself. Our evidence
has shown that this is particularly the case in families where children are caring
for parents with mental illness. Protocols have not been sufficiently clearly
defined to help professionals ensure that, "regardless of initial contact – health,
education or social services – families with young carers will be routed
appropriately for services" (SSI, 1996, p 15).

The Department of Health continues to emphasise the need for and
importance of "local procedures and practice guidance to help professionals
work together in supporting young carers" using "clear protocols" (Dearden
and Becker, 2000b, p 178). One way of developing triggers for the onset of
young caring would be not only to recognise and understand the importance
of the association between young caring and parental impairment, but also the
many contexts which influence the nature and extent of caring responsibility
among children. Therefore, we must recognise that in some families children
will care for parents with a range of illnesses and disabilities as well as for
siblings, grandparents and other co-resident relatives. More significantly, and
in a wider context, the degree and extent of children's caring responsibility can
be greatly influenced by factors such as the level of informal and formal support,
the nature of expressed needs, as well as the degree of care recipient autonomy.
This in turn will be influenced by the care recipient's ability to work or earn
money, the nature and extent of community support and understanding (thus,
a parent's experience of stigma and discrimination also need to be considered).

...hese ways we can see how a more empathic approach to young carers, ...the people for whom they care, would be one that embraced a systemic ...pproach. Schuff and Asen describe a systemic approach as one which "views children and families in the many different contexts of which they are part" (1996, p 135). This approach would recognise the relationship between young caring and parental mental impairment. A key development here would be to formulate a 'mapping' procedure in which young carers' experiences could be located and stratified in a more systemic sense.

Mapping the young caring experience

What has been consistently missing from policy and practice guidance has been a model or device that recognises the gradation or diversity of the young caring experience when parents have mental health problems. Mapping the young caring experience in the ways in which we suggest here (see Boxes 5.1 and 5.2) would enable professionals to identify and determine needs, priorities and the nature and level of support required. The mapping process itself assumes the adoption of a more family-centred approach and one which also promotes enhanced inter-agency communication and information sharing (see Box 5.2). Although this holistic (systemic) approach might, in practice, raise questions among professionals about which family member is their primary client or responsibility, in theory and heuristically, the model is based on the premise that looking at the individual in the context of the family, and other settings, is essential in order to treat service users effectively and deliver positive outcomes. Such an approach was recognised and implemented by only a handful of professionals in our research, primarily young carers project workers.

At the very least it is the responsibility particularly of the front-line professional – the 'street level bureaucrat' – to recognise the triggers for caring in families and to map or grade young carers' experiences as a means of deciding which type of help they should receive. Boxes 5.1 and 5.2 illustrate how adopting a systemic approach to young caring requires professionals to play a key role in locating young carers somewhere on the X axis (caring role), while considering a range of factors including, and most significantly, the (nature and severity of) the parental condition (the Y axis). Later in this chapter we 'map' three cases from our sample of 40 families (Boxes 5.3 and 5.4) to illustrate how the mapping process might work in practice. Before any mapping can be implemented, professionals need some general awareness of who young carers are and what they do.

Box 5.1 shows that, in order for professionals to identify and locate young carers in the mapping process, they must first consider a range of factors. In terms of placement on the Y axis (the nature of illness), the process does not simply rely on professionals assessing and grading the nature and severity of parental mental ill health. Rather, it also relies on a systemic approach which considers the Y axis in relation to other factors, such as the degree of personal (parental) autonomy and independence, the nature and effectiveness of informal

Box 5.1: Mapping the young caring experience: recognition and identification

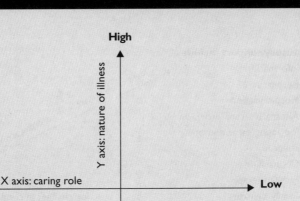

Mapping the X axis (caring role)
Factors:

- nature of caring responsibility (consider: physical, emotional, intimate, nursing, domestic, general duties)
- extent of responsibility (consider: duration of caring activity, when caring occurs – through the night, early morning, etc – levels of tasks involved)
- level and availability of alternative support (consider: informal support: other siblings, family members, neighbours, friends, etc; formal support services)
- level of expressed need (consider: what young carers say they need as children and as carers: will needs change? Possible future needs)

Mapping the Y axis (nature of illness/disability)
Factors:

- nature and severity of condition (consider: physical or mental illness, physical disability, chronic or terminal illness, long term, short term or episodic in nature)
- degree of personal autonomy (consider: role and availability of informal carers, partner, children, extended family; availability of formal support; level and effectiveness of these)
- level of expressed need (consider: what families say they need, evidence of social exclusion, systemic approach – housing, economic needs, employment, benefits, etc)

and formal support networks, as well as the level of expressed need. It is important to point out that this exercise is to map the place of *children* on the axis, not their parents. However, it is not possible to map children without reference to their parents' illness, which itself must be located within a broader health and social context.

Thinking about the X axis (caring role), it is equally important to recognise factors such as the nature of caring responsibilities among children, the extent

Box 5.2: Mapping the young caring experience: assessment and support

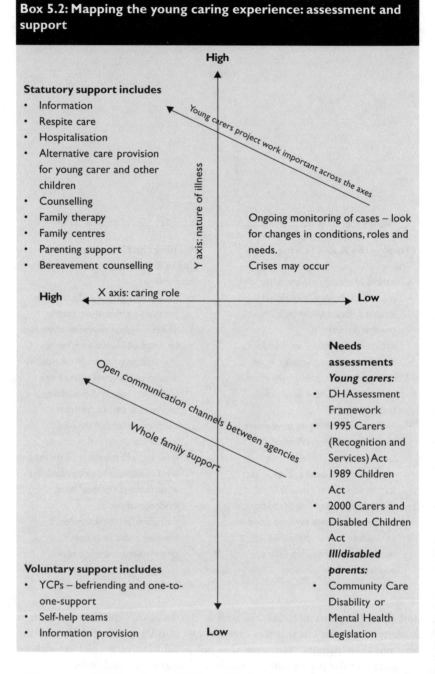

Statutory support includes
- Information
- Respite care
- Hospitalisation
- Alternative care provision for young carer and other children
- Counselling
- Family therapy
- Family centres
- Parenting support
- Bereavement counselling

High

Young carers project work important across the axes

Y axis: nature of illness

Ongoing monitoring of cases – look for changes in conditions, roles and needs.
Crises may occur

High ← X axis: caring role → **Low**

Open communication channels between agencies

Whole family support

Needs assessments
Young carers:
- DH Assessment Framework
- 1995 Carers (Recognition and Services) Act
- 1989 Children Act
- 2000 Carers and Disabled Children Act

Ill/disabled parents:

Voluntary support includes
- YCPs – befriending and one-to-one-support
- Self-help teams
- Information provision

- Community Care Disability or Mental Health Legislation

Low

of these responsibilities, the availability of alternative support networks and the effects and outcomes of caring on children and young people (Box 5.1). Although included in these factors are the regularity and extent of caring responsibility, these issues alone will not indicate the nature or degree of need among young carers, or indeed, by themselves, influence young carers' eventual placement along the X axis. It is also important to consider some of the effects of caring on children and these can only properly be assessed when professionals listen to young carers themselves. Regularity of care and the extent of caring responsibilities are important, but not simply in a policy sense. A young person's caring responsibilities may not be particularly onerous in terms of time or frequency – referred to in the Carers (Recognition and Services) Act as 'regular' or 'substantial' – but the impact of caring may be considerable and the outcomes negative. For example, a child who lends 'emotional' support to a schizophrenic lone parent may have particular associated problems which locate the young carer higher on the X axis than the *amount* of caring responsibility might at first indicate.

Adopting a systemic and holistic approach to young caring in this way by 'mapping' their experiences would, importantly, reduce the need for professionals to make (often difficult and complex) snapshot judgements about parenting capacity. Although this has been cited in policy as a central factor in assessment procedures for young carers (Dearden and Becker, 2000b; DH, 2000), understanding 'parenting capacity', especially in the context of parental mental illness, can often prove a complex issue, and certainly more problematic than the term itself infers. In practice, it can be difficult for professionals to determine and accurately define the parameters of parental capacity. As Göpfert et al have argued, professionals often have to rely on expectations or standards about what, for example, "a [good] parent might be like and often using a checklist format" (1996, p 272). Furthermore, Zetlin et al have argued that parenting requirements are often based on middle-class standards or assumptions. Therefore, "the skills that constitute adequacy of any parent have yet to be agreed upon" (1985, p 70).

The issue is further clouded when factors such as parental mental impairment are considered, where symptomatic behaviours themselves can often be interpretated as evidence of inadequate parenting. And yet many commentators have argued that behavioural outcomes in this respect should not necessarily be conflated with risk to children or seen as evidence of 'poor' parenting. Thurman argues, for example, that "lack of performance by an individual does not necessarily mean lack of competence on the part of that individual" (1985, p 39). In practice, decisions about parenting capacity are often made at the extreme end of the spectrum when evidence of serious neglect or abuse requires child protection procedures to be implemented (see Göpfert et al, 1996). Given that parenting capacity is one of the domains included in current assessment frameworks in the context of parental mental ill health (DH, 2000; Horwath, 2000), a systemic approach to young caring would perhaps be more appropriate and effective. In this sense a more systemic perspective should also, as Scuff and Asen have argued, "be sensitive to cultural and ethnic issues and *take into account the meaning of symptomatic behaviours*" (Schuff and Asen, 1996, p 144; emphasis added). In other words, professionals should not assume that 'bizarre' behaviour in parents *necessarily* poses a threat to their children.

In practice, contradictions may present themselves when implementing mapping procedures for young carers. For example, some young carers may figure high on the X axis (caring role) in terms of the amount of time and frequency of care undertaken. In terms of other factors, such as the level of expressed need and the impacts of caring, however, their eventual placement might be at the lower end of the axis. This is why it is important for professionals not just to consider X and Y axes principally and other factors parenthetically, but to consider the *range* and *interaction* of all factors relating to caring, impairment and their outcomes for children, parents and other family members. This can only occur with effective communication between young carers, their families and the relevant welfare professionals.

Certainly empirical evidence to date would suggest that we are more likely to see a high correlation between an elevated placement on the X (caring role) axis with a high placement on the Y (nature of illness) axis. Most research has tended to highlight correlations between cases at the high end of both axes (see Bilsborrow, 1992; Aldridge and Becker, 1993a, 1994; Newton and Becker, 1996; Dearden and Becker, 2000a). Clearly, however, there will be cases that do not follow these patterns and the case studies attempt to emphasise these differences (see Box 5.3). However, little or no empirical evidence to date indicates cases that figure high on the X axis and low on the Y axis (for example, a child providing 'high' levels of care for a parent with very 'low' levels of illness). Although it may be possible to think hypothetically about examples in this respect, research to date does not provide us with them. Furthermore, examples of cases such as these might indicate in practice the need for looking at such cases with concern, not as examples of young caring, but of children whose labours were fundamentally being exploited.

It is important to consider the mapping process as fluid and subject to change. Although the most ideal scenario would be to have all cases occurring as low correlations, and professionals should move constantly to this end, they should also be aware of the potential for 'movement' up or down the axes – hence the need for close monitoring of cases (see Box 5.2). It may be that in many cases (and this is the reason the Y axis is a crucial factor in the mapping process) the nature and severity of the parental condition has a direct influence on a young carer's placement and movement on the map in terms of the X axis. This can sometimes occur regardless of the influence of other factors, and may be particularly true of severe and enduring mental health conditions. Our evidence has shown that parents affected by bipolar disorders and schizophrenia, for example, often experience quite rapid symptomatic changes over short periods of time. Such transitions, if left untreated or inadequately supported, can have severe consequences both for families and for children when they care, and may mean that children move quite rapidly from a relatively 'low' position of care provision to higher levels where their own needs increase.

In our sample of 40 families, 11 parents reported that their illness and symptoms had deteriorated since the first interview; another five had become more dependent on alcohol; two had attempted suicide; ten had been hospitalised; and 13 described new physical health problems (see Chapter Two, Box 2.3). These dramatic changes in parental health (the Y axis) would have an impact on the level of children's caring responsibilities (the X axis), and without adequate monitoring of these changes would more likely lead to negative outcomes not only for parents but also for their children who care.

The *quality* of support services available to mentally ill parents will also have a mediating impact on children's position on the X axis. For example, had the parents in our sample whose situations had worsened received compensatory support services from health and social care agencies, then children's positioning on the caring (X) axis may not have moved at all, or the level of their caring roles could even have been *reduced*. In the absence of service provision, however, that is flexible and responsive to *changes* in parental conditions and needs, children, as co-resident carers, would often take on *higher* levels of caring responsibility. It is important also to look at other factors such as housing conditions, the nature and extent of community support, the availability of other family members and income issues, and so on, since these factors also have an impact on where children are placed along the X axis, and where they may move to when situations and conditions change.

The case studies (see Boxes 5.3 and 5.4) attempt to illustrate the diversity of the young caring experience and help readers understand more clearly how to map young carers' experiences. For example, Case One figures low on the X (caring) and Y (nature of illness) axes. This is because the young carer's age, her understanding about mental health issues, her ability to support her mother effectively during times of crisis, as well as the fact that her mother's support needs are low, all point to a low placement for the young carer. Her placement five years earlier, however, would have been considerably higher on the X axis.

In the same way, Case Two also figures relatively low on the X axis (caring role), particularly because of Paula's age, the availability of alternative informal support from her mother and Paula's low level of caring responsibility. However, in respect of the Y axis (nature of illness), her placement is higher up the scale because of her father's lack of formal support and unstable condition. Therefore, Paula's placement indicates a need for more immediate and improved support and services for the *parent* as well as for Paula herself.

Case Three figures high on the X axis because of the amount of caring, both domestic and emotional, that Alison has to undertake. She also worries about her mother a great deal but the only source of support Alison has received for herself has been from the young carers project. Her mother is relatively well supported, although her condition is severe and often has serious consequences for herself and for Alison. Alison requires further support in her own right.

Box 5.3: Case studies

Case One

Ruth is 18 years-of-age and lives alone with her mother, Gwyn, who has manic depression, agoraphobia as well as a physical health condition (fibromyalgia). Ruth is in full-time employment and 'looks after' her mother during crises when her mother's manic depression escalates. Gwyn is on medication, which is effective most of the time. She has had several hospital admissions, all voluntary, and Ruth has been able to stay with her mother at the hospital during these times. Gwyn is actively involved with local mental health groups, and both she and Ruth are very knowledgeable about Gwyn's condition. Gwyn has good formal and informal support, although support for Ruth has been inadequate in the past. Ruth says she does not need any support for herself now, but needed it in the past. Although both have said they have had to fight for services and support in the past their current levels of support are good.

Case Two

Paula is 17 years-of-age and lives with her parents and two younger sisters. She is training to be a radiographer while also doing some part-time work. Her father, Robert, has paranoid schizophrenia as well as a physical health problem (diabetes). Paula cares for her father when her mother is out. She also looks after her younger sisters sometimes. Although Paula's mother is the main carer, Paula offers emotional support to her father. He says she does not know the extent of her emotional caring in this respect as he tries to keep some of the worse aspects of his illness from his children (particularly the voices he hears which have resulted in several suicide attempts in the past). Although Robert is on medication, this does not always control his illness. He is also currently trying to obtain CPN support because his new doctor, he says, refuses to help him get psychiatric support. Robert says he feels on the edge of suicide much of the time. Paula has never been assessed or included in discussions with professionals but says she does not need any support for herself now. Robert says the whole family needs additional support.

Case Three

Alison is 16 years-of-age and she lives alone with her mother, Ann, who has psychotic depression. Alison is currently in full-time further education. However, in the past, Alison's schooling was affected because she was worrying so much about her mother and could not concentrate on her schoolwork. For three years Alison has done all the cooking, cleaning and other domestic chores in the house, as well as administering medication to her mother and providing emotional support. Ann is on medication but these have side effects such as amenorrhoea and lactation. She has heard voices since she was a child and she has also attempted suicide on a number of occasions. Ann says the support she receives for herself is 'good', although the family has only just received homecare and Alison still undertakes a great deal of domestic care. Alison attends a local young carers project and she says the staff are 'very supportive'. However, Alison has not received a formal needs assessment.

Box 5.4: Mapping the case studies

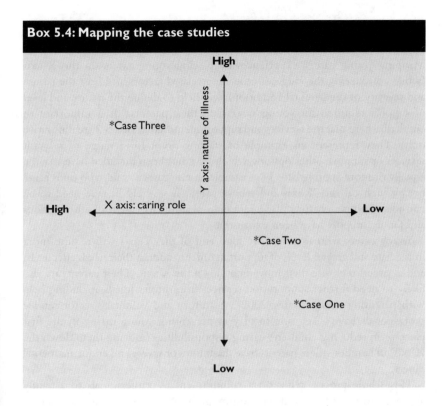

Assessment

We can see then how and why the mapping process is an important stage in the assessment process and how it might inform decisions about services and support to young carers *and* parents. In practice it requires professionals to recognise the triggers for caring, identify and locate young carers in the mapping process, and monitor and refer cases where necessary, particularly where family circumstances change quite rapidly. In our sample of 40 families it is notable that the circumstances of most families changed considerably between the first and second interview but services remained largely static and unresponsive to these changes.

Once professionals become more widely aware of young caring and can recognise cases, and when effective mapping procedures are implemented, then various policy options and interventions also become germane. Therefore, a child who has been recognised and identified (in the mapping process) as a 'young carer' and who figures fairly highly on the X axis could also, in policy terms, be considered to be a 'child in need' with specific rights under children's and carers' legislation. As we have already shown, this would then require professionals to utilise the relevant law and policy guidance to meet these children's/young carers' needs. In this way, mapping procedures converge and coincide with assessment and support systems (Box 5.2).

Support

Mapping young carers' experiences by placing young carers on the X axis (while considering the range of other interrelated factors, not least the nature and severity of the parental condition), will help to define the nature and level of support required for young carers and their parents. It is important to emphasise here that the services and support identified in Box 5.2 are illustrative only. They represent an example or starting point for a range of relevant services or support; other options, which have not been included here, may be equally or more appropriate. For example, in rare cases a child who finds him/herself high on the X axis and whose parent is severely ill may need to be considered ultimately for a placement in local authority care if all other options and family support have been exhausted.

Young carers who figure at the high end of the X axis will require more immediate and greater levels of support in order to address their needs effectively, and in order to ensure their movement down the X axis. Their parents are also likely to need further support and services from professionals, including help with parenting needs (Wates, 2002). Statutory and voluntary sector service professionals have a key role to play in preventing young caring in the first place or in reducing children's caring responsibilities (moving them down the X axis) in families where parents have disabilities or severe and enduring mental illness.

This whole process relies on a commitment by professionals to a family approach to assessment and service provision. A focus on children alone or parents in isolation undermines the usefulness of the mapping procedure and will in reality lead to negative outcomes for families as a whole. Furthermore, inter-agency work is also important across and between voluntary and statutory organisations, and between adult and children's services.

The responsibility of professionals to monitor cases has been underlined in much of the recent research and policy on young carers (see Becker et al, 1998). However, although the monitoring of cases in this respect is important at all levels, it becomes a crucial response midway and upwards through the X axis, particularly as we have seen how changes and crises can occur quite dramatically in cases where parents have severe and enduring mental health problems.

Conclusions

The usefulness of the model we have presented in this chapter is that it enables professionals involved with young carers, parents with mental illness, or families as a whole, to make informed judgements about the needs of young carers in these families. These judgements are based on a wide range of interrelating factors associated with caring levels and responsibilities, the nature and severity of parental mental illness, the support systems available to children and parents, the outcomes for both, to name but a few. Young carers placed high on the X axis (as a consequence of assessments that define their own support needs as high) need to be assisted in such a way as to reduce their caring responsibilities (or ideally to prevent them entirely) and bring young carers down the X axis. This will require consistency and continuity in services and support for both young carers and their parents if children's caring responsibilities are truly to be reduced or prevented.

Mapping procedures also enable professionals to identify the support needs of parents even though they are not specifically placed on the map. As we have already pointed out, the nature and extent of parental mental illness, and the services that parents receive, have consequences for young carers' placement on the X axis. Fundamentally, the needs of parents cannot be considered or responded to in isolation from the support needs of their children who take on caring responsibilities, and vice versa. Therefore, mapping also allows professionals to make judgements about the support needs of young carers and their parents in these situations. Professionals must consider the *interdependent* needs of children and parents, rather than, as our evidence has shown, treating them in isolation – either from an adult-focused or child-centred perspective. Crucially, of course, this will require professionals to consult with all family members about needs and services. Our evidence has shown that far too often professionals fail to include young carers in important discussions.

It is hoped that professionals, working with any family where there is parental mental illness and where children take on caring responsibilities, will be able to map the child's position on the caring, X axis, and make informed judgements about what support that child *and* their parent may require. Again we emphasise that the aims should be to prevent caring responsibilities that have negative outcomes for children's health and wellbeing from developing in the first place or becoming institutionalised within families.

While the mapping device offers a practical way forward for professionals, the position of parents with mental illness and children who care for them must also be placed within a broader socio-political context. So, for example, crucial issues about income levels, housing conditions, employment, social capital and so on, also have major implications for the quality of life, wellbeing and living standards of both mentally ill parents and young carers. A truly systemic approach would consider all of these factors as well as how they relate to the needs of parents with mental illness and children who care in these families. The quality of housing, the adequacy of benefits and the environments that families live in may be as important as the nature and severity of parental mental illness in determining outcomes for young carers and their parents. This requires professionals, and all of us concerned, to recognise the deficiencies of a medical model and the need for a broader social model of illness, disability *and* caring. This refocusing is required in order to meet more adequately the expressed needs of parents with severe and enduring mental illness and the children who care for them.

Bibliography

Alderson, P. (1995) *Listening to children: Children, ethics and social research*, Essex: Barnardos.

Aldridge, J. and Becker, S. (1993a) *Children who care: Inside the world of young carers*, Loughborough: Young Carers Research Group.

Aldridge, J. and Becker, S. (1993b) 'Punishing children for caring', *Children and Society*, vol 7, no 4, pp 277-88.

Aldridge, J. and Becker, S. (1994) *My child my carer: The parents' perspective*, Loughborough: YCRG.

Aldridge, J. and Becker, S. (1995) 'The rights and wrongs of children who care', in B. Franklin (ed) *Children's rights: A handbook of comparative policy and practice*, London: Routledge, pp 119-30.

Aldridge, J. and Becker, S. (1996) 'Disability rights and the denial of young carers: the dangers of zero-sum arguments', *Critical Social Policy*, no 48, pp 55-76.

Aldridge, J. and Becker, S. (1998) *The handbook of young carers projects*, London: Carers National Association.

Aldridge, J. and Becker, S. (2001) 'Children who care: rights and wrongs in debate and policy on young carers', in B. Franklin (ed) *The new handbook of children's rights: Comparative policy and practice*, London: Routledge, pp 208-22.

Anthony, E.J. (1970) 'The impact of mental and physical illness on family life', *American Journal of Psychiatry*, vol 127, no 2, pp 138-46.

Arnaud, S.H. (1959) 'Some psychological characteristics of children of multiple sclerotics', *Psychosomatic Medicine*, vol 21, no 1, pp 8-22.

Audit Commission (1986) *Making a reality of community care*, London: HMSO.

Audit Commission (1994) *Finding a place: A review of mental health services for adults*, London: HMSO.

Baker, S. and MacPherson, J. (2000) *Counting the cost: Mental health in the media*, London: MIND.

Baldwin, M. (2000) *Care management and community care: Social work discretion and the construction of policy*, Aldershot: Ashgate.

Barnett, B. and Parker, G. (1998) 'The parentified child: early competence or childhood deprivation?', *Child Psychology and Psychiatry Review*, vol 3, no 4, pp 146-56.

Becker, S. (ed) (1995) *Young carers in Europe: An exploratory cross-national study in Britain, France, Sweden and Germany*, Loughborough: YCRG in association with the European Research Centre.

Becker, S. (2000) 'Young carers', in M. Davies (ed) *The Blackwell encyclopaedia of social work*, Oxford: Blackwell, p 378.

Becker, S., Aldridge, J. and Dearden, C. (1998) *Young carers and their families*, Oxford: Blackwell Science.

Becker, S., Dearden, C. and Aldridge, J. (2001) 'Children's labour of love? Young carers and care work', in P. Mizen, C. Pole and A. Bolton (eds) *Hidden hands: International perspectives on children's work and labour*, Brighton: Routledge Falmer, pp 70-87.

Becker, S. and MacPherson, S. (eds) (1988) *Public issues, private pain: Poverty, social work and social policy*, London: Carematters Books/Insight.

Becker, S. and Silburn, R. (1999) *We're in this together: Conversations with families in caring relationships*, London: Carers National Association.

Bibby, A. and Becker, S. (2000) *Young carers in their own words*, London: Calouste Gulbenkian Foundation.

Bilsborrow, S. (1992) *'You grow up fast as well...' Young carers on Merseyside*, Liverpool: Carers National Association, Personal Services Society and Barnardos.

Bleuler, M. (1978) *The schizophrenic disorders: Long term patient and family studies*, New Haven: University Press.

Bodnar, J.C. and Kiecolt-Glaser, J.K. (1994) 'Caregiver depression after bereavement: chronic stress isn't over when it's over', *Psychology and Ageing*, vol 9, no 3, pp 372-80.

Bowlby, J. (1977) 'The making and breaking of affectional bonds', *British Journal of Psychiatry*, no 130, pp 201-10.

Bowlby, J. (1980) *Attachment and loss. Vol 3: Loss, sadness and depression*, London: Hogarth Press.

Brook Chen, A. and Baker, G. (2001) *Composition and statistical monitoring of 24 young carers projects in London*, London: London Young Carers Workers Forum.

Bryman, A. (1989) *Research methods and organization studies*, London: Unwin Hyman.

Buck, F.M. and Hohmann, G.W. (1983) 'Parental disability and children's adjustment', in E.L. Pan, T.E. Backer and C.L. Vash (eds) *Annual review of rehabilitation*, New York: Springer Publishing Co, pp 203-41.

Cawson, P. (2002) *Child maltreatment in the family: The experience of a national sample of young people*, London: NSPCC.

Cawson, P., Wattam, C., Brooker, S. and Kelly, G. (2000) *Child maltreatment in the United Kingdom: A study of the prevalence of child abuse and neglect*, London: NSPCC.

Chase, N.D. (1999) 'Parentification: an overview of theory, research, and societal issues', in N.D. Chase (ed) *Burdened children*, California: Sage, pp 3-33.

Cleaver, H., Unell, I. and Aldgate, J. (1999) *Children's needs – parenting capacity: The impact of parental mental illness, problem alcohol and drug use, and domestic violence on children's development*, London: The Stationery Office.

Connors, C.K., Himmelhock, J., Goyette, C.H., Ulrich, R. and Neil, J.F. (1979) 'Children of parents with affective illness', *American Academy of Child Psychiatry*, vol 18, no 4, pp 600-67.

Coolican, H. (1996) *Introduction to research methods and statistics in psychology*, (2nd edn), London: Hodder and Stoughton.

Crabtree, H. and Warner, L. (1999) *Too much to take on: A report on young carers and bullying*, London: The Princess Royal Trust for Carers.

Cytryn, L., McKnew, D.H., Bartko, J.J., Lamour, M. and Hamovitt, J. (1982) 'Offspring of patients with affective disorders II', *Journal of the American Academy of Child Psychiatry*, vol 21, no 4, pp 389-91.

Deacon, D.N. (1999) 'Young carers and old hacks', *The Journal of Young Carers Work*, no 2, pp 9-11.

Dearden, C. and Becker, S. (1995) *Young carers: The facts*, Sutton: Reed Business Publishing/Community Care.

Dearden, C. and Becker, S. (1998) *Young carers in the UK: A profile*, London: Carers National Association.

Dearden, C. and Becker, S. (1999) 'The experiences of young carers in the UK: the mental health issues', *Mental Health Care*, vol 2, no 8, pp 273-6.

Dearden, C. and Becker, S. (2000a) *Growing up caring: Vulnerability and transition to adulthood – young carers' experiences*, Leicester: Youth Work Press.

Dearden, C. and Becker, S. (2000b) 'Young carers: needs, rights and assessments', in J. Horwath, (ed) *The child's world: Assessing children in need, the reader*, London: Department of Health, NSPCC, University of Sheffield, pp 173-82.

DeChillo, N., Matorin, S. and Hallahan, C. (1987) 'Children of psychiatric patients: rarely seen or heard', *Health and Social Work*, vol 12, no 4, pp 296-302.

Department of Health (DH) (1989a) *Caring for people: Community care in the next decade and beyond*, London: HMSO.

DH (1989b) *Working for patients*, London: HMSO.

DH (1991) *The Children Act 1989: Guidance and regulations. Volume 2 – family support, day care and educational provision for young children*, London: HMSO.

DH (1992) *The health of the nation*, London: HMSO.

DH (1993) *The secretary of state's ten point plan for developing safe and successful community care*, London: DH.

DH (1994) *The health of the nation: Key area handbook – mental illness*, London: HMSO.

DH (1996a) *Carers (recognition and services) Act 1995: Policy guidance and practice guide* (LAC (96)7), London: DH.

DH (1996b) *Building bridges: A guide to arrangements for inter-agency working for the care and protection of severely mentally ill people*, London: HMSO.

DH (1996c) *The NHS: A service with ambitions*, London: HMSO.

DH (1996d) *The spectrum of care: Local services for people with mental health problems*, London: DH.

DH (1997) *Developing partnerships in mental health*, London: The Stationery Office.

DH (1998a) *Modernising mental health services: Safe, sound and supportive*, London: The Stationery Office.

DH (1998b) *Modernising social services: Promoting independence, improving protection, raising standards*, London: The Stationery Office.

DH (1998c) *The government's response to the children's safeguards review*, London: The Stationery Office.

DH (1998d) *Partnership in action: New opportunities for joint working between health and social services*, London: The Stationery Office.

DH (1998e) *Quality protects: Framework for action*, London: The Stationery Office.

DH (1999a) *National service framework for mental health*, London: The Stationery Office.

DH (1999b) *Modernising the care programme approach*, London: DH.

DH (2000) *Framework for the assessment of children in need and their families*, London: The Stationery Office.

DH (2001) *Children looked after by local authorities, year ending 31 March 2000, England*, London: DH.

DH (2002) *Draft Mental Health Bill* (Cm 5538-I), London: DH.

DH, HO and DfEE (Department of Health, Home Office and Department for Education and Employment) (1999) *Working together to safeguard children: A guide to inter-agency working to safeguard and promote the welfare of children*, London: The Stationery Office.

DH and The Welsh Office (1998) *People like us – The report of the review of the safeguards for children living away from home*, London: The Stationery Office.

Department of Health and Social Security (DHSS) (1971) *Hospital services for the mentally ill*, London: HMSO.

Elliott, A. (1992) *Hidden children: A study of ex-young carers of parents with mental health problems in Leeds*, Leeds: Leeds City Council Mental Health Development Section.

Eurostat (1997) Unpublished tabulations provided by Eurostat from the 1994 European Community Household Panel.

Falkov, A. (1996) *Fatal child abuse and parental psychiatric disorder: A study of working together. 'Part 8' reports*, London: DH.

Falkov, A. (1997) 'Parental psychiatric disorder and child maltreatment part II: extent and nature of the association', *Highlight*, no 149, London: National Children's Bureau.

Falkov, A. (1998) *Crossing bridges: Training resources for working with mentally ill parents and their children*, London: DH.

Feldman, M.A. (1986) 'Research on parenting by mentally retarded persons', *Psychiatric Clinics of North America*, vol 9, no 4, pp 777-96.

Feldman, M.A., Case, L., Towns, F. and Betel, J. (1985) 'Parent education project I: development and nurturance of children of mentally retarded parents', *American Journal of Mental Deficiency*, vol 90, no 3, pp 253-8.

Feldman, M.A., Stiffman, A.R. and Jung, K.G. (1987) *Children at risk in the web of parental mental illness*, New Brunswick and London: Rutgers University Press.

Frank, J., Tatum, C. and Tucker, S. (1999) *On small shoulders: Learning from the experiences of former young carers*, London: The Children's Society.

Germino, B.B. and Funk, S.G. (1993) 'Impact of a parent's cancer on adult children: role and relationship issues', *Seminars in Oncology Nursing*, vol 9, no 2, pp 101-6.

Göpfert, M., Webster, J. and Seeman, M.V. (eds) (1996) *Parental psychiatric disorder, distressed parents and their families*, Cambridge: Cambridge University Press.

Göpfert, M., Harrison, P. and Mahoney, C. (1999) *Keeping the family in mind: Participative research into mental ill-health and how it affects the whole family*, Liverpool: North Merseyside Community Trust, Imagine, Barnardo's, Save the Children.

Gorell Barnes, G. (1996) 'The mentally ill parent and the family system', in M. Göpfert, J. Webster and M.V. Seeman (eds) *Parental psychiatric disorder, distressed parents and their families*, Cambridge: Cambridge University Press, pp 42-59.

Green, A.E., Maguire, M. and Canny, A. (2001) 'Mapping and tracking vulnerable young people', *Findings*, York: Joseph Rowntree Foundation.

Gregory, R. (1989) 'Political rationality or incrementalism?', *Policy and Politics*, no 17, pp 139-53, (reproduced in M. Hill [ed] *The policy process: A reader*, Hemel Hempstead: Prentice Hall/Harvester Wheatsheaf, pp 175-91).

Griffiths, Sir R. (1988) *Community care: Agenda for action*, London: HMSO.

Hatfield, A.B. (1978) 'Psychological costs of schizophrenia to the family', *Social Work*, vol 23, no 5, pp 255-9.

Hill, M. (ed) (1993) *The policy process: A reader*, Hemel Hempstead: Prentice Hall/Harvester Wheatsheaf.

Hill, S. (1999) 'The physical effects of caring on children', *The Journal of Young Carers Work*, no 3, pp 6-7.

HM Government (1946) *National Health Service Act 1946*, London: HMSO.

HM Government (1948) *National Assistance Act 1948*, London: HMSO.

HM Government (1957) *Report of the Royal Commission on the law relating to mental illness and deficiency*, London: HMSO.

HM Government (1959) *Mental Health Act 1959*, London: HMSO.

HM Government (1970a) *Local Authority Social Services Act*, London: HMSO.

HM Government (1970b) *Chronically Sick and Disabled Persons Act 1970*, London: HMSO.

HM Government (1975) *Better services for the mentally ill*, London: HMSO.

HM Government (1980) *National Health Service Act*, London: HMSO.

HM Government (1983) *Mental Health Act 1983*, London: HMSO.

HM Government (1986) *Disabled Persons (Services, Consultation and Representation) Act 1986*, London: HMSO.

HM Government (1989) *Children Act 1989*, London: HMSO.

HM Government (1990) *NHS and Community Care Act 1990*, London: HMSO.

HM Government (1995a) *Carers (Recognition and Services) Act 1995*, London: HMSO.

HM Government (1995b) *Disability Discrimination Act 1995*, London: HMSO.

HM Government (1995c) *Mental Health (Patients in the Community) Act 1995*, London: HMSO.

HM Government (1996) *Community Care (Direct Payments) Act 1996*, London: HMSO.

HM Government (1997) *The new NHS: Modern, dependable*, London: The Stationery Office.

HM Government (1999) *Caring about carers:A national strategy for carers*, London: The Stationery Office.

HM Government (2000a) *Carers and Disabled Children Act 2000*, London: The Stationery Office.

HM Government (2000b) *Care Standards Act 2000*, London: The Stationery Office.

HM Government (2001) *Building a strategy for children and young people*, London: Children and Young People's Unit.

Hetherington, R., Baistow, K., Katz, I., Mesie, J. and Trowell, J. (2002) *The welfare of children with mentally ill parents: Learning from inter-country comparisons*, Chichester: Wiley.

Holzhausen, E. (1999) 'Developments in government's young carers policies', *The Journal of Young Carers Work*, no 2, pp 7-9.

Horwath, J. (ed) (2000) *The child's world: Assessing children in need, the reader*, London: Department of Health, NSPCC, University of Sheffield.

Howell, R. (1998) 'Q: when is a project not a project? A: when "joint finance" has expired', *The Journal of Young Carers Work*, no 1, pp 7-9.

Hudson, B. (1989) 'Michael Lipsky and street level beauracracy: a neglected perspective', in M. Hill (ed) (1997) *The policy process:A reader* (2nd edn), London: Prentice Hall.

Imrie, J. and Coombes, Y. (1995) *No time to waste: The scale and dimensions of the problem of children affected by HIV/AIDS in the United Kingdom*, Ilford: Barnardo's.

Inman, K. (2002) 'Role reversal', *The Guardian*, Society Supplement, 2 January.

Jones, P. (2000) 'What causes schizophrenia?', Paper presented at the 'Enduring Mental Illness' conference, Nottingham, 1-2 May.

Kavanagh, S. and Knapp, M. (1996) 'At the crossroads of health policy, health economics and family policy: whose interest to provide a family-oriented service?', in M. Göpfert, J. Webster and M.V. Seeman (eds) *Parental psychiatric disorder, distressed parents and their families*, Cambridge: Cambridge University Press, pp 335-47.

Keith, L. and Morris, J. (1995) 'Easy targets: a disability rights perspective on the "children as carers" debate', *Critical Social Policy*, nos 44/45, pp 36-57.

Landells, S. and Pritlove, J. (1994) *Young carers of a parent with schizophrenia: A Leeds survey*, Leeds: Leeds City Council Department of Social Services.

Larsson, G. and Larsson, A. (1982) 'Health of children whose parents seek psychiatric care, *Acta Psychiatrica Scandinavia*, vol 66, part 2, pp 154-62.

Levin, P. (1997) *Making social policy: The mechanisms of government and politics, and how to investigate them*, Buckingham: Open University Press.

Lindblom, C. (1959) 'The science of muddling through', *Public Administration Review*, vol 19, no 2, pp 79-88.

Lindblom, C. (1980) *The policy making process* (2nd edn), Englewood Cliffs: Prentice Hall.

Lipsky, M. (1980) *Street-level bureaucracy: Dilemmas of the individual in public services*, New York: Russell Sage Foundation.

Lynch, E.W. and Bakley, S. (1989) 'Serving young children whose parents are mentally retarded', *Infants and Young Children*, vol 1, pp 26-38.

Maher, J. and Green, H. (2002) *Carers 2000: Results from the care module of the General Household Survey 2000*, London: The Stationery Office.

Mahon, A. and Higgins, J. (1995) '...A life of our own', young carers: An evaluation of three RHA funded projects in Merseyside*, Manchester: University of Manchester Health Services Management Unit.

Marlowe, J. (1996) 'Helpers, helplessness and self-help: "Shaping the silence": a personal account', in M. Göpfert, J. Webster and M.V. Seeman (eds) *Parental psychiatric disorder, distressed parents and their families*, Cambridge: Cambridge University Press, pp 135-151.

Marsden, R. (1995) *Young carers and education*, London: London Borough of Enfield, Education Department.

Meltzer, H., Gill, B., Petticrew, M. and Hinds, K. (1995) *The prevalence of psychiatric morbidity among adults living in private households* (OPCS surveys of psychiatric morbidity in Great Britain report 1), London: OPCS.

Meredith, H. (1991) 'Young carers: the unacceptable face of community care', *Social Work and Social Sciences Review*, Supplement to vol 3, pp 47-51.

Ministry of Health (1951) *Report of the departmental committee working party on social workers in the mental health services*, London: HMSO.

Ministry of Health (1959) *Report of the departmental committee working party on social workers in the local authority and welfare services*, London: HMSO.

Ministry of Health (1962) *Hospital plan for England and Wales*, London: HMSO.

Ministry of Health (1963) *Health and welfare: The development of community care*, London: HMSO.

Morris, J. (1995) 'Easy targets: a disability rights perspective on the "young carers" debate', in SSI, *Young carers: Something to think about*, London: DH.

Mumoz, M. (1998) *Young carers and their families in Westminster*, London: Westminster Carers Service.

Murray, R.M. (2000) 'Schizophrenia is (not simply) a neurodevelopmental disorder', Paper presented at the 'Enduring Mental Illness' conference, Nottingham, 1-2 May.

Newton, B. and Becker, S. (1996) *Young carers in Southwark: The hidden face of community care*, Loughborough: YCRG.

Newton, B. and Becker, S. (1999) *The capital carers: An evaluation of capital carers young carers project*, Loughborough: YCRG.

O'Hagan, K. (1993) *Emotional and psychological abuse of children*, Milton Keynes: Open University Press.

O'Neill, A. (1988) *Young carers: The Tameside research*, Tameside: Tameside Metropolitan Borough Council.

O'Neill, A.M. (1985) 'Normal and bright children of mentally retarded parents: the huck finn syndrome', *Child Psychiatry and Human Development*, vol 15, part 4, pp 255-68.

ONS (Office for National Statistics) (1996) *Young carers and their families*, London: The Stationery Office.

Olsen, R. (1996) 'Young carers: challenging the facts and politics of research into children and caring', *Disability and Society*, vol 11, no 1, pp 41-54.

Olsen, R. (1999) 'Young carers and the "disability" response: identifying common ground', *The Journal of Young Carers Work*, no 2, pp 4-7.

Orvaschel, H., Walsh-Allis, G. and Ye, W. (1988) 'Psychopathology in children of parents with recurrent depression', *Journal of Abnormal Child Psychology*, vol 16, no 1, pp 17-28.

Orvaschel, H., Weissman, M.M. and Kidd, K.K. (1980) 'Children and depression: the children of depressed parents; the childhood of depressed patients; depression in children', *Journal of Affective Disorders*, vol 2, no 1, pp 1-16.

Page, R. (1988) *Report on the initial survey investigating the number of young carers in Sandwell secondary schools*, Sandwell: Sandwell Metropolitan Borough Council.

Parker, G. and Olsen, R. (1995) 'A sideways glance at young carers', in Social Services Inspectorate *Young carers: Something to think about*, London: DH, pp 63-74.

Parker, G. (1992) 'Counting care: numbers and types of informal carers', in J. Twigg (ed) *Carers: Research and practice*, London: HMSO, pp 6-29.

Parker, G. (1994) *Where next for research on carers?*, Leicester: Nuffield Community Care Studies Centre.

Perkins, R. (2000) 'Recovery and service provision: the individual's journey', Paper presented at the 'Enduring Mental Illness' conference, Nottingham, 1-2 May.

Philo, G. (ed) (1996) *Media and mental distress*, Harlow: Addison Wesley Longman.

Philo, G. and Secker, J. (1999) 'Media and mental health', in B. Franklin (ed), *Social policy, the media and misrepresentation*, London: Routledge, pp 135-45.

Philo, G., Secker, J., Platt, S., Henderson, L., McLaughlin, G. and Burnside, J. (1994) 'The impact of the mass media on public images of mental illness: media content and audience belief', *Health Education Journal*, no 53, pp 271-81.

Poole, R. (1996) 'General adult psychiatrists and their patients' children', in M. Göpfert, J. Webster and M.V. Seeman (eds) *Parental psychiatric disorder, distressed parents and their families*, Cambridge: Cambridge University Press, pp 3-6.

Pound, A. (1996) 'Parental affective disorder and childhood disturbance', in M. Göpfert, J. Webster and M.V. Seeman (eds) *Parental psychiatric disorder, distressed parents and their families*, Cambridge: Cambridge University Press, pp 201-218.

Powell, E. (1961) 'Address to the annual conference', *MIND Annual Report 1961*, London: MIND.

Read, J. and Clements, L. (2001) *Disabled children and the law*, London: Jessica Kingsley Publishers.

Rieder, R.O. (1973) 'The offspring of schizophrenic parents: a review', *Journal of Nervous and Mental Diseases*, vol 157, no 3, pp 179-90.

Ritchie, J. (1994) *The report of the inquiry into the care and treatment of Christopher Clunis*, London: HMSO.

Roberts, D. (1996) 'The child grown up: "On being and becoming mindless": a personal account', in M. Göpfert, J. Webster and M.V. Seeman (eds) *Parental psychiatric disorder, distressed parents and their families*, Cambridge: Cambridge University Press, pp 185-9.

Rosenberg, S.A. and McTate, G.A. (1982) 'Intellectually handicapped mothers', *Children Today*, vol 11, no 1, pp 24-6.

Roy, R. (1990) 'Consequences of parental illness on children: a review', *Social Work and Social Sciences Review*, vol 2, no 2, pp 109-21.

Sameroff, A.J. and Zax, M. (1973) 'Perinatal characteristics of the offspring of schizophrenic women', *Journal of Nervous and Mental Disease*, vol 157, no 1, pp 191-9.

Sayce, L. (1995) 'Response to violence: a framework for fair treatment', in J. Crichton (ed) *Psychiatric patient violence*, London: Duckworth, pp 127-50.

Schilling, R.F., Schinke, S.P., Blythe, B.J. and Barth, R.P. (1982) 'Child maltreatment and mentally retarded parents: is there a relationship?', *Mental Retardation*, vol 20, no 5, pp 201-9.

Schuff, G.H. and Asen, K.E. (1996) 'The disturbed parent and the disturbed family', in M. Göpfert, J. Webster and M.V. Seeman (eds) *Parental psychiatric disorder, distressed parents and their families*, Cambridge: Cambridge University Press, pp 135-51.

Schulsinger, H. (1976) 'A ten-year follow-up of children of schizophrenic mothers clinical assessment', *Acta Psychiatrica Scandinavia*, vol 53, pp 371-86.

Schumaker, K.L. (1995) 'Family caregiver role acquisition: role-making through situated interaction', *Scholarly Inquiry for Nursing Practice: An International Journal*, vol 9, no 3, pp 211-29.

Scottish Executive (2001) *Men and women in Scotland: A statistical profile*, Edinburgh: Scottish Executive.

Seebohm Committee (1968) *Report of the committee on local authority and allied social services*, London: HMSO.

Seifer, R. and Sameroff, A.J. (1981) 'Adaptive behaviour in young children of emotionally disturbed women', *Journal of Applied Developmental Psychology*, vol 1, no 4, pp 251-76.

Smith, G. and May, D. (1980) 'The artificial debate between rationalist and incrementalist models of decision making', *Policy and Politics*, no 8, pp 147-161, (reproduced in M. Hill [ed] (1993) *The policy process: A reader*, Hemel Hempstead: Prentice Hall/Harvester Wheatsheaf, pp 163-74).

SSI (Social Services Inspectorate) (1995) *Young carers: Something to think about*, London: DH.

SSI (1996) *Young carers: Making a start*, London: DH.

SSI (2000) *A jigsaw of services: Inspection of services to support disabled adults in their parenting role*, London: DH.

Sturges, J.S. (1977) 'Talking with children about mental illness in the family', *Health and Social Work of Rehabilitation*, vol 2, no 3, pp 88-109.

Sturges, J.S. (1978) 'Children's reactions to mental illness in the family', *Social Casework*, vol 59, no 9, pp 530-6.

Thurman, S.K. (ed) (1985) *Children of handicapped parents: Research and clinical perspectives*, Orlando: Academic Press.

Vernon, S. (1998) *Social work and the law*, London: Butterworths.

Ward, H. and Rose, W. (eds) (2002) *Approaches to needs assessment in children's services*, London: Jessica Kingsley Publishers.

Wates, M. (2002) *Supporting disabled adults in their parenting role*, York: YPS.

Weissman, M.M. and Paykel, E.S. (1974) *The depressed woman: A study of social relationships*, Chicago: University of Chicago Press.

West, M.L. and Keller, A.E.R. (1991) 'Parentification of the child: a case study of Bowlby's compulsive care-giving attachment pattern', *American Journal of Psychotherapy*, vol 45, no 3, pp 425-31.

Wilson, C., Nairn, R., Coverdale, J. and Panapa, A. (2000) 'How mental illness is portrayed in children's television – a prospective study', *British Journal of Psychiatry*, vol 176, pp 440-3.

Winters, K.C., Stone A.A., Weintraub, S. and Neale, J.M. (1981) 'Cognitive and attentional deficits in children vulnerable to psychopathology', *Journal of Abnormal Child Psychology*, vol 9, no 4, pp 435-53.

Woods, N.F., Yates, B.C. and Primino, J. (1989) 'Supporting families during chronic illness', *IMAGE: Journal of Nursing Scholarship*, vol 21, no1, pp 46-50.

Zetlin, A.G., Weisner, T.S. and Gallimore, R. (1985) 'Diversity, shared functioning and the role of benefactors: a study of parenting by retarded persons', in S.K. Thurman (ed) *Children of handicapped parents: Research and clinical perspectives*, Orlando: Academic Press, pp 69-95.

Identifying parents with mental ill health and young carers in research procedures: a methodological discussion

A number of small-scale studies in the late 1980s and early 1990s pointed to young caring as a growing social issue, rather than a private one. Although later research tried to estimate the extent of the problem using quantitative research methods, this often proved problematic in identifying and gaining access to large numbers of 'vulnerable' respondents.

Increasingly, researchers adopted qualitative methods aimed at smaller numbers of young carers in order to gain further insight into hitherto neglected areas of study and to provide "information to guide future developments" (Page, 1988, p 32). These qualitative approaches complemented the conclusions of some of the earliest studies on young carers where an emphasis on 'the numbers game' (O'Neill, 1988) was seen as less useful than looking at particular cases in some depth:

> One has to look at the size of the problem in the context of the severity of impacts on individuals .... It is arguably more important to identify each individual case than might be true for the [survey] as a whole. (O'Neill, 1988, p 3)

Adopting qualitative methods of investigation proved useful for our purposes, not just because such methods have been tried and tested in the field over some considerable time, but also because qualitative approaches place more emphasis on *context* and *process* rather than a reliance on preordained tools or instruments. In this case, questionnaire surveys would have been unlikely to uncover the kind of information needed to guide our further understanding of the nature of young caring in the context of parental mental ill health. Furthermore, qualitative approaches give priority to "the perspectives of those being studied rather than the prior concerns of the researcher" (Bryman, 1989, p 135).

Our intention was to conduct in-depth semi-structured individual interviews with three respondent groups:

- young carers;
- co-resident relative(s) with a severe and enduring mental health problem;
- key welfare professionals in contact with these families.

We made the decision to approach children (and their families), not with questionnaires or structured research instruments, but with open-ended questions using semi-structured interview techniques (what Bryman refers to as 'type 3' interview-based studies). Here, the interviewer "uses a schedule but recognises that departures will occur if interesting themes emerge from what respondents say and in order to get their version of things" (Bryman, 1989, p 149).

We also planned to return to the families ten months after the initial interview so that any changes that might have occurred in their family circumstances, their needs and their personal and professional relationships might be identified. We recognised that some mental health conditions can often cause rapid cyclical changes in behaviour and we wanted to monitor these, as well as any changes in outcomes for families. We also wanted to record any differences in professional approaches made to these families after the first round of interviews had taken place. We hoped that the data generated by the two-phase interview process would enable us to gain further insight into the particular experiences and needs of children when they care for a parent with a mental illness. Furthermore, we hoped to gain deeper understanding about the nature of family and professional relationships in this context, as well as the type of caring undertaken by children, and how this might (or might not) change.

It transpired that most of the interviews took place in family homes (others were conducted, by request, over the telephone). The interview setting was dictated by both the expressed needs of the family (as this was where most parents and children felt comfortable) and, to some extent, by the nature of the illnesses themselves. For example, a number of parents' mental illnesses precipitated antisocial or reclusive-type behaviour. In some cases agoraphobia had occurred, with the effect that the use of external (that is, outside the family home) interview environments were entirely inappropriate.

Troubleshooting

Although the two-phase fieldwork was successful in terms of the qualitative methods used and the amount and quality of data obtained, some practical issues arose in respect of obtaining and stratifying the sample that we feel should be explained for a number of reasons:

- they pinpoint the particular problems of locating and identifying a sample – and gaining access to respondents – where the nature of the subjects for study in and of themselves make sample selection more difficult;
- they serve a useful pedagogic purpose for other social researchers in their future planning and organisation of research studies of this kind;
- they underline the necessity, which may occasionally arise, for redefining a sample.

Our original intention had been to stratify by gender, age, race, diagnostic category and who the young carers cared for.

From sample selection to transcription

Our intention was to examine the experiences and needs of children caring for a co-resident family member with a *severe and enduring mental health problem*. It was the distinct and particular nature of the conditions involved that proved problematic in the sample selection process. The criteria we adopted for determining whether someone had a 'severe and enduring' mental health problem was by reference to whether or not they were receiving support under the Care Programme Approach (CPA) (see Appendix B: 1991 (i), 1999 (ii), 1999 (iii)). Only adults on the CPA (especially the enhanced level) were to be included in our study. This too had its implications: some families were rejected because they were not on the CPA.

We had originally intended to select and interview 50 families, including the young carer, the parent(s) with mental health problems, and the key professionals in contact with these families. Although early forecasts for sample selection were promising, indicating a large number of families from which we might select, these initial 'ball park' figures were reduced considerably once the research process got underway. This also had some impact on the stratification process. Below we set out the phases of research, from sample selection to transcription.

The phases of research

1. Initial approach to identified sources for sample selection. (We approached 120 young carers projects and around 40 NSF projects. All projects were asked if they were in contact with families who fit our criteria and to give an estimate of the number of families who might be willing or able to participate in the study.)
2. Sources to return figures to research team.
3. Research team contacts sources to discuss sample and methods of approach to potential respondents.
4. Sources approach respondents to participate in study.
5. Sources contact research team with numbers of respondents for sample and contact details.
6. Research team contacts respondents for further discussion and to make arrangements for interview.
7. Interviews agreed (or abandoned) and date for interviews to take place confirmed.
8. Interviews conducted and recorded for transcription.
9. Tapes transcribed and analysed.
10. Stages 6-9 repeated ten months later for second round of fieldwork.

While recognising that "a truly representative sample is an abstract ideal unachievable in practice" (Coolican, 1996, p 59), obtaining a representative, stratified sample became of secondary consideration in our efforts to obtain the requisite numbers of respondents, that is, the 50 young carers, 50 co-resident relatives and 50 key professionals. Indeed, there was a considerable reduction in the numbers of *potential* sample families indicated by project workers initially (47 projects suggested a possible 750 parent and young carer respondents) and the *actual* number of families finally secured (40 families, 80+ parents and young carers interviewed). This contraction occurred for a number of key reasons:

- time lapse (between Phases 1 and 3 above);
- discrepancy between identification (Phase 2) and agreement (Phase 7);
- concerns by project staff about the impact of the research process (Phase 3);
- the impact of the condition of the respondent, and other factors, on the research process (all phases).

Time lapse

- Inevitably, there will be time delays between the initial approach made to sample sources in Phase 1 and follow-up requests for respondents to be involved in the sample (Phase 4) in order to allow sources to meet the deadline for replies and for all the necessary arrangements (and safeguards) to be put in place.

Although the time between these phases was only a matter of weeks in our study, some potential sample families defaulted in this time. The nature and status of parents' mental health often impaired their ability to make firm decisions and to plan ahead. One of the reasons that severe and enduring mental health conditions have featured in so few studies on young carers to date is no doubt due in part to the inherent difficulties involved in gaining access to respondents with these types of illnesses. This is especially the case when agreement to participate depends so much on symptomatic outcomes of illnesses themselves at any given time.

There can also be misunderstandings among sources about sample selection criteria. This was certainly true in our study where many young carers project workers, for example, had not fully understood that parents were to be included in the study. (Interestingly, this reflects these workers' own assumptions. We presented our research as a study of children caring for a parent with severe mental illness, and many workers assumed that only the young carers' perspectives would be sought by the research team. This was despite the fact that our project literature clearly stated that parents and professionals would also be interviewed.)

The time between Phases 3 and 4 (in our case, the time between asking project workers to approach families and the approach being made) can be prolonged as it often involves extra work for sources who may already have quite heavy caseloads. In our study it was also necessary during these phases for project staff to implement their own procedures for formally approaching families. This was done, generally, in order to safeguard client confidentiality and to ensure family stability was not undermined. For example, one young carers project had identified a possible nine families who they thought met the criteria and who might be willing to participate in the study. However, in order to comply with the project's confidentiality policy, the families could only be approached by project staff who had with them an accompanying letter from the research team. This letter had to include a reply slip for the families to sign and confirm their willingness to participate in the study. As a result, in the absence of a more direct and personal approach by the research team, no family replied to the letter.

Discrepancy between identification and agreement

- Between the phases of identification of respondents by sources (Phase 2) and agreement by the respondents (Phase 7), changes to previous agreements and defaults can occur.

For our study changes occurred during these phases because some project workers, having discussed the study criteria in more detail with the research team, realised that the families they had in mind were not in fact suitable. Furthermore, and perhaps more commonly, some families who were approached refused to participate in the study. Refusals like this can be explained in a number of ways, including the state of the parent's health at the time or their uncertainty about the possible outcomes of the research process itself (for themselves and for their families). Although getting parent respondents to agree to be interviewed in the first place was often difficult, conversely, once agreement had been reached and interviews arranged, they often talked openly and intimately about their experiences and needs.

A further obstacle here was that, to be included in the final sample, both the parent and the child had to agree to be interviewed. Although *permission* initially had to be sought from the parent for the child to participate in the study, *agreement* had to come from both. Therefore, inter-family indecision and disagreement sometimes prevented either interview from taking place. In these situations, families were not selected for the sample.

Concerns about the impact of the research process

- Sources can be concerned about the impact on respondents of participation in research processes.

Project staff were often uncertain about the effects on parents (and children) of talking in depth about their illnesses and experiences, as well as their children's involvement in caring. Therefore, in many cases a great deal of groundwork had to be done prior to project workers approaching families to participate in the study (Phase 4). This involved members of the research team attending team meetings to discuss issues such as confidentiality, post-interview support strategies and research procedures. Project workers were also often uncertain about introducing a relatively 'unknown' variable (the researcher) into families that had only recently been 'stabilised'.

This raises an important methodological point relating to the sample selection process. During the sample selection period, it became clear that project workers were, in many respects, implementing their own stratification of the sample by making a personal and professional judgement about whether certain families were 'suitable' or stable enough to withstand the interview process. As one project worker said:

> "Across the county, there are others [families] that we just wouldn't even approach ... because it is just so unstable and you know and maybe we shouldn't ... struggle with how we make these distinctions, maybe we shouldn't make those judgements, maybe we should throw this open to everybody, but at the same time, I suppose we felt this sense of responsibility towards saying, you know, this could well have some huge impact."

This 'cherry picking' approach to sample selection by sources may have meant that only the 'best' or most resilient cases were actually interviewed, and that these were not necessarily families with the greatest needs or in periods of greatest transition or crisis. Although some project workers clearly recognised the impacts of such appraisals in terms of the study, their ultimate concern was the emotional stability of the families concerned. However, considering the often rapid cycle of change that families can experience as a result of the onset or incidence of mental ill health, it is just as possible that, from the time families were approached by project staff (Phase 4) and the interviews taking place (Phase 8), these families had different or additional needs and problems.

The impact of the condition of the respondent, and other factors, on the research process

- The nature of the respondent's condition can influence the research process. And in the triangle of communication – between sources and respondents, sources and the research team, and the research team and respondents – a range of problems can emerge that affect successful research outcomes.

It was particularly true of our study that the condition of the affected parent and how this manifested itself was a key factor in the success of all the phases of research. (Depending on the nature of the diagnosis, this manifestation could be rapid behavioural changes, suicidal tendencies, paranoia, delusions and so on.) Therefore, problems arose in respect of securing and maintaining agreements with families to participate in the two-round interview process. Project workers also reported similar problems in sustaining agreements and contact with the families. Sometimes families would be willing to be interviewed during Phase 4 but would have changed their minds by Phase 7. A sudden change in the state of parents' mental health (or even their medication) could threaten the smooth operation of all phases of the research process. Sometimes, maintaining contact with respondents was complicated by other, more practical issues. These issues included respondents who, due to an unexpected crisis of illness, were unable to talk on the telephone, telephones being cut off due to non payment of bills, and some families moving house or having only temporary residencies with friends or relatives between the rounds of research.

Within the triangle of communication, problems arose that made the successful transition from sample selection to transcription and analysis more complex. Sometimes weeks of failed telephone calls to families by the research team would result in regression to earlier phases. For example, at Phase 6 the research team occasionally had to revert to Phase 3 because families could no longer be contacted. In our study, both the research team and project workers experienced similar communications problems with families, as the following correspondence (from project manager to researcher) illustrates:

> "I too have been trying to phone [parent] having received a message to phone her urgently. Her mobile must be switched off. She doesn't have a landline. There is another crisis there at the moment, [young carer] has gone to older sister for a few days."

[Two weeks later]

> "I have had trouble getting hold of [parent] who is having problems again at the moment and have not been able to get through. Her mother, [the young carer's grandmother] has a phone and I did speak to her last week and she said her daughter [parent respondent] wasn't answering the phone. Hopefully she will be better again. I'm going to [young carer's] school tomorrow and will check if she's in – though she is hardly attending at the moment. I know [the grandmother] is fairly fed up with her daughter at the moment and says her mental health problems began when she was in her late teens and she is 43 now."

> "[Another parent] often doesn't pick up the phone, but does 1471 and tends to phone back. Always difficult contacting people with mental health problems."

Delays also occurred between Phases 6 and 8, usually because of changes to family schedules, the state of health of the care recipient, or the family simply changed their minds about taking part in the interview. 'Doorstep' refusals also occurred. These were usually due to an unexpected crisis or deteriorating mental health. In some cases the respondent did not feel able to cope with the interview process on the day.

It is worth remembering also that a number of respondents were co-morbid or had combinative mental and physical health conditions. One interview took nearly three months to arrange as the parent had severe depression and was also regularly hospitalised with a chronic bowel condition. The interview was eventually conducted – at the respondent's request – at her bedside.

Second-round sample selection

After all of these methodological and process difficulties, it must be remembered that our research design included a second phase of fieldwork interviews with parents, young carers and professionals. Phases 6 to 9 had to be repeated some ten months after the first round of fieldwork, and it is not surprising, therefore, that many of the difficulties described above also became a feature of this second phase.

Although the second-round sample should have included all families (and key professionals) who participated in the first round of interviews, inevitably some attrition occurred. Of the 40 families involved in the initial interview process, 28 participated in the follow-up fieldwork. This 30% attrition rate can be accounted for in a number of ways. First, some parents (four cases) refused to take any further part in the research, and did not want their children to participate either. Second, some of the families had split up (six cases), which meant some young carers had left home (through natural transitions) or parental relationships had broken down and families had moved on. Third, the fact that so many families had split up meant that making contact with the families once again was difficult, and we were unable to contact two families throughout the second-round communication process.

Key workers were not re-interviewed where families were not included in the second round of fieldwork. Of the 28 families who did participate, only nine professionals were interviewed (see Chapter Four of this volume). This was because 14 professionals had left or were no longer the particular respondent family's key worker; two refused to participate again in the research process; one professional was on sick leave, and a further key worker was on secondment at the time the second-round fieldwork was underway. Although the attrition rate for the professional respondents seems high, it must be remembered that 12 key workers were not included in the second phase of research because 12 families had opted out or were unavailable.

We re-interviewed families even when their key worker had changed (in 14 cases, as we have said). This was because the changes that had occurred in these families' lives during the ten months between interview phases were important in terms of our data collection and analyses. When these changes also indicated a new or different key worker, then the families' experiences of service interruptions or changes were also important to record.

It must be pointed out that the difficulties experienced in selecting and interviewing our final sample of families had no necessary relationship with the potential or actual number of families where a parent has a severe and enduring mental health problem, and where their children provide care for them. The fact that it was difficult to recruit and maintain a sample for *research purposes* did not mean that these families were few in number. Rather, there is evidence from our sources and from our estimates (see Chapter One of this volume) that such families abound, but, as we have seen, this can translate into a relatively small sample when it comes to *conducting* the research itself. This, in its own way, says a great deal about the vulnerability of these families and their fears, anxieties and circumstances.

The issues we have raised here relate to the various phases of research, and are not intended to highlight the negative aspects of researching 'vulnerable' respondent groups, especially parents with severe and enduring mental health problems and children who care for them. Rather, they aim to underline the complexities involved in gaining access to such respondents (in this case both the parents and young carers) and to advocate the need for patience, understanding and sensitivity when implementing and managing research strategies in such cases.

Furthermore, in cases such as these, where both subject groups are likely to be difficult to identify and recruit for participation in fieldwork, it is possible that some adjustments to sample stratification and numbers will be necessary. In our case, where the sample selection process became problematised by a range of factors, not least the difficulties involved in gaining access to the families themselves, it was necessary to reduce the original sample size by ten families. In such instances it becomes more useful to think not in terms of pre-determined, specified numbers of respondents, but rather to apply the concept of saturation: to continue to recruit families and conduct interviews until the information and data obtained becomes largely repetitive. At which point it may transpire that the efforts (time, money, resources and so on) to recruit more respondents produces little, if anything, 'new' in terms of findings.

Young carers and parents with severe mental illness: a chronology and guide to relevant law and policy

A note on the chronology and guide

Law and policy provide the framework for professional interventions and practices with children caring for parents with severe mental illness. Since the Second World War, many laws and 'policies' have been introduced and developed by government concerning vulnerable children, young carers, adult carers, and people with mental health problems, although very few are specifically and directly concerned with children caring for parents with severe mental illness.

Here, we present a chronology and guide to the key pieces of legislation and policy that have relevance to *young carers looking after parents with severe mental illness*. Starting with relevant law and policy initiatives from the 1940s, we follow these developments through to the current day.

There is always a fine line to be drawn between including (and regarding it as relevant and appropriate), and excluding an entry. This judgement is less difficult with regards to the law. We have included entries on legislation which specifically refer to young carers, vulnerable children and adults with mental illness (most of the community care legislation also refers to this latter group). These legal entries are concerned with the law in England. There are differences in the legal framework of Wales, Scotland and Northern Ireland.

In terms of what to include as 'policy', we have been helped by Levin's (1997, p 19) categorisation. Levin suggests that a policy can be recognised because it has certain attributes. 'Policy' denotes *belongingness*; that is, a policy belongs to someone or some body. Policy also has *status* and *authority*, and denotes *commitment* on the part of policy makers to get things done. Finally, a policy also possesses the attribute of *specificity*. Some stated intentions are quite specific, others less so. The less specific a policy, the more options it leaves open when it comes to translating the policy into action. The more specific it is the closer it is to being a single blueprint for action. A policy must have at least some degree of specificity for it to be distinguishable from other policies. Each of the 'policy' entries in the chronology has these four attributes.

The chronology does not refer to other developments (for example, academic debates) or to other documents (for example, research reports/research findings on young carers, or mental health reports). The relevant research and key texts are referred to in other chapters of the book, or elsewhere in our work (see for example, Becker et al, 1998 for a review of the law and policy as it relates to young carers in general).

Some of the entries in the chronology are deliberately brief. The most relevant entries, however, contain detailed information and guidance on the law and policy, highlighting its importance for our focus on children caring for parents with severe mental illness.

Chronology and guide

1946
1946 National Health Service Act introduces major changes in mental health policy, including:

- the Minister of Health becomes the central authority for mental health;
- local authorities acquire wide powers and some duties for prevention, care and aftercare;
- care and treatment to be available as of right to all regardless of ability to pay (HM Government, 1946).

1948
1948 National Assistance Act enables local authorities to make arrangements to promote welfare of "persons aged eighteen and over, who are blind, deaf or dumb (or who suffer from mental disorder of any description) and other persons who are substantially and permanently handicapped by illness, injury or congenital deformity or such other disabilities as may be prescribed by the minister" (HM Government, 1948, s 29 (1)).

1951
Report of the departmental committee working party on social workers in the mental health services (Mackintosh Report) defines the roles of social work in the mental health field (Ministry of Health, 1951).

1957
The report of the royal commission on the law relating to mental illness and deficiency (Percy Report) recognises that advances in medical knowledge and the advent of social services demands changes in medical methods applied to mental illness as well as to the organisation of mental health services. This also leads to a comprehensive review of mental health law (HM Government, 1957).

1959

(i) *1959 Mental Health Act* lays down the statutory duties and functions of health and social services in the treatment of mentally disordered people. All types of hospital can now take any mentally ill patient whether on a compulsory order or informal basis. Informal treatment, where possible, is to be favoured. The Act omits to define 'mental illness' preferring instead to opt for a broader concept of mental disorder: "mental disorder means mental illness, arrested or incomplete development of mind, psychopathic disorder, and any other disorder or disability of mind" (HM Government, 1959, Part 1, s 4(i)).

(ii) *Report of the departmental committee working party on social workers in the local authority health and welfare services* (Younghusband Report). This gives further definition to the newly developing role of social worker in relation to health services (Ministry of Health, 1959).

1961

Minister of Health, Enoch Powell, addresses MIND annual conference. The 'water towers' speech confirms government policy to close down the old-style mental institutions (Powell, 1961).

1962

Hospital plan for England and Wales White Paper (Ministry of Health, 1962). This marks the official end of the policy of institutional segregation of mentally ill people and the beginning of community care. Targets for the reduction of hospital beds are set.

1963

Health and welfare: The development of community care (Ministry of Health, 1963) provides government guidance on inter-agency working arrangements necessary for the development of community care services.

1968

Report of the ministry of housing and local government committee on local authority and allied personal social services (Seebohm Report) recommends that unified social services departments should be established by local authorities to provide a single point of entry for social work and other family and community welfare services (Seebohm Committee, 1968).

1970

(i) *Local Authority Social Services Act* (HM Government, 1970a) expands social services departments and widens the remit of the social work profession.

(ii) *1970 Chronically Sick and Disabled Persons Act* (HM Government, 1970b). Section One requires local authorities to identify the needs of those persons identified in Section 29 of the 1948 National Assistance Act (including people who suffer from mental disorder of any description) and to publish information about the services it provides for these service users. Section Two places local authorities under a duty to provide a range of services for these people where they are satisfied that this is necessary to meet their needs. These services include:

* practical assistance in the home;
* assistance in arranging adaptations to the home;
* the provision of additional facilities designed to secure greater safety, comfort or convenience;
* the provision of a telephone and any special equipment necessary to enable the person to use it.

1971

Hospital services for the mentally ill (DHSS, 1971), a health service circular, underlines the thrust of existing policy, including:

* the integration of psychiatry with general medicine;
* the further reduction of in-patient beds;
* the development of day patient and out-patient services;
* the shift to local authorities of responsibility for residential and social care.

1975

Better services for the mentally ill White Paper (HM Government, 1975) sets out the government's policy framework for future service development, proposing local-based care, encompassing hospital services, residential accommodation and community services.

1979

Margaret Thatcher elected Prime Minister, ushering in a new approach to social policy, state intervention and the role of the private sector in providing welfare-related services.

1980

National Health Service Act (HM Government, 1980) abolishes area health authorities and introduces district health authorities, which are also given powers to make grants to social services and voluntary organisations.

1983

1983 Mental Health Act (HM Government, 1983). The Act:

- makes provision in relation to people who have a 'mental disorder' (see Box B.1);
- specifies procedures for the compulsory admission of patients to hospital;
- defines the position and rights of patients while in hospital;
- defines the circumstances of their treatment;
- defines procedures for their continued detention and for their discharge.

It also creates the Mental Health Act Commission.

Box B.1: 'Mental disorder' and 'mental illness' under the 1983 Mental Health Act

The four categories of mental disorder are *mental illness, severe mental impairment* (both of these are considered to be major disorders), *mental impairment* and *psychotic disorder* (both of which are considered to be minor disorders). *Mental illness* is *not* defined by the 1983 Mental Health Act, although the other three categories are:

Severe mental impairment: "a state of arrested or incomplete development of mind which includes severe impairment of intelligence and social functioning and is associated with abnormally aggressive or seriously irresponsible conduct".

Mental impairment: defined in the same terms except that the word "significant" is used instead of the word "severe".

Psychotic disorder: "a persistent disorder or disability of mind (whether or not including significant impairment of intelligence) which results in abnormally aggressive or seriously irresponsible conduct" (HM Government, 1983, s1(2); see also Vernon, 1998, pp 187-238).

Section 1(3) of the Act specifies that a person cannot be classified as mentally disordered "by reason only of promiscuity, or other immoral conduct, sexual deviancy or dependence on alcohol or drugs". Consequently, in this volume we do not include dependence on alcohol or drugs *by itself* as an indicator of mental disorder or mental illness.

1986

(i) *1986 Disabled Persons (Services, Consultation and Representation) Act* (HM Government, 1986). Section Four states that a local authority shall decide whether the needs of a disabled person (including anyone who suffers from a mental disorder of any description) call for the provision by the authority of any services in accordance with Section 2(1) of the 1970 Act. Section Eight of the Act provides that the assessment of services for the disabled person must take the abilities of carers into account:

> "Where: a disabled person is living at home and is receiving a substantial amount of care on a regular basis from another person (who is not employed to provide such care ...), and it falls to a local authority to decide whether the disabled person's need calls for the provision of any services under any welfare enactment – the local authority shall in deciding the question, have regard to the ability of that person to continue to provide such care on a regular basis".

The Act does not define 'carer', and carers of any age are therefore entitled to benefit from it.

(ii) *Making a reality of community care* (Audit Commission, 1986) is critical of the fragmented nature of mental health services, the relationship between health and social services, and the perverse incentives that are working against community-based care.

1988

Community care: Agenda for action (Griffiths Report) recommends that:

- the main responsibility for planning community care at local level should lie with local authority social services departments;
- responsibility for community care within central government should rest with a clearly designated minister;
- local authorities should act as organisers and purchasers of services, but not primarily as providers;
- earmarked resources should be transferred to local authorities to finance their new responsibilities (Griffiths, 1988).

The report suggests that local authorities have a specific role to play. They should be responsible for:

- identifying and assessing the community care needs of vulnerable adults, including those with mental health problems;
- arranging the support such people require, including all residential care as well as home-based and day care;

- maximising choice and competition through developing the role of the private sector and the mixed economy of care;
- supporting informal carers and informal networks.

While the Griffiths Report recognises the primary importance of family carers, the report fails to acknowledge that in some households care giving may be done by children.

1989

(i) *Caring for people: Community care in the next decade and beyond* White Paper (DH, 1989a) outlines six primary objectives of community care policy:

1. to promote the development of domiciliary, day and respite services to enable people to live in their own homes wherever feasible and sensible;
2. to ensure that service providers make practical support for carers a high priority;
3. to make proper assessment of need and good care management the cornerstone of high quality care;
4. to promote the development of a flourishing independent (private) sector alongside good quality public services;
5. to clarify the responsibilities of agencies and so make it easier to hold them to account for their performance;
6. to secure better value for taxpayers' money by introducing a new funding structure for social care.

Chapter Seven of the paper focuses on services for people with a mental illness. The chapter:

- reaffirms the government's support for a policy of locally-based services;
- emphasises that the number of hospital beds should be reduced only as a consequence of the development of new services;
- requires that all district health authorities have instituted, in collaboration with social services departments (SSDs), a Care Programme Approach (CPA) by April 1991;
- agrees with the Griffiths Report that SSDs should continue to be responsible for providing social care to those with a mental illness who require it;
- establishes a mental illness specific grant to be paid to SSDs;
- recognises the important contribution of the voluntary sector and encourages this to develop further;
- wants the private sector to have a greater role, perhaps in building hospitals and other forms of accommodation;
- recognises the need to do something about homeless mentally ill people – those who have lost touch with services;

- recognises the need for greater cooperation between agencies and sectors, especially health and SSDs.

(ii) *Working for patients* White Paper (DH, 1989b) gives hospitals the authority to apply to become self-governing NHS hospital trusts. Trusts are able to provide services under contract for any health purchaser regardless of location as well as for the private sector.

(iii) *1989 Children Act* (HM Government, 1989). Social services authorities are under a general duty, by virtue of s17(1), to safeguard and promote the interests of children "in need" and in furtherance of this duty they are "empowered to provide a wide range of services". This Act is important because many young carers can (and have) been considered to be 'children in need' under this Section, and are thereby entitled to support from local authorities (see Box B.2).

> ### Box B.2: 'Children in need' under the 1989 Children Act
>
> Section 17(10) of the 1989 Children Act provides that a child shall be taken to be 'in need' if
>
> > "(a) he is unlikely to achieve or maintain, or to have the opportunity of achieving or maintaining, a reasonable standard of health or development without the provision for him of services by a local authority ...; or (b) his health or development is likely to be significantly impaired, or further impaired, without the provision for him of such services; or (c) he is disabled".
>
> The Act provides local authorities with a power to assess children in need (paragraph three of Schedule Two to the Children Act) and the 1989 Children Act Guidance (Volume Two: Family support) (DH, 1991) clarifies what is required in such assessments.
>
> When a child has been identified as 'in need', the Children Act specifies that a range of support services should be made available. Section 17(1) states that:
>
> > "It shall be the general duty of every local authority ... (a) to safeguard and promote the welfare of children within their area who are in need; and (b) so far as is consistent with that duty, to promote the upbringing of such children by their families, by providing a range of services appropriate to those children's needs".
>
> The Act requires that a range of services be provided to help to keep families together. In some cases this could also include cash payments, or services to other members of the family where this will safeguard or promote the child's welfare.

Essentially, local authorities must safeguard the welfare of any child in need, including young carers who are defined in this way, and promote the upbringing of such children by their families by providing a range and level of services appropriate to those children's needs. These services can include advice, guidance, counselling, help in the home, and family centres, and can be provided for the family of the child in need or any member of the family should this safeguard the child's welfare. Local authorities can provide these services directly or arrange for them to be provided by, for example, a voluntary or private organisation. They are also required to publicise the help available to families in need.

1990

1990 NHS and Community Care Act (HM Government, 1990) establishes the legislative framework for the restructuring of both the NHS and community care system. Section 47(1) places a duty on local authorities to carry out an assessment of an individual's needs for community care services (including people with mental health problems and any services provided under Section 117 of the 1983 Mental Health Act). Section 46 requires local authorities to publish community care plans after wide-ranging consultation with various stakeholders.

1991

(i) Care Programme Approach (CPA) to be implemented by health authorities, jointly with social services. The CPA is one of the cornerstones of the government's mental health policy. It provides a framework for the care of people with severe mental illness outside hospital by introducing 'systematic arrangements' for assessment and after-care to ensure that people being treated in the community receive the health and social care they need. The essential elements of CPA include:

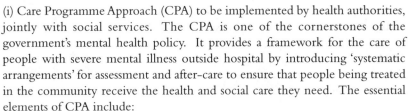

- a systematic assessment of health and social care needs;
- an agreed care plan;
- allocation of a key worker;
- regular review of the patient's progress.

By June 1996 all health authorities had reported that the CPA was in place.

(ii) Social services departments to have in place new complaints procedures and inspection units.

(iii) A Mental Illness Specific Grant is introduced to assist implementation of community care by helping local authorities to expand social care provision for people with mental health problems. Since then it has funded a wide range of innovative schemes as well as core services.

1992

(i) Social services required to have published their first community care plan by April.

(ii) *Health of the nation* White Paper (DH, 1992) outlines the government's strategic objectives to reduce ill health, social disability and death caused by mental illness, and to "improve significantly the health and social functioning of mentally ill people". For the first time mental health was confirmed as a first-rank Department of Health policy priority, and it has remained so ever since.

1993

(i) Social services to have established their own assessment and care management procedures for all vulnerable people who look to the authority for support, and have in place their charging and paying arrangements for contracting and purchasing. First transfer of social security to social services.

(ii) *The secretary of state's ten-point plan for developing safe and successful community care* (DH, 1993) incorporates:

• supervised discharge and supervision registers;
• new standards of care for people with schizophrenia;
• better mental health service planning;
• better training for CPA key workers.

1994

(i) *Finding a place: A review of mental health services for adults* (Audit Commission, 1994) identifies:

• deficiencies in current arrangements and proposes better management of community care;
• better targeting on those most severely mentally ill;
• better integration of hospital and community services, working to common criteria.

(ii) Supervision registers introduced to ensure that people with a severe mental illness who may be a significant risk to themselves or others receive appropriate and effective care in the community. The registers identify and provide information on service users who are – or are liable to be – at risk to themselves (through suicide or serious self-neglect) or others (through violence).

(iii) Publication of the Clunis Report (Ritchie, 1994), a major public enquiry into a high-profile homicide that had caught the attention of the media and others. The recommendations of this report had a deep and lasting impact on subsequent policy developments.

(iv) *The health of the nation: Key area handbook – mental illness* (DH, 1994). This confirmed mental health as one of the Department of Health's five key priority action areas.

1995

(i) *1995 Carers (Recognition and Services) Act* (HM Government, 1995a) (implemented in April 1996), gives carers of any age – including young carers – the right to an assessment of their "ability to provide and to continue to provide care". Social services are required (if so requested by a carer) to carry out this assessment of the carer at the same time as it assesses or reassesses the person for whom care is provided (the carers' assessment is therefore linked to the cared-for persons' assessment). The Act applies to carers who "provide a substantial amount of care on a regular basis". Circular LAC (96)7 (DH, 1996a) states that it is "for local authorities to form their own judgement about what amounts to 'regular' and 'substantial' care". Carers who do not provide substantial or regular care should also have their views and interests taken into account when an assessment is undertaken. 'Care' includes physical caring tasks as well as emotional care and general attendance to ensure the service user comes to no harm.

(ii) *Young carers: Something to think about* (SSI, 1995). The first document specifically on young carers from the Department of Health. It focuses on policy issues concerned with:

- the identification of young carers and definitions;
- a whole family approach which emphasises the need for adequate services for ill or disabled parents;
- an appropriate focus on the child's needs;
- the importance of multi-agency working.

The report's 'Action checklist' on the Whole Family Approach states that professionals should:

> Start with the needs of the family/disabled or ill parent, and see what needs remain for the child; work with the child as part of the family unit; acknowledge the rights of the child including to information, to be listened to and to stop physically caring; recognise that poverty and disabling environments, services and attitudes can limit adults' ability to parent; acknowledge the distinction between parenting and parental activity; recognise that time spent on counselling, talking and therapeutic work can prevent inappropriate and expensive crisis responses; focus more

on support for children in need rather than on protection of children at risk; acknowledge young carers' legitimate concerns about professionals' attitudes and insensitivity and their fear of professional intervention; remember 'families do their best'. Start with the family's solution and work with any dilemmas and contradictions. (SSI, 1995, p 16)

(iii) *1995 Disability Discrimination Act* (HM Government, 1995b). Part III of the Act deals with discrimination in the provision of goods, facilities and services. Since December 1996, it has been unlawful for a service provider to refuse unjustifiably to provide a service to a disabled person (including people with a mental disorder) on the same terms as available to other people. From October 1999, service providers have to take reasonable steps to change policies, practices or procedures that make it impossible or unreasonably difficult for disabled people to use a service. Further provisions come into force from 2004 which state that service providers will have to take reasonable steps to remove, alter or provide reasonable means of avoiding physical features that make it impossible or unreasonably difficult for disabled people to use a service.

(iv) *1995 Mental Health (Patients in the Community) Act* (HM Government, 1995c) provides, by amendment to the 1983 Mental Health Act, for supervised discharge orders for certain patients discharged from hospital following detention for treatment under the Act. It also establishes a new category of patients that are subject to compulsory after-care in the community, including powers for health and social services authorities to require patients to live at a specified place and attend for medical treatment.

1996

(i) *Building bridges: A guide to arrangements for inter-agency working for the care and protection of severely mentally ill people* (DH, 1996b). This publication provides detailed advice to promote delivery of effective and coordinated services for severely mentally ill people and offers examples of good practice in inter-agency working. This report is a direct government response to the recommendations of the Clunis Report (see 1994 (iii)).

(ii) *The NHS: A service with ambitions* (DH, 1996c) sets out the government's aims to achieve a high quality integrated health service organised and run around the health needs of individual patients.

(iii) *The spectrum of care: Local services for people with mental health problems* (DH, 1996d) describes the full range of specialist skills and settings which should be available to people with severe mental illness – in their own homes, in supported accommodation or in a hospital setting, whichever is most appropriate.

(iv) *1995 Carers (Recognition and Services) Act: Policy guidance and practice guide* (DH, 1996a) points out that 'regular' care should be distinguished from 'frequent' care. Regular connotes an event which recurs or is repeated at fixed times or uniform intervals. It also states that:

> Some users with mental health or substance misuse problems or with conditions such as neurological disorders, dementia, cancer or HIV/AIDS will have care needs which vary over time but may present regular and substantial burdens for carers. (DH, 1996a, para 7)

The guidance also clarifies various items relating to carers, including what is meant by 'regular and substantial care' and the importance of assessing not just existing carers but those 'intending' to provide care. It emphasises the importance of primary care staff, including GPs and community nurses, in recognising the needs of users and carers. It also emphasises that:

> Local authorities should ensure that it becomes part of routine practice to inform any carer who appears to be eligible under this Act of their right to request an assessment. (DH, 1996a, para 20)

The guidance also refers specifically to children with caring responsibilities (see Box B.3).

Box B.3: Guidance on young carers

Paragraph 22 of the Policy and Practice Guidance LAC (96)7 states that:

"Where the carer is a child the impact of caring may be different as it may affect the child's health and development by the restrictions that providing regular and substantial care might place on the child's educational and leisure opportunities. This should be carefully considered as part of the assessment. It is equally important that the assessment focuses on how best to enable an ill or disabled parent (or other family member) to live independently so that the parent's ability to parent is supported rather than undermined. Consideration should be given as to whether the child is a 'child in need' under the Children Act 1989".

With regards to the assessment of young carers, Paragraph 15.5 states:

"If it appears to the care manager that a child or young person is providing regular and substantial care and the young carer does not request an assessment, the care manager should still consider whether there is a need to assist or relieve the child either through the provision of community care

---

services for the user or through the provision of services to promote the welfare of the child. There may be some young carers who do not provide substantial and regular care but their development is impaired as a result of their caring responsibilities. In such situations local authorities will wish to consider whether they should exercise their existing duties towards children in need". Young carers who are assessed under the Carers Act are able to access services under the 1989 Children Act.

The Practice Guide (DH, 1996a, p 12) sets out the following guidelines:

• listen to the child or young person and respect their views;
• give time and privacy to children who may need this in order to talk about their situation;
• acknowledge that this is the way the family copes with disability or illness;
• acknowledge parents' strengths;
• beware of undermining parenting capacity;
• consider what is needed to assist the parent in his or her parenting role;
• consider the needs of the child(ren) arising from the caring responsibilities;
• consider whether the caring responsibilities are restricting the child's ability to benefit from his/her education;
• consider whether the child's emotional and social development are being impaired;
• remember children must be allowed to be children;
• provide information on the full range of relevant support services, young carers groups and contact points for advice or information on specific issues.

(v) It becomes mandatory for local authorities to assess the level of need for children's services in their area and draw up a children's service plan. The plan will be prepared by the Social Services Department in liaison with health and education authorities, certain voluntary organisations, the police, probation service and other relevant bodies. It should reflect the medium–term strategic planning process by projecting three years ahead, being reviewed regularly in the interim.

(vi) *1996 Community Care (Direct Payments) Act* (HM Government, 1996) empowers local authorities to provide cash payments for some of those assessed as needing community care services. For example, a disabled parent may use a direct payment to purchase personal assistance to enable them to get up in the morning in time to take their children off to school.

(vii) *Young carers: Making a start* (SSI, 1996) confirms the need for a flexible, coordinated social services approach that crosses the boundary between community care and children's services. It points to the importance of coordination of social services with education and health professionals, who may be the first to identify the problems of young carers and their families.

1997

(i) *Developing partnerships in mental health* Conservative Green Paper (DH, 1997) restates government's commitment to developing partnerships in the care of people with severe mental illness. Outlines options for structural change, but these are overtaken – and forgotten – amid the activities of the forthcoming general election.

(ii) Tony Blair and New Labour win general election and embark on a reform and 'modernising agenda' for social welfare.

(iii) *The new NHS: Modern, dependable* White Paper (HM Government, 1997) introduces new initiatives, including Health Improvement Programmes, Health Action Zones, a new NHS Charter, Primary Care Groups, Primary Care Trusts, National Service Frameworks, a National Institute for Clinical Excellence, a new system of clinical governance in the NHS, and a Commission for Health Improvement.

1998

(i) *Modernising mental health services: Safe, sound and supportive* (DH, 1998a) sets out the government's new vision for mental health services for adults. It argues that care in the community has failed and focuses on issues of public concern about violence associated with mental illness. Modern mental health services must provide care that is:

- *Safe* – to protect the public and provide effective care for those with mental illness at the time they need it;
- *Sound* – to ensure that patients and service users have access to the full range of services which they need;
- *Supportive* – working with patients and service users, their families and carers to build healthier communities.

The report identifies the 'failures' of current mental health policy and practice. Failure is due to:

- inadequate care, poor management of resources and under-funding;
- the proper range of services not always being available to provide the care and support people need;
- treatments, antidepressants, new anti-psychotic drugs and psychological therapies for severe mentally ill people not reaching those who need them;
- patients and service users not remaining in contact with services;
- the overburdening of families who have willingly played a part in providing care;
- problems in recruiting and retaining staff;

- an outdated legal framework which fails to support effective treatment outside hospital;
- the failure of the 1983 Mental Health Act to provide an adequate framework for dealing with those who present a risk to the public.

The report recommends that modern mental health services will assess individual needs, deliver better treatment and care whether at home or in hospital, enabling 24-hour access to services, ensuring public safety, and managing risk more effectively; modern mental health services will have a firm base in primary care. Primary Care Groups will work closely with specialist teams to integrate service planning and delivery. Information systems will support the delivery of care and the management of resources, and there will be close partnerships with education, employment and housing. Patients, service users and carers will be involved in their own care, and in planning services. Services will be delivered in the most efficient and cost effective way with clear guidance from the National Institute for Clinical Excellence. Secure hospital services will be improved. Public protection will remain the first priority at all times.

Reform will be underpinned by substantial new investment – £700m over three years (1999-2002). This new investment will be in return for reform and improvements in service delivery, efficiency and cost effectiveness. The new investment will provide extra beds of all kinds, better outreach services, better access to anti-psychotic drugs, 24-hour crisis teams, more and better trained staff, regional commissioning teams for secure services, and development teams. Performance will be monitored through the new performance assessment frameworks for health and social care, complemented by external inspections. A new Mental Health National Service Framework will determine models and national standards (published September 1999).

(ii) *Modernising social services* Social Services White Paper (DH, 1998b) identifies six main problems with the current system of social services:

- failure to protect the most vulnerable;
- lack of coordination;
- inflexibility;
- a lack of clarity in roles;
- inconsistency;
- inefficiency.

It proposes that local authorities should lose their inspection functions and new independent bodies should be established. National standards and rules for care services should be introduced, as should a General Social Care Council to regulate and train staff. Performance-linked funding is required, as are requirements for greater compatibility on eligibility criteria and on charging policies.

(iii) *People like us – The report of the review of the safeguards for children living away from home* (Utting Report) presents a "woeful tale of failure" at all levels to provide a secure and decent childhood for some of the most vulnerable children in society. It shows that, in far too many cases, children are harmed rather than helped in care. Failings are not just the fault of individuals but also of the whole system itself (DH, The Welsh Office, 1998). The government's response (DH, 1998c) is published later that year.

(iv) *Partnership in action: New opportunities for joint working between health and social services* (DH, 1998d) suggests new ways in which health and social services should be allowed to work together, including a transfer of funds between sectors and pooled budgets.

(v) Quality Protects launched (DH, 1998e). Quality Protects is a three-year programme to transform the delivery and management of children's services. The initiative comprises the publication of a set of government objectives for children's services, a framework for the preparation of new Quality Protects Action Plans by local authorities, and guidance for local councillors. In addition, the government commits £350 million additional resources over three years to social services in the form of a special grant for children's services.

Quality Protects has a strong concentration on better outcomes, for which targets will be set. The key changes are:

- the reform and renewal of the public care system;
- improving the education of looked after children;
- increasing the choice of placements for looked after children;
- improving services for care leavers;
- radical improvements to procedures to prevent dangerous people from working with children;
- stronger emphasis on inter-agency working and the corporate responsibility of local authorities;
- better safeguards for children and young people in all settings away from home.

A key objective of Quality Protects is "To ensure that children whose parents have specific needs arising out of disability or health conditions enjoy the same life chances as all other children in the locality". This is particularly relevant to young carers. Other objectives are outlined in Box B.4.

Box B.4: The objectives of Quality Protects

The Quality Protects programme sets out eight national objectives, each of which is accompanied by a list of sub-objectives. The objectives are intended to be clear, affordable and enforceable. Social services departments will be required to develop effective systems to measure their performance in achieving them. While the government is particularly concerned with service provision to looked after children, its objectives are intended to cover all those children and families who receive help of any kind which is funded or part funded by SSDs. This will include young carers and their families in many instances.

The objectives of Quality Protects are to ensure that:

• children are securely attached to carers capable of providing safe and effective care for the duration of childhood;
• children are protected from emotional, physical, sexual abuse and neglect;
• children in need generally, and looked after children in particular, gain maximum life chances from educational opportunities, healthcare and social care;
• young people leaving care, as they enter adulthood, are not isolated and participate socially and economically as citizens;
• referral and assessment processes discriminate effectively between types and levels of need and produce a timely service response;
• children with specific social needs arising out of disability or a health condition are living in families or other appropriate settings in the community where their assessed needs are adequately met and reviewed;
• resources are planned and provided at levels which represent best value for money, allow for choice and different responses for different needs and circumstances.

1999

(i) National carers strategy, *Caring about carers* (HM Government, 1999), commits the government to a number of initiatives to improve the situation and support of all carers, including a grant for respite care services. A separate chapter on young carers recommends that:

• local authorities should identify children with additional family burdens;
• respite care services should be developed;
• there needs to be awareness raising and improved training for professionals;
• the national curriculum should contain relevant material;
• there should be a designated link person in every school;
• enhanced counselling services for young carers should be developed;
• there should be more young carers projects.

The document observes that:

> Under the Carers (Recognition and Services) Act 1995, young carers can ask for an assessment of their needs. But many are not aware that this is possible. Some local authorities are reluctant to advertise this fact because of their concern about raising expectations. With the help of the voluntary sector, the statutory services should ensure that young carers are not expected to carry inappropriate levels of caring responsibility. To achieve this, disabled or ill parents need support to maintain their independence and to carry out their parenting responsibilities.

(ii) *National service framework for mental health* (DH, 1999a) sets national standards, based on clinical evidence, and sets out best practice for promoting mental health and treating mental illness. It promises national and regional support for health and social services and establishes the progress that should be made within certain timescales. Seven standards require health and social services to:

- promote mental health for all and combat discrimination against people with mental health problems;
- identify the needs of patients with mental health problems and ensure they are offered effective treatments;
- ensure all services are available around the clock;
- ensure that all mental health service users on the CPA receive care which prevents or anticipates crisis and reduces risk;
- provide a hospital bed or suitable alternative bed for those who need it in an environment close to home that protects them and the public;
- make sure carers who look after someone on the CPA have their own caring, physical and mental health needs assessed on an annual basis;
- reduce the level of suicide.

Standard Six, 'Caring about carers', aims to ensure that health and social services assess the needs of carers who provide regular and substantial care for those with severe mental illness, and provide care to meet their needs. It recognises that:

> The families of individuals with severe mental illness may have to contend with demanding behaviour, extra financial burdens, restrictions upon their social and family life, and occasionally a risk to their own safety. The needs of those caring for people with severe mental illness or dementia are especially high.... [Additionally] extreme crimes of violence, manslaughter and murder are much more likely to be committed against family members or carers than against a stranger. Carers need to know what to do in a crisis, and to be assured that prompt action will be taken. (DH, 1999a, p 70)

Standard Six also recognises the specific contribution made by young carers and the importance of assessing young carers' needs and providing them with adequate support (see Box B.5).

Box B.5: What the 1999 National service framework for mental health says about young carers

About half of those with severe mental illness live with family or friends, and many others receive considerable support from them. Carers of service users, including young carers, should be involved in their own assessment and care planning process, which takes account of the state of their own mental and physical health needs, and ability to continue to care. (DH, 1999a, p 69)

There is evidence that carers of people with severe mental illness are not getting the services they need to support them, or to ensure that their own health is maintained. Young carers are a particularly vulnerable group. Few authorities had implemented the Carers (Recognition and Services) Act within their mental health services when inspected recently by the Social Services Inspectorate. (DH, 1999a, p 70)

Where the person with mental illness is a parent, health and local authorities should not assume that the child or children can undertake the necessary caring responsibilities. The parent should be supported in their parenting role and services provided so that the young carers is able to benefit from the same life chances as all other children, and have the opportunity for a full education, and leisure and social activities. The young carer's plan should take account of the adverse impact which mental health problems in a parent can have on the child. (DH, 1999a, p 72)

All individuals, including young carers, who provide regular and substantial care for a person on the CPA should have an assessment of their caring, physical and mental health needs, repeated on at least an annual basis. They should also have their own written care plan which is given to them and implemented in discussion with them (implemented for young carers from April 2002). Standard Six outlines the roles and responsibilities of social services, GPs, primary-care teams and others with regards to assessing and meeting carers' needs and establishes the 'milestones' from which progress to meet this standard can be evaluated.

(iii) *Modernising the care programme approach* (DH, 1999b). The government reaffirms its commitment to the CPA as *the* framework for care coordination and resource allocation in mental healthcare, but outlines the need for reform. Proposed changes take account of available evidence and recent experience to make CPA "an even more efficient and effective system of care co-ordination".

The proposed changes include the following:

- CPA will be integrated with Care Management in all areas to form a single care coordination approach for adults of working age with mental health problems;
- Each health and social services mental health provider must jointly identify a Lead Officer with the authority to work across all agencies to deliver an integrated approach to the CPA and Care Management;
- Two levels of CPA must be introduced – Standard and Enhanced;
- The requirement to maintain a supervision register will be removed (from April 2001);
- The key worker will be known as the Care Coordinator;
- Review and evaluation of care planning should be regarded as ongoing processes;
- Local service providers should ensure that a system is in place to collect data on all service users;
- Local audit should assess the quality of CPA implementation not just numbers.

(iv) *Working together to safeguard children* (DH, HO and DfEE, 1999) sets out how all agencies and professionals should work together to promote children's welfare and protect them from harm, abuse and neglect (replacing a previous version issued in 1991). It has specific things to say about children living with mentally ill parents (see Box B.6).

Box B.6: What *Working together* says about children living with parents with mental illness

Mental illness in a parent or carer does not necessarily have an adverse impact on a child, but it is essential always to assess its implications for any children involved in the family. Parental illness may markedly restrict children's social and recreational activities. With both mental and physical illness in a parent, children may have caring responsibilities placed upon them inappropriate to their years, leading them to be worried and anxious. If they are depressed, parents may neglect their own and their children's physical and emotional needs. In some circumstances, some forms of mental illness may blunt parents' emotions and feelings, or cause them to behave towards their children in bizarre or violent ways. Unusually, but at the extreme, a child may be at risk of severe injury, profound neglect, or even death .... The adverse effects on children of parental mental illness are less likely when parental problems are mild, last only a short time, are not associated with family disharmony, and do not result in the family

---

> breaking up. Children may also be protected when the other parent or a family member can help respond to the child's needs. Children most at risk of significant harm are those who feature within parental delusions, and children who become targets for parental aggression or rejection, or who are neglected as a result of parental mental illness. (DH, HO and DfEE, 1999, paras 2.22-23)

It goes on to state that:

> All professionals working in mental health services in the statutory, voluntary and independent sectors, should bear in mind the welfare of children, irrespective of whether they are primarily working with adults or with children and young people. They are likely to become aware of a broad range of children's needs in their daily work. All mental health professionals should be aware of the legislation concerning child protection and informed about their local child protection procedures and the workings of the ACPC, and of their responsibilities for safeguarding children. (DH, HO and DfEE, 1999, para 3.39)

> Adult mental health services have a responsibility in safeguarding children when they become aware of or identify a child at risk of harm. Close collaboration and liaison between the adult mental health services and children's welfare services are essential in the interests of children. (DH, HO and DfEE, 1999, paras 3.45-46)

2000

(i) The government's *Framework for the assessment of children in need and their families* (DH, 2000) provides a systematic basis for collecting and analysing information to support professional judgements about how to help children and families in the best interests of the child. Practitioners should use the framework to gain an understanding of:

- a child's developmental needs;
- the capacity of parents or caregivers to respond appropriately to those needs, including their capacity to keep the child safe from harm;
- the impact of wider family and environmental factors on the parents and child.

The framework specifies how assessments of all children, especially children in need, should be carried out. A companion volume of Practice Guidance contains detailed information on the manner in which the framework should be applied. The accompanying reader, *A child's world* (Horwath, 2000), contains specific reference to the ways in which the framework should be applied to young carers.

The framework emphasises that:

- young carers should not be expected to carry inappropriate levels of caring which have an adverse impact on their development and life chances;
- an assessment of family circumstances is essential;
- young carers can be assessed under the Carers Act and consideration must be given as to whether they are a child in need under the Children Act;
- young carers can receive help from local and health authorities;
- the central issue is whether a child's welfare or development might suffer if support is not provided to the child or family;
- services should be provided to promote the health and development of young carers while not undermining the parent.

 (ii) *2000 Carers and Disabled Children Act* (HM Government, 2000a) gives carers over the age of 16 years (and caring for someone over the age of 18) new rights:

- carers may request an assessment of their own needs, even if the person receiving care does not wish to have an assessment;
- local authorities may provide services for carers in their own right;
- carers may receive vouchers for short-term breaks;
- carers may receive direct payments in lieu of services for which they have been assessed.

The Practice Guidance to the Act sets out to promote services and other provisions that are designed to sustain the caring relationship in a manner that is in the interests of all parties. Support for carers is essential to their own wellbeing and also of those to whom care is provided. People should receive support that they feel is most appropriate to their needs. In some cases, a cash payment in lieu of services may be more appropriate so that carers can make their own arrangements and pay someone of their own choosing.

Local authorities are able to charge carers for services that are provided to them, subject to a means test (they cannot charge carers for services belonging to the person they are caring for). Authorities are not *required* to charge for non-residential community care services – whether they do so or not is a matter for their discretion.

Carers under the age of 16 will need to access assessments and services through the 1995 Carers (Recognition and Services) Act or the 1989 Children Act.

(iii) *2000 Care Standards Act* (HM Government, 2000b) establishes the National Care Standards Commission in England and the Care Standards Inspectorate for Wales, both to regulate and inspect services against national minimum standards. The Act also establishes Social Care Councils to regulate the social care workforce including social work.

(iv) *A Jigsaw of services* (SSI, 2000) finds that disabled parents are usually not identified as a relatively discrete group of service users. The focus of workers appeared to be either on the children in the family or on the impact of the adult's disability on their own personal needs. Work was rarely focused on the whole family and how to support and help the parents in the discharge of their parental duties. Best practice suggests that a disabled adult's care plan arising from a multi-professional needs-led assessment would include service provision for parenting tasks, if appropriate, and services would be provided from the relevant skilled workers or agencies. There needs to be a cultural and practical shift in the approach to working with disabled parents. It needs to be underpinned by:

- a recognition of the right of disabled people, within the bounds of current legislation, to be supported in fulfilling their roles and responsibilities as parents;
- knowledge of child welfare principles described in the 1989 Children Act;
- needs-led assessment which focuses on the whole family and, when necessary, incorporates the views of a range of professionals;
- protocols, practical arrangements and strategies to improve inter-divisional/ corporate/inter-agency work at an individual and strategic level.

2001
The government consultation document, *Building a strategy for children and young people* (HM Government, 2001) sets out the government's vision for all children and young people and how they can best reach their full potential, and what support they require from different agencies. Specialist workshops with young people, including young carers, are held across England.

2002
(i) Social Care Institute of Excellence launched to:

- establish and disseminate a knowledge base of 'what works' in social care;
- provide guidelines on efficient and effective social care practice and service delivery;
- disseminate the above through creating effective partnerships – in particular closer working relationships between health and social care are advocated.

(ii) Draft Mental Health Bill (DH, 2002) proposes, among other things, a new legal framework for the compulsory treatment of people with mental disorders. Compulsory treatment can be used where it is necessary for the health or safety of a patient. People with dangerous and severe personality disorders can be detained even if they argue their conditions are untreatable.

Index

Page references for tables and boxes are in *italics*; those for notes are followed by n

Also available from The Policy Press

Mental health services and child protection
responding effectively to the needs of families
Nicky Stanley, Bridget Penhale,Denise Riordan, Rosaline S. Barbour and Sue Holden
Paperback £15.99 US$25.00 tbc
ISBN 1 86134 427 9
234 x 156mm 128 pages tbc
September 2003 tbc

Child welfare
Historical dimensions, contemporary debate
Harry Hendrick
Paperback £18.99 US$29.95
ISBN 1 86134 477 5
Hardback £55.00 US$59.95
ISBN 1 86134 478 3
234 x 156mm 304 pages
February 2003

Champions for children
The lives of modern child care pioneers
Bob Holman
Paperback £14.99 US$25.00
ISBN 1 86134 342 6
Hardback £45.00 US$55.00
ISBN 1 86134 353 1
216 x 148mm 232 pages
October 2001

Children, family and the state
Decision-making and child participation
Nigel Thomas
Paperback £18.99 US$29.95
ISBN 1 86134 448 1
234 x 156mm 256 pages
October 2002

For further information about these and other titles published by The Policy Press, please visit our website at:
www.policypress.org.uk

To order titles, please contact:
Marston Book Services
PO Box 269 • Abingdon
Oxon OX14 4YN • UK
Tel: +44 (0)1235 465500
Fax: +44 (0)1235 465556
E-mail: direct.orders@marston.co.uk